St Antony's Series

General Editor: **Jan Zielonka** (2004–), Fellow of St Antony's College, Oxford

Recent titles include:

Fiona Macaulay
GENDER POLITICS IN BRAZIL AND CHILE
The Role of Parties in National and Local Policymaking

Stephen Whitefield (*editor*)
POLITICAL CULTURE AND POST-COMMUNISM

José Esteban Castro
WATER, POWER AND CITIZENSHIP
Social Struggle in the Basin of Mexico

Valpy FitzGerald and Rosemary Thorp (*editors*)
ECONOMIC DOCTRINES IN LATIN AMERICA
Origins, Embedding and Evolution

Victoria D. Alexander and Marilyn Rueschemeyer
ART AND THE STATE
The Visual Arts in Comparative Perspective

Ailish Johnson
EUROPEAN WELFARE STATES AND SUPRANATIONAL GOVERNANCE OF
SOCIAL POLICY

Archie Brown (*editor*)
THE DEMISE OF MARXISM-LENINISM IN RUSSIA

Thomas Boghardt
SPIES OF THE KAISER
German Covert Operations in Great Britain during the First World War Era

Ulf Schmidt
JUSTICE AT NUREMBERG
Leo Alexander and the Nazi Doctors' Trial

Steve Tsang (*editor*)
PEACE AND SECURITY ACROSS THE TAIWAN STRAIT

C. W. Braddick
JAPAN AND THE SINO-SOVIET ALLIANCE, 1950–1964
In the Shadow of the Monolith

Isao Miyaoka
LEGITIMACY IN INTERNATIONAL SOCIETY
Japan's Reaction to Global Wildlife Preservation

Neil J. Melvin
SOVIET POWER AND THE COUNTRYSIDE
Policy Innovation and Institutional Decay

Julie M. Newton
RUSSIA, FRANCE AND THE IDEA OF EUROPE

Juhana Aunesluoma
BRITAIN, SWEDEN AND THE COLD WAR, 1945–54
Understanding Neutrality

George Pagoulatos
GREECE'S NEW POLITICAL ECONOMY
State, Finance and Growth from Postwar to EMU

Tiffany A. Troxel
PARLIAMENTARY POWER IN RUSSIA, 1994–2001
A New Era

Elvira María Restrepo
COLOMBIAN CRIMINAL JUSTICE IN CRISIS
Fear and Distrust

Ilaria Favretto
THE LONG SEARCH FOR A THIRD WAY
The British Labour Party and the Italian Left Since 1945

Lawrence Tal
POLITICS, THE MILITARY, AND NATIONAL SECURITY IN JORDAN, 1955–1967

Louise Haagh and Camilla Helgø (*editors*)
SOCIAL POLICY REFORM AND MARKET GOVERNANCE IN LATIN AMERICA

Gayil Talshir
THE POLITICAL IDEOLOGY OF GREEN PARTIES
From the Politics of Nature to Redefining the Nature of Politics

E. K. Dosmukhamedov
FOREIGN DIRECT INVESTMENT IN KAZAKHSTAN
Politico-Legal Aspects of Post-Communist Transition

Felix Patrikeeff
RUSSIAN POLITICS IN EXILE
The Northeast Asian Balance of Power, 1924–1931

St Antony's Series
Series Standing Order ISBN 0–333–71109–2
(*outside North America only*)

You can receive future titles in this series as they are published by placing a standing order. Please contact your bookseller or, in case of difficulty, write to us at the address below with your name and address, the title of the series and the ISBN quoted above.

Customer Services Department, Macmillan Distribution Ltd, Houndmills, Basingstoke, Hampshire RG21 6XS, England

Gender Politics in Brazil and Chile

The Role of Parties in National and Local Policymaking

Fiona Macaulay

in association with
St Antony's College Oxford

60796251

10-11-07

First published 2006 by
PALGRAVE MACMILLAN
Houndmills, Basingstoke, Hampshire RG21 6XS and
175 Fifth Avenue, New York, N.Y. 10010
Companies and representatives throughout the world

PALGRAVE MACMILLAN is the global academic imprint of the Palgrave Macmillan division of St. Martin's Press, LLC and of Palgrave Macmillan Ltd. Macmillan® is a registered trademark in the United States, United Kingdom and other countries. Palgrave is a registered trademark in the European Union and other countries.

ISBN-13: 978–0–333–73614–2
ISBN-10: 0–333–73614–1

This book is printed on paper suitable for recycling and made from fully managed and sustained forest sources.

A catalogue record for this book is available from the British Library.

Library of Congress Cataloging-in-Publication Data
Macaulay, Fiona, 1962–
   Gender politics in Brazil and Chile : the role of parties in national and local policymaking / Fiona Macaulay.
      p.   cm. — (St. Antony's series)
   Includes bibliographical references and index.
   ISBN 0–333–73614–1
   1. Women in politics—Brazil.   2. Women in politics—Chile.
   3. Political parties—Brazil.   4. Political parties—Chile.   5. Partido dos Trabalhadores (Brazil)   6. Chile. Servicio Nacional de la Mujer.
   I. Title.   II. St. Antony's series (Palgrave Macmillan (Firm))
   HQ1236.5.B6M33 2005
   320'.082'0981—dc22   2005049993

10   9   8   7   6   5   4   3   2   1
15   14   13   12   11   10   09   08   07   06

Printed and bound in Great Britain by
Antony Rowe Ltd, Chippenham and Eastbourne

For Adrian and Joseph

Contents

PART II CHILE

List of Tables

Glossary

AD	*Acción Democrática* (Democratic Action, Venezuela)
ADM	*Assessoria dos Direitos da Mulher* (Women's Advisory Unit, Brazil)
APRA	*Alianza Popular Revolucionaria Americana* (American Popular Revolutionary Alliance, Peru)
ARENA	*Aliança Renovadora Nacional* (Alliance for National Renovation, Brazil)
autónomas	independent feminists
bancada feminina	women's parliamentary caucus, Brazil
CEDAW	Convention on the Elimination of all Forms of Discrimination Against Women
CEM	*Coordenadoria Especial da Mulher* (Women's Co-ordinating Committee, Brazil)
CEMA-Chile	*Centros de Madres* (Mothers' Centres, Chile)
CEN	*Comissão Executiva Nacional* (Workers' Party National Executive Committee, Brazil)
CESCO	*Consejo Económico y Social Comunal* (Social and Economic Council, Chile)
CFEMEA	*Centro Feminista de Estudos e Assessoria* (Feminist Research and Advisory Centre, Brazil)
CIDEM	*Centro de Información de los Derechos de la Mujer* (Women's Rights Information Centre, Chile)
CMD	*Concertación de Mujeres por la Democracia* (Alliance of Women for Democracy, Chile)
CNDM	*Conselho Nacional dos Direitos da Mulher* (National Council on Women's Rights, Brazil)
CODECO	*Consejo de Desarrollo Comunal* (Local Development Council, Chile)
conselhos	state or municipal-level advisory councils on women's rights, Brazil
COPEI	*Comité de Organización Política Electoral Independiente* (Christian Democratic Party, Venezuela)
CUT	*Central Unica dos Trabalhadores* (Trade Union Confederation, Brazil)
DN	*Diretório Nacional* (Workers' Party National Directorate, Brazil)

EOP	Equal Opportunity Plan
FA	*Frente Amplio* (Broad Front, Uruguay)
FMLN	*Frente Farabundo Martí de Liberación Nacional* (Farabundo Martí National Liberation Front, El Salvador)
FSI	Female Success Index (the relative performance of female compared to male candidates)
FSLN	*Frente Sandinista de Liberación Nacional* (Sandinista National Liberation Front, Nicaragua)
gremialista	corporatist, communitarian form of social organization based on guilds and civic associations, Chile
IBAM	*Instituto Brasileiro de Administração Municipal* (Brazilian Institute for Municipal Administration)
Intendente	regional governor, Chile
MDB	*Movimento Democrático Brasileiro* (Brazilian Democratic Movement)
MFA	*Movimento Feminino pela Anistia* (Women's Amnesty Movement, Brazil)
MOL	Municipal Organic Law
MVR	*Movimiento Quinta República* (Fifth Republic Movement, Venezuela)
NGO	non-governmental organization
OMM	*Oficina Municipal de la Mujer* (Municipal Women's Office, Chile)
PAN	*Partido Acción Nacional* (National Action Party, Mexico)
PB	participatory budget, Brazil
PC	*Partido Comunista* (Communist Party, Chile)
PCdoB	*Partido Comunista do Brasil* (Communist Party of Brazil)
(P)DC	*Partido Demócrata Cristiano* (Christian Democratic Party, Chile)
PDS	*Partido Democrático Social* (Social Democratic Party, Brazil)
PDT	*Partido Democrático Trabalhista* (Democratic Labour Party, Brazil)
PFL	*Partido da Frente Liberal* (Liberal Front Party, Brazil)
PJ	*Partido Justicialista* (Peronist Party, Argentina)
PLN	*Partido de Liberación Nacional* (National Liberation Party, Costa Rica)
PMDB	*Partido do Movimento Democrático Brasileiro* (Party of the Brazilian Democratic Movement)
PN	*Partido Nacional* (National Party, Chile)
poblaciones	shantytowns, Chile
pobladoras	women shantytown dwellers, Chile

políticas	party women
PP	*Partido Popular* (Popular Party, Brazil)
PP(B)	*Partido Progressista Brasileiro* (Brazilian Progressive Party, a 1995 fusion of the PPR and PP, renamed the *Partido Progressista* in 2003)
PPD	*Partido por la Democracia* (Party for Democracy, Chile)
PPR	*Partido Progressista Reformador* (Progressive Reform Party, Brazil)
PPS	*Partido Popular Socialista* (Popular Socialist Party, Brazil)
PR	*Partido Radical* (Radical Party, Chile)
PRD	*Partido de la Revolución Democrática* (Party of Democratic Revolution, Mexico)
PRI	*Partido Revolucionario Institucional* (Institutional Revolutionary Party, Mexico)
PRODEMU	*Fundación para la Promoción y Desarrollo de la Mujer* (Foundation for Promoting Women's Development, Chile)
promoción popular	the advancement of ordinary people's interests, Chile
PS	*Partido Socialista* (Socialist Party, Chile)
PSB	*Partido Socialista Brasileiro* (Brazilian Socialist Party)
PSDB	*Partido da Social Democracia Brasileira* (Party of Brazilian Social Democracy)
PT	*Partido dos Trabalhadores* (Workers' Party, Brazil)
PTB	*Partido Trabalhista Brasileiro* (Brazilian Labour Party)
RN	*Renovación Nacional* (National Renovation, Chile)
SERNAM	*Servicio Nacional de la Mujer* (National Women's Service, Chile)
SNM	*Secretaría Nacional de la Mujer* (National Women's Secretariat, Chile)
SNM	*Secretaria Nacional de Mulheres do PT* (Workers' Party National Women's Secretariat, Brazil)
SPM	*Secretaria Especial de Políticas para as Mulheres* (Special Secretariat for Policies on Women, Brazil)
temporeras	female seasonal agricultural workers, Chile
UDI	*Unión Democrática Independiente* (Independent Democratic Union, Chile)
UN	United Nations
UP	*Unidad Popular* (Popular Unity, Chile)

List of Brazilian States

AC	Acre
AP	Amapá
CE	Ceará
DF	Distrito Federal (Federal District)
ES	Espírito Santo
GO	Goiás
MA	Maranhão
MG	Minas Gerais
MS	Mato Grosso do Sul
PA	Pará
PB	Paraíba
PE	Pernambuco
PI	Piauí
PR	Paraná
RJ	Rio de Janeiro
RN	Rio Grande do Norte
RO	Rondônia
RS	Rio Grande do Sul
SC	Santa Catarina
SE	Sergipe
SP	São Paulo

Acknowledgements

This book would not have been possible without the assistance of very many individuals and organizations. First and foremost, I would like to thank Alan Angell, for his tremendous support, both intellectual and practical, and for his persistent, gentle nagging over several years until I finally produced the goods. I also appreciate the encouragement of Professors Leslie Bethell, Director of the Centre for Brazilian Studies, University of Oxford, and James Dunkerley, Director of the Institute for the Study of the Americas, University of London, in which institutions I have been employed as a researcher and lecturer over the last five years. My colleagues in both places, in particular Maxine Molyneux, Rachel Sieder, Mahrukh Doctor and Kathryn Hochstetler, have also provided me with much-appreciated motivation and stimulation.

I must also express my gratitude to all the unsung librarians, secretaries and assistants – nearly all women – in innumerable archives and institutions whose patience, cheery helpfulness, and collusion were a lifeline during the more frustrating moments of fieldwork. I thank in particular the following: in Brazil: the Workers' Party, Fundação Perseu Abramo, Instituto Brasileiro de Administração Municipal, Centro Pastoral Vergueiro, the São Paulo state council for women's rights, Centro de Informação Mulher, Conselho Nacional dos Direitos da Mulher, and CFEMEA; in Chile: SERNAM, ISIS International, Servicio Electoral, FLACSO, Centro de Estudios de la Mujer, Instituto de la Mujer, Instituto Libertad and the Library of Congress.

The staff of the Workers' Party and of SERNAM were mercifully tolerant of my requests for countless interviews and obscure documents. I hope my study will be of interest and use to both. For her inspiration and assistance I thank especially Tatau Godinho, who headed the PT women's secretariat for several years. I extend gratitude also to my many interviewees in both countries, including party and women's movement activists, politicians, academics, NGO researchers, and local government officials. They gave graciously of their time, and their experience and insights form the heart of this study.

CEDEC and the political science departments of the University of São Paulo and of the Catholic University in Santiago generously extended facilities to me as a visiting researcher. In the UK, funding was provided by the Economic and Social Research Council, the University of Oxford's Interfaculty Committee for Latin American Studies, Committee for Graduate Studies and St Antony's Carr and Stahl funds.

During the three periods of fieldwork, I was fortunate to have the friendship of María Lourdes González, Charmaine Levy, Dominique Fournier, Margaret Power, Carolina Fresard, Sonia Sobral, Igor Fuser, Morris Kachani, Gabriel Felipe de Souza, Mário Tato, Cláudio Couto Gonçalves, Maurício Rands Barros and Wilma Keller. Over the years, Wilma provided me with a home-from-home in São Paulo. Sadly, she died in August 2002 after a long and courageous battle with cancer, before this book was completed and without seeing Lula elected president. In Oxford, Laurence Davis, Louise Haagh, Pamela Lowden, Celso Ribeiro, Renate Dwan, Elizabeth Joyce and Tony King all shared in the pain of writing. Nina Laurie at Newcastle University provided a much-needed job to fund writing up once my grant ran out. I am also grateful to Jelke Boesten, Jenny Herbst, Montserrat Relancio and Jussara Bordin for tracking down information and processing data.

Sections of Chapters 3 and 4 have appeared as a chapter entitled 'The purple in the rainbow: gender politics in the PT' in Gianpaolo Baiocchi (ed.), *Radicals in Power: the Workers' Party (PT) and Experiments with Urban Democracy in Brazil*. I thank Zed Press for their kind permission to reproduce those parts.

Finally, I thank my family for their support, especially my mother who, as a party activist and leader in her local Conservative Party, must have stimulated my early interest in the relationship between party politics and gender issues. This book is dedicated to my partner, Adrian Salmon, and to our son Joseph. Adrian could probably recite the text backwards, given the number of times he has patiently read, copy-edited and formatted it. Joe's arrival may have slowed down the process of writing the book, but he has also brought me a great deal of joy and the challenge of thinking through gender relations every day. Now I will have more time to play.

FIONA MACAULAY

Introduction

This book is a comparative study of how party politics have filtered women's movement demands for political voice and state resources in two Latin American countries, Brazil and Chile. The country case studies have been selected to illuminate this central research concern from complementary vantage points. The Brazil case focuses on a specific *party*, the Workers' Party (*Partido dos Trabalhadores* – PT) and the municipal and state (provincial) administrations that it controlled prior to entering national government in 2003, whilst the Chilean case centres on a governmental *institution*, the National Women's Ministry (*Servicio Nacional de la Mujer* – SERNAM). In the first case, we look from the party to the state, examining how one very distinctive political party became a key conduit for feminist policy initiatives and promotion of women's political participation. In the second case, we look in the other direction, from the state to the party system, investigating how SERNAM's gender policies have been bounded and shaped by party competition and the resurgence of the religious–secular ideological cleavage in Chilean politics. I chose these two asymmetrical cases because of the peculiarities and variables offered by the two countries' political and administrative histories. Brazil has a singular new party of the Left in the PT, but a party *system* that is far less institutionalized and differentiated, and individual parties that are organizationally and ideo-logically much weaker than their Chilean counterparts. Conversely, Chile has the continent's most institutionalized state gender policy mechanism, which has resisted party political depredations better than its Brazilian forerunner. To this I add another dimension, comparing the dynamics of party politics and gender policy at both national and sub-national level. Here too, the selection of the case material allows for a view through contrasting optics. Until 2003, the PT had governed only

1

at state and municipal level while the women's movement had simultaneously lost its foothold in central government and was concentrating its efforts through horizontal, decentralized networks, and seeking opportunities in the multiple arenas that a federal system of government offers. In Chile, by contrast, both the political power of the governing centre-left coalition and the policy activities of SERNAM remain highly concentrated in a centralized polity where the pace of decentralization has been glacial. This emphasis on the *spatiality* of gendered politics is one of the key contributions of this study.

The pairing of Brazil and Chile offers both strong parallels and polar contrasts. Both underwent a transition to democracy following a prolonged period of authoritarian rule. Brazilian military government lasted for over 20 years (1964–85), the Pinochet dictatorship in Chile for over 16 years (1973–90). In both countries well-organized and vocal women's movements emerged towards the end of military rule, joining forces with the pro-democracy movement and successfully lobbying the centre-left parties to persuade incoming democratic governments that women's rights should be actively promoted. Both set up governmental units to promote women's rights, but with widely different results. In both, significant left-wing parties played a key role in the democratizing polity, the historic Socialist Party in Chile and the much newer PT, born of the radicalism of the new social movements. On the other hand, Brazil's experience of mass, democratic politics had been severely limited, with a party system in continual flux whilst Chile had a long, and largely stable, constitutional and increasingly democratic history, with parties of considerable longevity. Under military rule party politics was maintained in Brazil, yet abolished in Chile. Brazil underwent a decade-long transition, whilst Chile's hinged on a simple plebiscite. The differences are also geographical and administrative: Brazil is a country of continental dimensions, with a federal system of government that accords a notable degree of administrative, political and fiscal autonomy to local government. The government of Chile's ribbon of territory continues to be concentrated in Santiago, despite an ongoing process of deconcentration. Beyond these factors there are plenty more contrasts of language, history, demographic composition, religion, social attitudes and political culture.

In order to understand how modern Latin American states have shaped gender relations through policy and legislation, feminists must look not only to the bureaucratic arenas and actors of the state, but also to the political ones, especially the political parties. Parties have presented women's movements in the region with both opportunities and obstacles.

They structure political choice through a near-monopoly on representation, mediate societal interests, act as gatekeepers between civil society and the state (both of which they penetrate to differing degrees) and as important filters to new legislation. As such, they form a key element of the institutional-political terrain that feminists and other social groups must negotiate in pursuit of changes in social policy, allocation of state resources, and full political citizenship.

Parties are complex organizations, differentiated by their ideology, ethos, and internal organization. Their behaviour also depends on their sphere of activity, whether focused on internal recruitment and control of members, on elections and wooing voters, on legislative bargaining, or on the bureaucracy of government. In these various arenas parties also generally act *relationally*, seeking both to find allies and to differentiate themselves from competitors. A party's ideology or its chosen course of action in parliament or in government are very often shaped and bounded by the activities of its peers and by the political conjuncture, which may prompt it, for example, to seek new electoral constituencies. All these factors influence the normative conceptions of gender relations that parties develop and express within their internal culture and practices, election manifestos and congressional voting record. This study examines how not just the ideologies, but also the *historical trajectories and organizational practices and cultures* of political parties in Latin America, taken individually and collectively, affect two dependent variables. The first variable is women's participation and representation in political life. It encompasses the conditions under which women have been able to exercise political voice, as voters, members, leaders and elected representatives of the political parties that structure political choice. The second concerns women's movement demands for policies, legislation and state agencies to promote gender equality and equity. Gender equality I define as socio-legal changes within a liberal rights framework, whilst gender equity refers to a distribution of public resources that recognizes *differences* between men's and women's life paths, interests and needs based on reproduction and the current sexual division of labour. These two variables are, of course, interrelated, for the extent and discursive framing of women's agency affect the way in which gender policy is demanded, designed and implemented by the political parties, the women's movement outside the parties, and by the feminist bureaucrats who often form the interface between movement, party and state.

This study is a response, in the first instance, to the notable absence of a gender perspective in the literature on parties, party systems and political-institutional arrangements in the region, which contrasts with the growing and sophisticated academic output in the countries of the geopolitical North.[1] As competitive politics replaced authoritarian regimes and unstable situations of civil conflict and militarized government in the last two decades, political parties came to the fore in political life as never before in Latin America. Neo-institutionalists began to bring back in not just the state, but also the political parties as key actors in this Third Wave of liberal, representative government (Mainwaring and Scully, 1995). If analyses of the 1960s and 1970s had considered many parties to be epiphenomenal, marginal to the greater processes of social change such as revolution, modernization, corporatism, bureaucratic authoritarianism, dependency or populism, parties were now increasingly regarded as vitally important agents of government, governance and citizenship, and stabilizers (or destabilizers) of the new democracies. Whilst parties make a crucial contribution to the process of democratic consolidation by 'shaping the political arena' (Mainwaring and Scully, 1995: 3) in which other actors operate, they are, equally, shaped by the institutional context in which they function. The new wave of interpretation also admits that some party systems have become over- rather than under-institutionalized, that parties may actually crowd out other actors and sectors in society from policymaking, and that ideology often plays a major, rather than a minor, role in party systems and competition. Parties may serve as much to control citizenship, participation, representation and democratic debate as to encourage and promote these undoubted public goods. However, few mainstream works of political science acknowledge the gendered character of political parties in the region and the complex ways in which they stratify political agency. In the past two decades, a literature has burgeoned on individual parties, party 'families'[2] and systems in the region, alongside investigations of other issues of institutional design and performance, such as presidentialism, executive–legislative relations, constitutional revision, and electoral systems. However, if we accept that political institutions are socially embedded, and both reflect and construct social values and behaviours, then we must conclude that a gender-ignorant analysis is an impoverished one as gender relations permeate political structures and processes at both the micro sociological and the macro institutional level.

This work also addresses a lacuna in the literature on the diverse activities of women's groups and movements in Latin America, which touches only tangentially upon political parties. Although the wave of gender quotas that has swept the continent since the mid-1990s has prompted analysis of the impact of the electoral system on women's political representation, scholars have so far largely neglected the internal workings of the individual parties that compete through these electoral systems as well as the interactions between allies and competitors within the party systems.[3] The democratic transitions saw women's groups both excited about the new opportunities to press their claims, and sceptical about the motivations of those parties that took up their banners. The fierce debates between the *autónomas* (independent feminists) and the *políticas* (party women) counterposed the ideal of movement independence against a fear of co-option and invisibility within the parties. As new spaces opened up within government structures, attention switched away from whether the women's movement should be for, in or against the parties, to a focus on how women's claims were negotiated within the state. This prompted a new literature on national women's mechanisms, on the emergence of new 'femocracies' (Watson, 1992), and on the national and regional campaigns to revise constitutional and legal gender norms. This study contends that we can understand a great deal more about how national and sub-national governments handle gender issues when we specifically examine the internal and interactional workings of the political parties that compose or oppose the government, and that act upon and within the state.

Outline of the book

Chapter 1 takes a broad historical and regional overview, considering how political parties and party competition in Latin America have framed and filtered women's claims for political and social rights over more than a century, ranging from the granting of female suffrage, through to the gender quotas of the 1990s, the establishment of national state gender mechanisms, changes in legal norms, and the design of social programmes, at both national and local levels.

The next three chapters examine the case of Brazil. Chapter 2 analyzes the extent of party political influence on women's representation at all levels of political life, on the national-, state- and municipal-level women's councils, and on constitutional and legal reforms. It also highlights how the women's movement has organized in a dense set of policy networks in order to work through and around such a highly permeable party system. Chapter 3 focuses specifically on the PT, its gendered foundations, the evolution of the party programme and approach to gender issues. It explores why and how the PT has promoted more women as candidates and party leaders than any other party in Brazil, spearheaded gender-progressive legislation and revived the national women's unit. Chapter 4 analyzes how the new municipal institutional arrangements have been used by feminists within PT administrations to experiment with new forms of gender policy consultation and mainstreaming. It also contemplates the degree to which the PT's much-vaunted innovations in social participation and justice have extended to gender equity policies and a gendered understanding of the municipality.

The next three chapters deal with the Chilean case. Chapter 5 explores how a highly structured, competitive and differentiated party system has conditioned women's political agency, and examines how Chile's recent history has produced a number of radically opposed projects for polity, society and economy that have frequently sought to mobilize women as a support constituency through state agencies. Chapter 6 traces the development of SERNAM, its relationship to the political parties of both government and opposition, and demonstrates how party political conflict is played out on the terrain of gender relations. Chapter 7 considers the political and bureaucratic obstacles and opportunities that have confronted SERNAM in translating national gender policies to regional and municipal level in a highly vertical administrative system and polity, where new spaces of civic participation have been slow to appear. The concluding chapter pulls the strands together and provides an explicit comparison between the two country case studies along a number of variables.

1
Gendered and Gendering Parties

In order to contextualize the Brazilian and Chilean cases, this chapter surveys the various ways in which Latin America's political parties have shaped the two interlinked dependent variables of this study: women's political participation and the formation of state gender policy. Parties are both *gendered* organizations that reflect the gender ideology of their membership and leaders through their internal culture and practices, and *gendering* institutions that act as gatekeepers, framing, encouraging or restricting women's political agency as party supporters, activists, leaders, candidates and representatives, and (re)producing normative conceptions of gender relations through their electoral campaigns, party policies and legislative activity. Much analysis focuses only on ideology, especially the left–right axis, whereas I propose closer attention to three overlooked independent variables: the *intersection* of the left–right cleavage with the secular-religious one in the region's party systems; the *gendered political habitus* that develops within individual parties and how this is sustained by practices of gendered political *sociability*; and the *type* as well as the degree of party institutionalization. These variables, in combination, determine the *permeability* of individual parties and party systems to gender issues.

The chapter begins by examining how parties constitute a keystone of a gendered regime of representation, which is understood as a set of electoral, party and governance systems that varies from country to country and produces specific outcomes in terms of women and men's differentiated access to political voice and power. It then analyzes the ways in which party interests and ideology have influenced state gender policy, and concludes by considering the conduct of parties in the municipal arena, a terrain that has been posited as being, at least in theory, more conducive to women's political agency and progressive social policy.

7

Ideology and party system cleavages

Political parties do not generally exist in isolation; they are born, operate and mutate in the electoral and legislative arenas within a party *system*, which is itself formed to a degree in response to social and political cleavages. In Latin America these have included rural–urban, authoritarian–democratic, secular–clerical, and left–right divisions – the last two the most enduring (Coppedge, 1997). Parties develop their ideological alignment and policy positions partly in relation to external referents, making them members of a particular political family,[1] and partly in dynamic relation to their rivals, as Downs' model of spatial competition suggests (Downs, 1957). Both these underlying cleavages and conjunctural factors influence whether or not the parties differentiate themselves using gendered political discourse, styles of representation or distinct policy platforms. Indeed, Lipset and Rokkan's 1967 account of European social cleavages identified sex differences as one of the factors impinging on party politics conducted through electoral competition. The *intersection* of the left–right and religious–secular cleavages helps to explain when, how and why parties deploy gender-ideological discourses for the purposes of both party system competition and their social and economic projects. The left–right cleavage is less likely to generate evidently gendered contests than the religious–secular one, given the focus on class and capital. Modernizing, secular conservative parties also have primarily economic concerns and are much less concerned with confining women within strict gender roles than are traditionalist, semi-confessional parties. Cleavages hinging on moral values invariably invoke gender relations through an emphasis on sexuality and the family. Whilst the left–right cleavage has faded, the secular–religious one has been enjoying a resurgence in Latin America, possibly precisely because of the constraints that hegemonic neo-liberalism places on economic policymakers of all hues, leaving politicians looking for new political markers.

Gendered political habitus and sociability

But ideology is not everything. Party histories and organizational development are equally, if not more, important factors. Panebianco's (1988) foundational thesis argues that a party's culture and organizational practices can be traced back to the particular circumstances attending its genesis, such as its original political orientation and social base. These historical continuities persist even when parties make ideological adjustments in reaction to external circumstances and realignments in the party system.

This book argues that a party's attitude to women's political agency and to gender relations derives from a number of originating factors such as the proportion of women among the party's founders and the strength of the party's base (voters, activists) in civil society organizations in which women play a numerically important role. Such factors create a *gendered political habitus* that may be understood, borrowing from Bourdieu, as a conditioning, ideational environment that creates a structural propensity to think and act in predetermined ways. Political parties occupy this wider universe of shared values that are hard, cognitively, to question – for example, the view that women constitute 'unnatural' political actors. These values in turn produce exclusionary institutional practices, such as holding meetings at times, in locales and in a manner that precludes women's participation. As Panebianco (1988: 4) notes 'the party itself is a producer of inequalities within its own structure'. However, within this universe parties are individuated, each differing from its domestic rivals and from the other members of their ideological 'family group' in its interpretation of this habitus as a result of particular institutional histories rooted in space and time. Thus Panebianco's path dependency and the structural aspects of habitus are not wholly deterministic; parties retain agency to react to demands for change made from outside or inside the party, such as those made by feminists. It does, however, help explain the slowness and unevenness of their responses, as well as gendered patterns of recruitment and even of electoral preference.

The particular habitus of each party is sustained by a political sociability that socializes new entrants and excludes those who do not conform to its practices. This sociability is employed in this study to denote a bond of party political common identity and belonging that derives from shared – and inevitably gendered – life experiences, identities, discourses and practices of association forged in specific social contexts and locations. For example, women found that their struggle for a presence within traditional socialist and social democratic parties often collided with the logic of an andro-centric party culture that privileged trade union and strike militancy over community activities as forms of political action, and often saw women as less appealing candidates for a largely male and manual-labouring electoral base. Even within an ideological grouping such as the Left, party origins and development generate visibly different organizational cultures; compare El Salvador's Farabundo Martí National Liberation Front (*Frente Farabundo Martí de Liberación Nacional* – FMLN) (armed struggle), Nicaragua's Sandinista National Liberation Front (*Frente Sandinista de Liberación Nacional* – FSLN) (armed struggle then revolutionary party of government), Uruguay's Broad Front (*Frente Amplio* – FA) (breakdown of two-party dominant rule), Chile's Socialist Party (organized labour movement) and Party for Democracy (*Partido por la Democracia* – PPD) (instrumental transition party), and Brazil's PT (labour and popular movements, in a party-led transition). This diversity affects the relationship between the party leadership, rank-and-file and wider political constituencies, all of which have gendered aspects. For instance, the FSLN and FMLN, as former guerrilla movements, developed a militaristic internal culture where bearing arms became the measure of leadership, thus effectively excluding many women activists. However, these previously closed bastions of homosociality are now being prised open through the introduction of new institutional rules, such as gender quotas, resulting in left-wing parties generally selecting and electing more women representatives.

The *forms* of internal party organization – the relationship between leadership and adherents, vertical or horizontal structures – also contribute towards creating distinct forms of political sociability, which in turn produce diverse modalities of women's incorporation. Many Latin American parties are what Duverger terms 'caucus' formations, splinter groups created by those already in power, whilst others are electoral-professional parties with little ideological definition. Communist, or Communist-style, parties tend to be vertically organized, hierarchical and cadre-led (for example, the FSLN and the Cuban Communist Party), whilst the older social democratic parties tend more towards the mass bureaucratic model built on pillars of organized interest group representation. Some parties are bureaucratized (the dominant parties in Chile, Uruguay, and Venezuela before the 1990s) whilst others, especially the more populist, present themselves as organic 'movements' operating with diffuse, horizontal networks, such as the Argentine Peronist Party (*Partido Justicialista* – PJ), and Venezuela's Fifth Republic Movement (*Movimiento Quinta República* – MVR). On the Left alone, some parties are highly unified (classically, Communist parties) whilst newer parties such as the PPD, PT, FA and Mexico's Party of Democratic Revolution (*Partido de la Revolución Democrática* – PRD) were born of broad coalitions and, in consequence, their degree of ideological and organizational coherence varies enormously. Factionalism, whether focused on personalist or power struggles or on ideological differences, creates an additional layer of internal competition for female political entrepreneurs to negotiate. Parties can also reflect the organizational features of the civil society groups that form their social base (socialist parties and unions, Christian Democratic parties and the Catholic Church, conservative parties and business interests) and in so doing, reflect the gender composition and attitudes of those bodies.

Degree and type of institutionalization

This study also hypothesizes that the intensity and type of party institutionalization matters, for reasons related both to the electoral system and to the character of the party system. I suggest that overly institutionalized party systems,[2] where parties penetrate all aspects of political life, dominate the channels of representation and make the cost to new entrants very high. It seems that under-institutionalized parties and party systems are more permeable – for example, to gender quota demands.

Sartori's measure of party system fragmentation is relevant here, as two- to three-party systems have tended to be stable to the point of over-institutionalization (Schedler, 1995), creating frustration among those excluded from the power-sharing arrangement (Uruguay, Colombia and Venezuela).

Individual parties may also be measured on an institutionalization scale. The Argentine Peronist Party is informally organized and weakly routinized, lacks a central authority structure, effective bureaucracy and stable internal rules and is therefore lacking in vertical institutionalization (Levitsky, 2003: 58). However, it has deep roots in society, with loyalty and votes fostered through its complex and fluid networks of base units, giving it powerful *horizontal* institutionalization. Conversely, strong vertical but weak horizontal institutionalization characterizes many centralized, electoral-professional parties. Some mass bureaucratic parties such as Venezuela's Democratic Action (*Acción Democrática* – AD) and Christian Democratic Party (COPEI) were strongly, perhaps excessively, institutionalized on both dimensions, creating a partyarchy that penetrated civil society to the point of suffocation, either co-opting groups, such as unions, or marginalizing them, in the case of women. I hypothesize that strong, but fluid, horizontal institutionalization is more conducive to the entry of women leaders at the base, but that strong vertical institutionalization, once the masculinized party habitus has been counteracted by new internal rules, such as a gender quota or creation of leadership posts, is eventually more propitious to women achieving lasting and effective influence on the party's gender policies.

Gender and political voice

How, in concrete terms, have women come to experience entry, voice and loyalty within the polities of the region? Comparative data show that the *Supermadre* ('supermother') argument (Chaney, 1979), whereby Latin American women have justified their entry into the public sphere by claiming to be the bearers of feminine, maternal qualities imported from the private, domestic sphere, is not universally valid. Activists and parties have additionally deployed other arguments such as democratic rights, the expansion of the talent pool, substantive interest representation, and the fairness of adequate descriptive representation. Moreover, discourses of 'politicized motherhood' mask the contribution that parties, gendered regimes of representation, and political history and culture have made to framing women's political agency within quite diverse party systems.

Women's suffrage

Debates over women's political rights began in Latin America as early as the mid-nineteenth century, yet it was not until 1961 that the female franchise was extended in the final country of the region, Paraguay. Party politics were incidental in countries where autocratic rulers such as Martínez in El Salvador (1932–44) and Odría in Peru (1948–56) granted women's suffrage in the hope of some personal advantage, or where parties were absent, extremely weak, fragmented, or co-opted (Brazil, Paraguay). In most cases, however, female franchise was conceded at moments of party political realignment. The ordering of politics through parties from the early nineteenth century onwards meant the very nature of party political competition – including the degree of party fragmentation and the character of the political cleavages – had a direct bearing on the timing, framing and sequencing of women's suffrage, with parties often contradicting their ideological position under the imperative of electoral competition.

The major post-independence political cleavage, between State and Church, generated a paradox. Although Latin American conservative parties were strongly associated with Catholic Church social values, they were also republican and engaged in the electoral arena; therefore new political constituencies were a valuable commodity. Thus, in Chile, Colombia, Uruguay, Nicaragua and Ecuador they ended up supporting legislation for women's suffrage as a necessary evil to stem the electoral advance of their secularizing Liberal Party rivals. They also heeded and appropriated arguments deployed by suffragists and the Church that women would use their spiritual superiority to moralize the 'dirty business' of politics. Although the Colombian Conservatives had vehemently opposed Liberal proposals to grant female suffrage, it was approved in a populist move by the dictator Rojas Pinilla (1953–7) after the wave of violence that exploded in 1948, as he considered that women would exercise a pacifying and civilizing maternal influence on a troubled polity (Luna, 2001).

The labour-based, socialist and progressive anti-clerical parties such as AD, Peru's American Popular Revolutionary Alliance (*Alianza Popular Revolucionaria Americana* – APRA), the Chilean Socialist and Radical parties, and Mexico's Institutional Revolutionary Party (*Partido Revolucionario Institucional* – PRI) were, as the Liberal parties, ideologically inclined towards female suffrage but nervous of clerical influence and the damage that women's political preferences might inflict on their electoral fortunes. Some eventually passed suffrage laws, but only after decades of campaigning and lobbying on the part of women. In a dominant-party system such as Mexico's, the PRI did not require women's votes to stay in power, and dragged its feet on the issue until the 1950s, despite Cárdenas's attempt to push through a women's suffrage bill in the 1930s.

Parties formed at moments of major party system realignment, such as the regional wave of democratization in the late 1940s, immediately courted women as an 'uncaptured' constituency. In Costa Rica, José Figueres Ferrer, founder of the National Liberation Party (*Partido de Liberación Nacional* – PLN), granted female suffrage at the end of the civil war in 1948, just after the Argentine Peronists had seized a similar opportunity left open by that country's Radical and Socialist parties. Both subsequently made women and workers central pillars of their electoral and social dominance, maintaining women as a core constituency through the enactment of quota laws, state institutions and social policies (Saint-Germain and Morgan, 1991). Semi-authoritarian parties or anti-party populist rulers of ambiguous ideological orientation, such as Perón in Argentina, Fujimori in Peru, Chávez in Venezuela, and the Somoza clan (González, 2001) that ran Nicaragua as a private fiefdom for 40 years, were adept at reaping the electoral benefits of women's continuing alienation from traditional labour-based parties and their more floating political loyalties.

'Ant's work': women inside the parties

Even before they won the vote, women were active within political parties with a few, such as Magda Portal (secretary-general of APRA) and Alicia Moreau (head of the Argentine Socialist Party), emerging as leaders. Some suffragists set up their own, short-lived parties to highlight women's marginal position within the political mainstream. However, female activists consistently found themselves relegated to the women's department whose primary purpose the centre-left parties regarded as recruitment, and the Right as a *cordon sanitaire* between the nation's women and the contaminating influence of masculine political activity. Some parties, such as the PRI and Bolivia's Nationalist Revolutionary Movement

(*Movimiento Nacionalista Revolucionario* – MNR), did not regard women as a relevant social category, or were suspicious of their political preferences, and subsumed them within the grassroots sectors. Women also found it very hard to exercise much agency within the rigid, formalized and impermeable structures of highly centralized parties such as those of Venezuela's partyarchy, which engulfed a previously active women's movement within low-status party bureaux (Friedman, 2000a).

Several parties, all labour-based but varying in ideological orientation, such as the PRI, Peronists, AD and COPEI, and Chile's Christian Democrats, adopted strongly corporatist or Leninist models of internal organization that mirrored the strategies employed to incorporate key social sectors – peasants, labour, and grassroots organizations – into hierarchical state-society relations once the party reached power. This type of organization tended to achieve high levels of penetration into society and party identification, and blurred the line between party and state in countries with hegemonic parties. Party women's organizations, such as the Federation of Cuban Women and the Nicaraguan Luisa Amanda Espinoza Women's Association (AMNLAE), combined various functions as tools of state sectoral policymaking, pillars of the national revolutionary project, and as a conduit for party-political recruitment, much as labour ministries did for working-class men. The Peronists even formed a parallel Women's Party, whose purpose was to recruit new members, bring out the vote, transmit Peronist ideology, and provide income generation, welfare, and cultural and educational services to local women (Bianchi and Sanchis, 1988); it is easy to see the relevance of Panebianco's 'genetic' interpretation of current party formations as a function of a party's organizational history. The party that gave women suffrage and established the continent's first unilateral party gender quota (candidacies were allocated equally to each of the three pillars of the 'movement') instituted the first statutory gender quota four decades later. However, in recent years the traditional women's departments have increasingly been criticized as reproducing a gendered division of labour within political institutions, and many have been replaced or supplemented with technical departments aimed at providing a forum for women to articulate their collective interests and inject a gender perspective into the party manifesto.

Gender and representation

Levels of women's representation in elected office remained very low in the postwar period, with the notable exception of Argentina under the

Peronists in the 1950s and the Cuban Communist Party,[3] rising only in the early 1970s in the Southern Cone. During the following years of prolonged authoritarian rule or civil conflict, the political arena became feminized by a variety of women's groups engaged in pro-democracy protests, countering repression and economic crisis, and keeping alight the flame of outlawed political parties. However, the return to democracy saw *lo político*, the traditional political society dominated by men, crowd out *lo social*, the domain of women, social movements and civil society. Transition in Chile, Argentina and Uruguay brought about a restoration of the historic political parties, and a remasculinization of national politics as male politicians returned from exile to their 'rightful' places; in the first post-transition elections Argentina elected only 4.3 per cent women deputies and Uruguay none. This prompted women to pay more attention to institutional arrangements and press for space within the parties in the 1990s (Waylen, 2003); by 2004, Latin America had an average 18.5 per cent female representation in national legislatures, just above the world average.[4] However, this aggregate figure hides significant variations resulting from both institutional differences in regimes of representation and party-level variables. For example, Costa Rica led the region with 35.1 per cent, whilst some of its Central American neighbours barely topped 10 per cent.

Electoral system

Political parties are both fashioned by, and act upon, the electoral system, which in turn creates incentives and constraints for the ideological positioning of parties, coalition formation, campaign conduct, female candidate selection and promotion, and the translation of voter preferences into the distribution of seats. The rise in women's representation was mainly produced by the quota laws of the 1990s, spearheaded by Argentina in 1991 and inspired by European experiences and the diffusion of the recommendations of international rights-based organizations through regional feminist networks (Htun and Jones, 2002). Latin American countries have generally opted not for the reserved legislative seats quota common in Asia and Africa, which guarantees women a percentage of seats, but rather for statutory legislation requiring all parties to reserve a minimum percentage of places, generally between 20 and 40 per cent, for women – or, in some cases, both sexes – on candidate lists. Some leftist parties have followed the predominant European model by voluntarily imposing unilateral quotas for their lists where there is no statutory legislation, or have reserved seats on their governing bodies, giving women more visibility and status, and thus greater likelihood of being selected as candidates or backed by the leadership in the party primaries. After Mexico's PRD adopted its leadership and candidate quotas in 1993, it elected proportionately more women to Congress than any other party. Parties backed these quotas for a diversity of reasons. In Argentina, the quota bill was introduced by a Radical senator but passed under a Peronist government, with both parties eyeing women voters, whilst in Costa Rica positive discrimination measures were promoted by the PLN, a party long associated with liberal modernization and social justice. Despite the absence of statutory quotas in the peace accords, levels of women's representation rose higher in El Salvador and Nicaragua than in Honduras or Guatemala primarily because the two former revolutionary parties adopted unilateral party quotas (FSLN 30 per cent and FMLN 35 per cent) in response to demands by their own women activists. Parties with a unilateral quota for candidate lists or leadership positions also exerted a contagion effect on national legislation (Costa Rica and Brazil) and on their rivals, for example in Mexico from the PRD to the PRI to the conservative National Action Party (*Partido Acción Nacional* – PAN) (Bruhn, 2003).

Nonetheless, some countries (Uruguay, Chile, Honduras, Guatemala, Venezuela and Colombia) still have no statutory party quotas due to opposition from the main political parties or from the electoral or constitutional courts. The longevity and vertically institutionalized character of the dominant parties makes them resistant to claims to representation by 'outsider' groups. It can also be very difficult to apply a quota to electoral systems such as Uruguay's, with its notoriously complex system of multiple sub-lists which creates intense intra-party competition and fragmentation. Party factionalism, when expressed formally in the sub-lists of Uruguay and the Argentine provinces, or informally in the allocation of winnable seats, effectively reduces the party magnitude (number of seats won in a district) and thus hinders the application of any quota.

These quota systems have brought mixed results due to the variations in the type of electoral systems and key details of institutional design (Htun and Jones, 2002). Closed-list proportional representation systems, with reasonable party and district magnitude (number of seats per district), a placement mandate in law (male and female candidates proportionally interspersed throughout the list), and mechanisms of enforcement, provide the ideal conditions for a statutory quota to translate directly into equivalent representation, which has occurred only in Argentina and Costa Rica (Rule and Zimmerman, 1994; Norris, 2004).

Female success index

The percentage of women that a party runs or elects in relation to its competitors is only one part of the story. Whilst the most effective statutory quotas eliminate male bias within parties in relation to candidate selection and promotion, in majoritarian elections or in open-list proportional systems, where voters can express a preference for an individual, party variables still affect the fate of female candidates. Gendered party cultures and sociability, the mode of selection (by decentralized party primaries or party hierarchy), the status of incumbents, the allocation of electoral resources and training among candidates, and the personal resources that candidates themselves bring can all affect the relative success rates of female and male candidates in a given party, a measure I term the *female success index* (FSI). The argument formerly employed by parties, that a low FSI was due to women's 'unelectability', is invalidated by recent opinion polls showing that voters now exhibit higher levels of trust in women politicians whom, for a number of reasons, they rate as more trustworthy, honest, competent, strong-minded, capable and responsible than men (Inter-American Dialogue, 2001). Institutional arrangements can combine with underlying sociological factors to produce gendered differences in political performance. For instance, women in the Costa Rican assembly reap much higher public approval ratings than their male counterparts as their bills enjoy double the success rate (81 per cent), which they themselves attribute to spending more time in committee and consultation. As Costa Rican legislators may not run for immediate re-election, male deputies dedicate time to tending their business and professional interests to which they will return, whereas the women treat politics as their sole occupation (Furlong and Riggs, 1999). Quotas are often not enough to overcome these differences and Costa Rica's Law of Women's Social Equality prompted the PLN to allocate 10 per cent of its public funding to encouraging women's political participation.

The party politics of gender policy

The last 25 years have seen an engagement of women's movements with the state witnessed previously only in the early decades of the twentieth century. The state, as a collection of institutions, practices and regulations, both produces and reproduces gender relations in many dimensions. Since colonial times in Latin America, legal codes and constitutions have set out men and women's differentiated juridical capacity, and levels of autonomy, responsibilities and rights in relation to property, family, marital relations, work, education and political voice. The new republics of the nineteenth century viewed the family as the lynchpin of their nation- and state-building projects. Embedded in, and identified with, the family, women performed key roles in the biological and social reproduction of human resources and new social values. In consequence, they became the target of state policies disciplining their domestic labour, reproductive choices, work outside the home and contribution to the social fabric, whatever the dominant ideology of the day. The fundamental political cleavage of the post-independence era – religion versus secularism – left its stamp in the penal and civil code provisions on divorce, reproductive rights, morality and sexuality. Similarly, the corporatist regimes that emerged as a result of the subsequent political cleavage between labour and capital left their imprint on the region's labour codes. But where gender policy was once the preserve of bureaucrats, now the demands of the organized women's movement are filtered through the lens of party political ideology and electoral competition. This section explores how party politics affects the establishment of gender policy units, and the introduction of constitutional and legislative reforms, whether these are *gender-progressive* (strategic, questioning the dominant division of labour and traditional gender socialization), *gender-static* (not questioning, but allowing practical gender needs to be met), or *gender-regressive* (actively challenging elements of the international gender rights regime).

State gender policy units

Since the 1970s, the United Nations has urged countries to set up national mechanisms for the advancement of women. In 1974, Costa Rica's PLN government established the Office of Programmes for Women and the Family within the Ministry of Culture, Youth and Sport and by 1999 every Latin American country had some national unit, many aimed at gender mainstreaming – that is, a cross-sectoral approach to integrating gender equity and equality concerns into all areas of public policy. Whilst in some cases the gender unit was the president's initiative, a means of signalling integration into international development practice and norms, in many others it resulted from the women's movement seizing a specific political opportunity, such as a democratic transition, to influence those parties coming into power. The political support and institutional resources the units receive, the degree of instrumentalization, and the orientation of their policies have been determined by aspects of the political environment, such as the party of government's ideological inclinations and degree of penetration of the state and civil society, the intensity and character of party competition, state capacity, and the degree of leverage that the women's movement can exert on the state and the party system.

Some parties have been receptive to a broadly feminist agenda in order to attract women voters and project an image of modernity. Those whose banner was one of profound social transformation – nineteenth-century liberals, *batllismo* in early twentieth-century Uruguay, revolutionary nationalism in Mexico, Socialist, Christian Democratic and Catholic integralist parties – have envisioned women either as diffusers of the new values or, in the case of reactionaries and conservatives, defenders of a tradition based on fixed sex-gender roles and social harmony. Others have been indifferent or had other priorities, such as socialist or revolutionary parties that interpreted gender claims as 'competing' with other oppression frameworks such as race and class, or with the 'defence of the revolution' (Cuba, Nicaragua and Mexico). The Left's gender policies have often been restrictively framed by notions of class interest, ignoring the issues that affect women in their everyday lives. In so doing they further alienated women voters, to whom the right-wing and Christian Democratic parties spoke much more effectively (Power, 2002). These different approaches correlate with what Htun (2003) calls the four normative traditions of gender and the state in Latin America – feminism, liberalism, Roman Catholicism and socialism. As a result, some state mechanisms are oriented towards welfare work with the family – only tackling women's practical gender needs within the current sexual division of labour and gender relations – whilst others attempt more structural changes.

Ideally, national women's mechanisms should be institutionally insulated from the influence of the governing party or president, electoral interests and changes of government. Some governments have adopted a gender agenda for quite cynical political motives. Whilst Fujimori (1990–2000) undermined Peru's democratic institutions, he appointed a record number of women ministers and senior bureaucrats, set up a gender department within the Ministry of Women and Human Development, a Parliamentary Women's Commission, a women's ombudsman and a ministerial advisory committee, passed legislation against gender violence, contracted out projects to feminist non-governmental organizations (NGOs) and confronted the Church hierarchy over its birth control programmes in order to project a radical, modernizing image (Blondet, 2002). Others, especially in party systems that are weakly ideological, have deactivated women's ministries, legally or through savage resources cuts, for fiscal or political reasons. However, in more polarized party systems, the women's unit may become a highly politicized and divisive battleground in party political struggles not just over women's votes but also over competing, and often totalizing, visions of the 'good society' and desirable sex-gender roles.

The Uruguayan National Women's Institute was established in 1987 by the liberal Colorado Party with a broad remit to co-ordinate policy, but was effectively deactivated for two years after the more conservative National Party took power in 1990, and recreated as the National Institute for the *Family* and Women. Until the re-election of the Colorados in 1995, it stopped functioning as an inter-ministerial council, and lost both its budget and its close ties to the generally left-leaning women's NGOs (Johnson, 2002: 105). The predecessors of Venezuela's National Institute for Women (INAMUJER) were also affected by shifting party, gender and developmental ideologies due to AD and COPEI's alternation in power (Friedman, 2000a). Since Chávez co-opted it into his national project of 'Bolivarian Revolution', women's organizations have become increasing vocal on both sides of the political divide, and such politicization may fatally discredit the agency.

Institutional location matters, both to enable the women's unit to promote gender mainstreaming effectively, and to avoid political contamination. However, the behaviour of the political leadership also gives out strong signals about the status and party politicization of these units. In 1985, Argentina's new democratic president, Alfonsín, set up a sub-secretariat for women within the Ministry of Health and Social Action, alongside parallel units for youth and for the elderly, disabled and children. Closely associated with his person, it did not survive his presidency. Its successor, the National Women's Council, established in 1992 in the president's office during Menem's Peronist government, initially received substantial support and funding until conflict over the United Nations (UN) Fourth World Conference on Women in Beijing led him to punish it through the imposition of draconian cuts in budget and mandate (Waylen, 2000). Similarly, Mexico's first national women's unit was set up under PRI President Zedillo in 1996. Although his successor, PAN President Fox, kept his promise to upgrade the unit, giving it more autonomy and a tenfold increase in its budget, its board was soon dominated by *panista* women, its appointed head a woman supported by an anti-abortion group, with a discourse reflecting the Catholic social conservatism of the governing party. In short, proximity to the president is a double-edged sword; it opens access to power, but also increases the likelihood of co-option and excessive identification with an individual or party.

Constitutional and legislative change

The 1979 UN Convention on the Elimination of all Forms of Discrimination Against Women (CEDAW) and the 1995 Beijing Conference's Platform for Action gave both the impetus and a blueprint to renewed judicial mobilization on the part of women's movements to remove anachronistic and discriminatory provisions from national (and subnational) constitutions and legal codes, and improve women's political, sexual reproductive, labour, family and human rights. Constitutions set out the definition of citizenship, the relationship between state and citizen, and the boundaries between private and public sphere. They are also regime markers, signalling a normative break with the preceding regime, with constitutional revision a key issue in political transitions. As a result, women's movements have lobbied to insert articles that explicitly outlaw sexual discrimination and extend women's rights. Often, mobilization around the drafting of a new constitution has marked a high point of networking and common cause amongst women's groups, which manage to elect to the constitutional assemblies a notable number of movement representatives, for example in Nicaragua (1985–6), Brazil (1987–8), Paraguay (1992), and Ecuador (1997–8). These are key junctures where the monopoly of political parties over representation relaxes and access expands for non-traditional political actors.

A huge amount of ordinary legislation has also been passed. Most countries now possess some form of electoral gender quota. Labour codes have been reformed to remove discriminatory prohibitions on women's work in particular situations, to define and outlaw sexual harassment, to give pregnant women and lactating mothers enhanced labour rights, and to prevent sex discrimination through unequal pay and intrusive investigation into women's reproductive history. Civil codes have been rewritten to restore full legal powers and rights to married women, both over their property and their children, and to protect women and their dependents in the case of divorce, widowhood or denial of paternity. The definition of sexual crimes has been rewritten in penal codes to make them offences against personal physical freedom and integrity rather than against public morals, and to eradicate all judgements on the victim's sexual history or honour. The region also produced its own legally binding statement of the state's responsibility in relation to domestic violence, in the 1994 Belém do Pará Inter-American Convention on the Prevention, Punishment and Eradication of Violence against Women. In national law, domestic violence has either been designated as a specific crime or else directed into advice and welfare centres, special police stations, and courts.

Dynamics of gender policy reform

Women's movements have also drawn on international gender norms as a strategic and discursive tool with which to disarm their domestic opponents. Although the region presents an apparent homogeneity in terms of the legal reforms undertaken, the local party political environment refracts and filters these transnational gender norms and affects how they are interpreted and applied. For instance, Uruguay is one of the few countries without an Equal Opportunities Plan because of the indifference of the historically hegemonic parties to all affirmative action proposals, including gender quotas. In the case of domestic violence, there appears to be a strong correlation between countries where the Catholic Church exerts strong influence on political parties, such as Chile and Peru, and the introduction of compulsory conciliation procedures that placed family unity above an individual woman's right to integrity.

The 're-clericalization' of politics in some Latin American countries has had clear implications for the terms of the debate surrounding gender issues (Blofield, 2001). After the assumption of John Paul II to the papacy in 1979, the Vatican took an aggressive stance on private sphere issues, and was supported in international arenas by a significant number of Latin American countries where conservative forces, such as Nicaragua's Liberal Party and El Salvador's Nationalist Republican Alliance (*Alianza Republicana Nacionalista* – ARENA), used reproductive rights and sexual mores to regain the moral high ground they had lost through their association with repressive regimes and corruption. At the 1994 Cairo International Conference on Population and Development, the Vatican and nine Latin American countries bracketed references in the Programme for Action referring to reproductive rights, sex education, abortion, contraception, the definition of the family and safe motherhood. A Papal communication sent to political leaders in advance of the Beijing conference contained arguments later rehearsed by several country delegations during the conference itself, with Argentina and Guatemala the Vatican's most vocal proxies (Franco, 1998). They objected to the *language* of the text, specifically to the terms 'gender', 'families' in the plural and 'reproductive rights', as if they felt that in eradicating the terminology, they could erase the social phenomena.[5] The anti-feminist backlash has seen conservative legislators take advantage of the widespread revision of legal texts to *retrench* gender discrimination, particularly around reproductive rights, which remain highly contentious. In a number of countries, attempts have been made to nullify existing provision for legal abortion[6] by changing the text of the Constitution, adding the words 'from the moment of conception' to the article guaranteeing the right to life. President Menem attempted to change the Argentine Constitution (in 1993) and Article 15 of the Civil Code (in 1999) to this effect. In January 1998, legislators in El Salvador succeeded in criminalizing all terminations, and altered the constitutional text accordingly the following year.[7] Guatemala, Nicaragua and Costa Rica all gave official status to the Day of the Unborn, whilst El Salvador's and Panama's legislators refused to sign the Optional Protocol to the CEDAW, arguing that it could facilitate abortion.[8]

The dynamics of legislating on gender issues are complex. Bills may be put forward by diverse executive bodies – such as the general ministries, the designated government mechanism for promoting women's equality, the president's office, even the president's wife – or by the legislature – whether by an individual deputy, a coalition of women deputies, a single party or coalition of parties, or the government or opposition benches. All of these variables determine the degree of support a bill will receive and the speed of its passage. For example, Costa Rica's gender quota proposals, sponsored by the 1986–90 PLN government, passed into law six years later, only after that party returned to power.

Some proponents of gender quotas advance a 'critical mass' argument that the more women are elected, the more likely they are to represent 'women's interests' and join together to push for key gender reforms. At the very least, they provide women's movements with a lobbying focus. There is something to be said for the politics of presence; Honduras's Equal Opportunities Law created a furore when male legislators passed it in substantially modified form[9] whilst their female colleagues were absent at a meeting of Central American parliamentarians (Clulow, 2003a). The same argument has prompted a rise in women in national government posts. In 2000, Costa Rica had five women ministers (30 per cent), whilst one-quarter of Colombia, El Salvador and Panama's cabinets were female.

However, the ease with which women legislators act individually and collectively on gender issues depends both on their individual profiles (party and grassroots activism, family ties), on the intensity of ideological conflicts, on whether gender issues form part of the core political cleavages in the party system and, finally, on the ability of organized women's movements to target legislators with clear reform proposals.

Where moral questions are highly party politicized, women legislators may adopt opposing views on issues such as reproductive rights. Conversely, in party systems that are weakly ideological, have a weak religious–secular cleavage, or are composed of parties driven more by personalism or rent-seeking, parties and politicians may be relatively malleable. In these cases, a well-organized women's movement in conjunction with a sympathetic party can set the legislative gender agenda, and legislators of different political stripes will have a higher propensity to collaborate on gender issues. However, in the absence of such agenda-setters, joint action is unlikely. For example, in Bolivia, a quota law raised the percentage of women deputies from 7.6 per cent in 1993 to 21.5 per cent in 2003, but the new women legislators have not coalesced as a group and prioritized gender issues (Costa Benavides, 2003).

In other cases, temporary coalitions form between women legislators around very specific issues on which there are no major divergences for, as Molyneux (2001) notes, the formulation of women's interests is highly context-specific. In the post-conflict situation in Central America, women's cross-party coalitions might have seemed unlikely because of the bitter ideological divisions of the civil wars. Yet, following the peace process in El Salvador, feminists managed to win the support of right-wing women on several issues such as gender quotas, responsible paternity and domestic violence, but not on abortion or economic rights (Hipsher, 2001: 150). Radical feminists, leftist and conservative women in Nicaragua came together in the 1996 National Women's Coalition to support women's candidacies and to agree upon a Minimum Agenda to be incorporated into the party platforms for the forthcoming elections (Blandón, 2001).

Although in Mexico and Argentina, where the two main parties are decades-long rivals, 'party loyalty frequently trumps gender identity' (Rodríguez, 1998: 8; Htun and Jones, 2002: 49), coalitions can still occur in highly institutionalized or divided party systems at particular junctures, such as transition to democracy (Uruguay, El Salvador), the writing of a new constitution, or the preparation process for international events. Costa Rica's bill on Women's Social Equality prompted representatives of the main two parties to work closely in a women's caucus, producing a raft of gender-progressive legislation (Figueres, 1998). It has also been argued that partyarchy squeezes to the margins women who then cast themselves as interlopers in the political system, impelling them to build broad coalitions outside the parties; for example, for reform of the Venezuelan Labour code (Friedman, 2002) and even, in the Chilean case, for regime change (Baldez, 2002). As Friedman (1998) points out, political opportunities are not gender-neutral, and political parties play a key role in the gendering of those conjunctures.

Together, the growing number of women legislators, feminist staff in the national and sub-national gender units, and organized women's groups form a potentially effective policy community through which to lobby both the parties and the state for gender-progressive policy and legislation (Watson, 1992). The tensions between the *políticas* and *autónomas* that were so marked at the time of transition have diminished. However, as so many feminists have moved into the state in various ways – into elected office, bureaucracy, and NGO service-providers – the relationship between the women's movement, the parties and the state requires constant renegotiation to maintain the balance between representation, effective mainstreaming within the state apparatus, and the strengthening of women's political claims.

A woman's place? Local government

So far, this chapter has examined the gendered dimensions of *whom* parties recruit as their electorate, leaders and representatives, and of *what* kinds of gender policies parties promote in government. We now turn to the gendered aspects of *where* party politics and policymaking are conducted. The actors, the interests at stake, the resources mobilized, and the patterns of political behaviour involved in politics and policy-making at local, national and international levels differ, and are inevitably place-sensitive and differently gendered as a result. This has been intensified by the decentralization process that has accompanied the consolidation of democracy in several countries.

Parties are spatially organized institutions, operating in distinct ways in a variety of arenas. This section considers how parties contribute to the gendering of the municipal arena through their ideology, organizational structures, permeability to local women's movements, modes of electoral competition and recruitment, and approaches to social policy. Gender relations are also constructed in specific places and spaces. Political discourses are structured around mental mappings of a topography of power, of a conflictive and contested masculine political arena versus the feminine safe haven of the private. The masculine political agent has historically been constructed as acting in the national political, public sphere, associated with macro-level issues of economy, state and nation. The feminine political subject, by contrast, has been framed as an actor within the social, local and private sphere, associated with home, neighbourhood, and the micro-management and reproduction of human capital and social values. These gendered spatial oppositions have proven to be enduring, from the suffrage movements of the early twentieth century to the new policy prescription of decentralization at the end of the century. An elective affinity between municipal government and women's agency has been proposed from a variety of perspectives – conservative, feminist and development-oriented – that invoke women as more caring, pragmatic and honest political actors, due to the proximity of both women and municipal government to the local community, a view that chimes with the regional cultural tropes of marianism[10] and complementarity but for which there is scant empirical evidence.

Political voice in the municipality

This association between the municipality and women's political agency was both reflected and reinforced by the decision of parties in some countries to introduce female suffrage in two stages, for fear of its social, moral and electoral consequences. In the municipal sphere, women could be protected from the malign, contaminating influence of national, masculine politics, whilst simultaneously producing a civilizing effect on local governance. Radical, secular and socialist parties were persuaded to grant municipal enfranchisement in Chile (1931), Peru (1933), and Mexico (1947), as a necessary and educational 'stage' that would offset the electoral advantage that women brought to Catholic and Conservative parties, and allow women to 'catch up' with men in their education and political consciousness.[11] Changes in the electorate also forced parties to reconsider their core constituencies; the PRI in Mexico needed women's votes and local legitimacy at a time of party reorganization and massive male out-migration (Ramos Escandón, 1998: 100). On the other hand, the federal structures of Brazil, Argentina and Mexico also provided political spaces that suffragists could more easily influence and, in all three, female franchise was first extended locally by enlightened provincial leaders.[12]

There are approximately 16,000 municipalities in Latin America, of which the vast majority have fewer than 100,000 inhabitants and are semi-rural or small urban centres. Women's representation remains highest at the lowest level of government, but only in those offices with least power; in Ecuador, women constitute 33 per cent of parish council members, 30 per cent of city councillors, and less than 3 per cent of mayors. Despite women's higher level of participation and leadership in informal neighbourhood-based associations and activities due to social and cultural factors, decentralization per se has not greatly increased their formal political presence. The percentage of female municipal legislators did not grow noticeably until the passage of decentralization legislation containing quota provisions (Ecuador) or quota laws covering municipal elections (Bolivia, Dominican Republic and Brazil). After Costa Rica introduced a 40 per cent statutory quota for all electoral lists, the proportion of women city councillors rose from 13 per cent in 1994 to an unprecedented 47.1 per cent in 2002. Likewise, Peru saw a rise from 7 to 24.8 per cent. However, in Mexico and Argentina electoral law and district magnitude vary from state to state, so quota laws were passed at the provincial level, leading to patchier compliance and a greater reliance on the political will of the local executive and political parties, and on local women's mobilization. By 2003, 13 Mexican states had passed quota laws whilst others were considering bills or provisions intended to encourage women's candidacies. By 1999, 22 of the 24 Argentine provinces had adopted quota laws (Jones, 1998) and in 1997 Buenos Aires City incorporated the national quota into its constitution (expanding it to include executive and administrative posts), increasing the proportion of women councillors from 6.7 to 35 per cent. Uruguay's lack of statutory quota underscores the party effect. Only the largest party (the Socialists) in the FA has an internal quota, but this resulted in the FA electing a much higher percentage of women councillors in Montevideo (36.8 per cent) compared to the Colorado Party (22.2 per cent) and the National Party (zero).

The percentage of women mayors has remained low and static, averaging 5.3 per cent by 2002 (Massolo, 2003), suggesting that the town hall is a poor training ground and springboard to higher office, particularly in centralized polities. Although in some countries there has been a slow rise (Argentina, Brazil, Chile, Colombia, Costa Rica, Paraguay), others have even witnessed a decline.[13] Selection and election of mayors are not affected by quotas, and the intensity of competition depends on political and institutional variables. The attitude of individual parties is in part a reaction to the local institutional environment, which reflects the relationship of provincial and municipal government to national political and administrative structures, and the prestige, power and resources available to local politicians. Their interest in local representation may range from rent-seeking and purely electoral ambitions, to implementation of innovative policies. Parties are also aware of the gendered character of the electoral messages transmitted in these contests, whether this is *continuismo*, clientelism, anti-corruption, managerial efficiency, or radical participation, which they require the face of the local party to embody. For example, in Mexico, it is not the left- or right-wing opposition but rather the party of the status quo, the PRI, that has elected the highest percentage of women mayors (Massolo, 1998).

Gender and municipal politics

In municipal government the political issues are different, the relationship with the electorate more intimate, social movements enjoy greater access, and the entry costs for newcomers and small parties are substantially lower. The historic centralism of most of the region's polities has ensured that local political bosses, even when devoid of formal powers, have maintained the municipality as a locus of clientelism, either to bolster their own individual power base as *caciques* or *coronéis*, or to orchestrate support for national politicians. For many types of parties, from the small, personalistic vehicles of local political bosses to the institutionalized national parties, electoral success depends upon widespread local penetration to get out the vote at the neighbourhood level. Parties therefore recruit women as key mobilizing agents whose presence and influence within local communities are critical to the maintenance of extensive party patronage networks, even when they are largely marginalized within national party leadership and representation structures. However, studies of local politics and gender issues have tended to focus on territorially-based, consumption-oriented social movements, stressing their autonomy, rather than on this kind of collaboration in and beyond the local state and party apparatus.

Highly institutionalized parties, such as the PRI, AD, COPEI, and Chile's Socialists and Christian Democrats, have operated highly formalized vertical and horizontal structures of national, provincial, municipal and neighbourhood committees, combined with a high degree of reach into civil society organizations such as unions, professional bodies and community groups. Meanwhile, populist movements or leaders tend to generate party structures that possess extensive horizontal rank-and-file networks. The PJ's historically weak routinization has helped, rather than hindered, its electoral success, as its flexible *movimientista* structure allowed it to mobilize women *en masse* first under the personal and charismatic leadership of its founding mother, Evita. By 1952, there were 3,600 women's 'base units' with half a million female members, organized in parallel to the mainstream, male-dominated, base units (Fraser and Navarro, 1980: 107–9; Bianchi and Sanchis, 1988: 90–1).[14] In the 1990s, the party substituted its (male-dominated) union-based structures with patronage-based territorial organizations in which women were more visible agents (Levitsky, 2003: 26). This 'Peronist problem-solving network' in the shantytowns, sustained by women combining the roles of brokers of clientelistic favours, social workers, soup kitchen organizers and party activists, supplied the new lifeblood of the party (Auyero, 2001: 132). The enduring paternal and maternal icons of Juan and Eva Perón had endowed Peronism with a quite distinctive gendered political habitus. Local women activists, often presidents of their local base unit, constantly reprise the role of Evita, as self-sacrificing 'mothers of the poor', a symbolic labour that combines clientelism with maternalist discourse and is very effective in securing the Peronist vote. This 'reproduction of mothering' by local female party leaders and brokers also reinforces spatial gender differences in the practice of party politics (Auyero, 2001: 138–9).

In more recent years, President Fujimori used control of food supplies and other forms of co-option to turn Peruvian women working in grass-roots survival and subsistence organizations into political clients of his semi-authoritarian regime (Blondet, 2002). In Venezuela, INAMUJER now reaches ordinary women through thousands of female-membership 'Bolivarian circles'. However, whilst its core agenda remained domestic violence and income generation, its activities have shifted from a critique of gender relations to solving individual problems, in a manner redolent of classic Peronist clientelism (Ellner and Hellinger, 2003: 49–50, 189).

Decentralizing gender policy

To what extent has decentralization, as part of the post-Washington consensus on state reform, enhanced the autonomy of local government and created new, multiple sites and arenas that allow women's groups to influence local agendas? It has certainly allowed the local policy agenda to encompass new topics, such as that of citizen security, into which a gender perspective is gradually being incorporated. The percentage of women in the municipal police in San Salvador has increased to 15 per cent and gender training is now offered to local law enforcement officials. Some decentralization laws and recently amended local government codes (in Chile and Bolivia) have also included explicit reference to the municipalities' duty to mainstream gender equity through local equal opportunities plans and gender planning. Some national women's units have a sub-national remit and have set up decentralized offices in a top-down process. By 2004, Costa Rica's National Women's Institute had created 58 Municipal Women's Offices (FUNDAPEM, 2004) and it now promotes local and regional Plans for Equality and Equity between Men and Women. Bolivia's Under-Ministry for Gender, Generational and Family Affairs is likewise required to influence that country's departmental and municipal development plans.

However, some countries have seen a bottom-up process initiated by local politicians and women's groups, with several capital cities spearheading the process of regionalizing and municipalizing women's units. Asunción's Women's Secretariat encouraged 16 of the 17 provinces to establish branches of the National Women's Secretariat by 2000. The Women's Institutes in eight of Mexico's provinces predate the national body, as did Brazil's. The Federal District's Institute also acquired a decentralized presence in each of the 16 sub-regions via the system of Integrated Women's Support Centres, and in 2002 won full legal status, funding and autonomy to pursue its policy agenda. Depending on the status of these local offices and the degree of political decentralization, this can allow simple diffusion and deconcentrated delivery of gender policy, or create new consultative forums. Virtually all of Costa Rica's municipalities have consultative Women's Councils attached to the town hall, with representation of local women's groups and municipal legislators.

The global policy community of feminist lobbyists, policymakers and politicians straddles a wide spatial range, and local government gender units assist the *glocalization* of international and national gender norms; that is, the trickle *down* and adaptation of these ideas to local circumstances. Provincial and municipal governments have been encouraged to endorse or produce their own versions of the CEDAW, the Beijing Platform for Action, and national equal opportunities programmes, either as a symbolic act or because federalism, as in Mexico, requires action at sub-national level. The Argentine national women's programme is implemented in 14 provinces, and the federal capitals of both Mexico and Argentina have their own equal opportunities plans.

The multiple spaces that a federal structure opens up for policy experimentation and plural politics can also allow successful local initiatives to trickle *up* and be replicated in national policy. For those parties likely to remain out of national government for the foreseeable future, particularly on the Left, local government offers an arena for opposition, demonstrating credibility, and showcasing experiments with new forms of popular democracy, accountability and delivery of high quality, accessible social services (Chavez and Goldfrank, 2004). Women's movements have successfully lobbied such sub-national political actors when national politicians have been unwilling to back gender equity legislation. In 1999, San Salvador became the first municipality to adopt a Municipal Gender Equity Policy, after the mayor endorsed a feminist platform presented to all candidates in the 1997 elections (Clulow, 2003b). The dynamism of Montevideo's Women's Committee, founded by the governing FA in 1991, highlighted the Colorado and National parties' inertia with regard to gender policy. The creation of new spaces of representation, such as participatory budget processes, can also amplify women's political voice. Neighbourhood councils set up by the FA had 44 per cent female representation (Chavez, 2004: 79), whilst the neighbourhood committees of the left-leaning city administration of Asunción in the mid-1990s adopted a 30 per cent gender quota for leadership positions. However, this requires active party backing; in Bolivia, where the percentage of women councillors has quadrupled due to a quota law, the proportion participating in municipal budget meetings has actually declined, despite the intent of the Popular Participation law.

On the downside, national gender-progressive policies may be resisted or contradicted at state or municipal level, with federalism actually slowing the trickle down of gender policies to local level. The Argentine domestic violence law applies only to the city of Buenos Aires, and there are variations in the legislation adopted by 21 provinces. The fluctuating political commitment within provincial government structures can also render the gender units institutionally vulnerable. Although by 2004 all but three of Argentina's 24 provinces had some form of gender unit, they encompassed a range of institutional forms from advisory council to second rank government body, subsumed within a department for human rights or human development.

Decentralization also allows party political conflict over gender to be conducted in multiple terrains. In Mexico, the only country where penal law varies at provincial level, 11 states allow terminations in cases of 'danger to women's health' and 'economic hardship', through liberalizing legislation introduced without fuss by the secularist PRI. However, the country's transition to competitive multi-party democracy has thrown the positions of the parties into relief along the long-standing secular–religious cleavage; whilst the PRD government in the Federal District, headed by feminist Rosario Robles, moved to expand abortion rights, in Guanajuato state politicians and activists from the Catholic PAN attempted to outlaw abortion completely, even in rape cases.

Where municipal women's offices form part of central government policy, they can become decoupled from their original design without active women's groups to use and support them. Costa Rica's municipal women's agencies found that limited resources, dependence on political will and constant negotiation with the different municipal actors created an unstable environment in which it is difficult to promote gender equality and equity. Local politicians diverted them into a predominantly welfare role dealing with issues such as domestic violence, meeting practical rather than strategic gender needs (FUNDAPEM, 2004).

Welfarism also frequently spills over into electoral clientelism. In the late 1980s, the United Left government of Lima instituted both a municipal Equal Opportunities Plan and the 'Glass of Milk' infant feeding programme, whilst APRA supported the Mothers' Clubs. However, these and the low-cost canteens were rapidly taken over by the Fujimori government, which needed an alternative political constituency. Venezuela's state- and municipal-level women's offices were the target of party co-option in the early 1990s (Friedman, 2000b: 70), whilst President Menem attended to his support base by investing US$14 million of federal funds in the creation of a network of provincial women's centres (Waylen, 2000; Htun, 2003: 128).

The following case studies of Brazil and Chile offer a detailed analysis of this ambivalent and multifaceted relationship between political parties and the women's movement, a relationship conducted in multiple terrains, both in spatial terms (national and local government) and in functional terms (the ballot, the state apparatus, inside the parties, in representative bodies). Whilst analyzing the specifics of the structural context of the party–institutional arena, the two cases will also show how both sides have adjusted to one another, with the feminist movement increasingly engaged with the parties as both gateway and obstacle to less gender-skewed representation and to state resources, and the parties more alert than ever to the demands of a locally and internationally established gender agenda.

Part I
Brazil

2
Porous Parties, Permeable State

In order to understand why it should have been a political party, the Workers' Party (*Partido dos Trabalhadores* – PT), rather than a government ministry that opened up new ground in gender legislation and policies in the 1990s, this chapter first outlines some of the peculiarities of the Brazilian party system, its development and underlying cleavages. It examines why the influence of the women's movement on the other parties has been so conjunctural and unreliable, as illustrated by the political problems encountered by the National Council on Women's Rights (*Conselho Nacional dos Direitos da Mulher* – CNDM). As the municipality and state are much more important spheres of government in a federal system, the chapter concludes by outlining how gender policy initiatives have emerged through the institutional spaces and instruments available in these sub-national arenas.

Transition and opportunity

The PT's engagement in gender issues is partly the result of advances made by the Brazilian women's movement in the 1980s, and also of the obstacles the latter encountered in getting a secure foothold in the state. The year 1975 represented a dual turning point for women in Brazil, marking the start of the UN Decade for Women and of a prolonged political thaw initiated by the military regime that would culminate, in 1985, in the indirect election of the first civilian president in two decades. Brazil's military dictatorship was distinct in several ways from Chile's, even while their projects of demobilizing society and taking control of the economy were apparently cognate. Firstly, Brazil's civilian–military technocracy actually intensified the state-led developmentalist policies of previous decades in order to move from import-substitution to export-oriented industrialization. This had the effect of creating enclaves of militant industrial workers that spawned first the 'new union' movement, and then a unique new left-wing force, the PT. Conversely, the neo-liberal agenda introduced in the 1970s in Chile did not start to take root in Brazil until the 1990s, under Presidents Fernando Collor de Mello and Fernando Henrique Cardoso.[1]

Secondly, the military did not abolish all party activity, but chose to create an artificial two-party system with a pro-government party, the Alliance for National Renovation (*Aliança Renovadora Nacional* – ARENA), and an 'official' opposition, the Brazilian Democratic Movement (*Movimento Democrático Brasileiro* – MDB), that could contest the posts of federal deputy, senator, state deputy, city councillor and mayor.[2] Thus, the transition was conducted via elections from 1974 onwards, forcing the women's movement into an early engagement with party political and electoral issues, and engendering fierce debates between and among the party women of the centre-left and the 'independents' of the movements. In the 1978 elections, the movement urged women to back sympathetic opposition candidates, and a number of feminists were elected at state and municipal level (Tabak, 1994: 132). The abolition of the two-party system in 1979 meant that in states such as São Paulo the movement became divided between the renamed Party of the Brazilian Democratic Movement (*Partido do Movimento Democrático Brasileiro* – PMDB) and new contenders on the Left (Alvarez, 1990: 147).[3]

Thirdly, the protracted character of the transition facilitated the steady growth of anti-regime groups and social movements that created cross-class coalitions and common agendas. A multiplicity of local grassroots groups, run or dominated by women, addressed issues of social reproduction such as childcare, cost-of-living, housing and healthcare (Machado, 1988; Corcoran-Nantes, 1993; Neuhouser, 1995), whilst others mobilized in trade unions, political parties and the Church, and those with a more feminist agenda focused on gender violence and reproductive rights. The opposition parties, the PMDB and Democratic Labour Party (*Partido Democrático Trabalhista* – PDT), won ten state governments in 1982, including the three largest, capturing feminist loyalties and affording the movement a toehold in the state apparatus *before* the transition was completed at national level. However, as the party system and the institutional arena underwent changes, by the 1990s the PT had become the party that most consistently adopted and promoted the feminist agenda.

Weak institutions: party and electoral systems

Party system

Brazil's party system has been marked by discontinuities. The regionally-based, exclusionary political system of the Old Republic ended in the centralized authoritarian period of the *Estado Novo* (1937–45), under President Getúlio Vargas, which banned all party activity. The Populist Republic (1946–64) saw several new parties[4] emerge in a limited democratic experiment terminated by the military government, which presided first over a two-party then a multi-party system. Of the current major parties, on the right the Liberal Front Party (*Partido da Frente Liberal* – PFL) and Progressive Party (*Partido Progressista* – PP) are the progeny of ARENA and its successor, the Democratic Social Party (*Partido Democrático Social* – PDS). The PMDB likewise originated in the military period and, in 1988, spawned on the centre-left the Party of Brazilian Social Democracy (*Partido da Social Democracia Brasileira* – PSDB), founded by advocates of a more principled and progressive agenda, including parliamentarianism. Remnants survive of the old pre-1964 populist Left, in the PDT[5] and the Brazilian Socialist Party (*Partido Socialista Brasileiro*),[6] and of the old orthodox Left, now divided between the Communist Party of Brazil (*Partido Comunista do Brasil* – PCdoB) and the Popular Socialist Party (*Partido Popular Socialista* – PPS).[7]

The party system in Brazil has been much criticized as inchoate, under-institutionalized and populated for the main part by unideo-logical, ill-disciplined parties with few organic roots in society.[8] Parties were created to support the ambitions of elite groups or individual politicians rather than represent the interests of organized sectors, and their political habitus was oriented around rent-seeking and clientelism (Mainwaring, 1999; Ames, 2001; Samuels, 2003). However, the permeability and protean quality of the system and its component parties have been both blessing and curse to the women's movement. The latter was not crowded out of the political arena by the return to democracy and a number of important women's networks grew and consolidated during the 1980s and 1990s. Nevertheless, the parties remained important gatekeepers between the state and demands for gender equity and equality.

Outside and inside the parties

Women's suffrage in Brazil was won by a group of mainly well-educated upper-class women who lobbied sympathetic politicians. It was never advocated by, or associated with, any specific political party, social institution or movement because, at a time of highly restricted political participation and elite bargaining, the popular vote did not determine access to power (Hahner, 1990). In 1932, women won the right to vote and run in local and national elections nationwide, but they voted only once, in the congressional elections of 1934, before the *Estado Novo* terminated electoral activity until 1945. The postwar parties also ignored women as an electoral constituency until the late 1970s. Unlike in Chile, left-wing President Goulart (1961–4) made no effort to call upon women to mobilize in support of his reforms, and studies of female protest against his government make scant mention of links to the conservative opposition parties (Simões, 1985).

Until the transition, women had little presence within the parties, reflecting the predominance of cadre or caucus organizational structures. Women's departments were sporadic, with no significant membership.[9] Nonetheless, in 1982 the PDS tried to compete with the PMDB for female votes by setting up its own 'women's movement'. Its gender ideology was conservative but vague, and self-proclaimed feminists in the party even demanded more female candidacies, higher representation in party leadership and executive posts, and state gender policies such as childcare (Alvarez, 1990: 162–5). This paradox underscores both the importance of women as a new electoral constituency at this juncture, and the extent to which the ideology of the Right in Brazil is centred on state power and is not oriented around issues in the domain of morality or values.

In the early 1980s, the PMDB's women's branch sheltered different political tendencies that disagreed about how best to involve women and address gender issues. The party's more fringe elements, such as the 8 October Revolutionary Movement (*Movimento Revolucionário do 8 de Outubro* – MR-8), and the banned Communist Party sought to co-opt grassroots women's groups into city- and state-wide 'federations', for largely sectarian purposes. Meanwhile, a number of middle-class intellectuals and professionals formed a study group to draw up gender policies, a strategy that bore fruit in 1982 when Franco Montoro was elected governor with the support of the city's housewives and a women's auxiliary set up by his wife and daughter. The party ran three feminists among its 12 women candidates that year and dominated the female presence in Congress until the end of the decade (Alvarez, 1990 166–71). However, by the late 1980s the PMDB had mutated into a classic 'catch-all' party, losing its more principled, social democratic members to the PSDB, and acquiring opportunistic ones from the Right,[10] and by 2002, it was the only major party without a women's department.[11] The PT's women's secretariat is now the most established and influential of such units.

Political cleavages: gender, religion and the party system

An analysis of the electoral base of the major Brazilian parties reveals little variation along the classic sociological dividing lines of race, class, religion and gender, which have been virtually irrelevant to competition and ideological differentiation in this party system (Samuels, 2004a). During the 1993 constitutional revision process, an attitudinal survey of deputies and senators concluded that while the centre-left was predictably consistent and supportive of extending women's rights, the Right was not necessarily hostile (CFEMEA, 1993).[12] It found little consensus within party blocs, ideological groupings or economic credos with respect to gender or 'private' realm issues such as sexuality, family and reproduction. Whilst the parties of the governing centre-right coalition of 1995–2002 voted consistently on President Cardoso's economic and structural reform agenda,[13] they generally opposed gender legislation only when it required financial commitments by the State, such as paid maternity and paternity leave, and the extension of pension and welfare rights to domestic and rural women workers.[14] Thus, deputies across the political spectrum, men as well as women, have generated legislative initiatives on gender rights. PSDB Senator Cardoso and his feminist stand-in, Eva Blay, were two of the first legislators to propose decriminalization of abortion, although this was never adopted as party or government policy.

Since the Second World War, party system cleavages have centred on three main axes: pro- and anti-Vargas, military rule, and state involvement in the economy. The first two have disappeared, the third persisting due to the late advent of neo-liberalism in Brazil. This generated a discernible left–right spectrum, but one mainly focused around economic, rather than moral, issues.[15] Historically, religious–secular political disputes have been of little relevance. The nineteenth-century Liberal Party expired with the Old Republic and the proto-fascist integralism of the 1920s was defeated by Vargas, an avowed atheist whose brand of state corporatism was functional and reflected few elements of Catholic social thought. Although the Church gained certain institutional privileges from his regime, it was at the cost of subordination to the state (Todaro Williams, 1976). In consequence, Brazil has never had a significant Christian Democratic or Church-associated party. In the twentieth century, the Catholic Church's political power became most visible in its oppositional stance to military rule in the 1970s and, unlike the Chilean Church, it went beyond criticisms of human rights abuses to embrace the principles of liberation theology, actively sheltering and supporting social movements and setting up radical Base Communities (Mainwaring, 1986; Della Cava, 1988). Neither the military government nor its party, ARENA, expended nearly as much energy as did the Chilean or Argentine regimes on educating women to be standard-bearers of traditional femininity and 'Western Christian values'. President Geisel (1974–9), a Lutheran, even pushed through a divorce bill in an attempt to undermine the Church and alienate it from the pro-divorce MDB. He also supported a woman's right to non-coercive family planning and established the women's health programme demanded by feminists (Htun, 2003: 68, 94). The rightward shift in the Vatican since the 1980s has had comparatively little impact, as the National Council of Bishops and much of the flock remained committed to social justice, a posture that at the ballot box primarily benefits the PT, a secular, pluralist party. The Parliamentary Catholic Group's members also range across the political spectrum, albeit being concentrated in the main parties.[16]

Meanwhile the born-again Christian movement is much more focused on questions of personal morality and salvation. The Pentecostal churches' social following and representation in Congress has grown enormously since the mid-1990s, and they control resources (TV and radio stations) that the Catholic Church lacks. However, the members of its parliamentary caucus are more dispersed, mainly across the smaller personalist parties associated with clientelist political practices.[17] Opinion polls show that parliamentary backing for public provision of legal abortion[18] rose steadily to over 87 per cent in 1999, with 78 per cent in support of limited decriminalization.[19] This reflects public opinion, even among Catholics. Less than 9 per cent oppose any form of liberalization, which is far fewer than the membership of either the Catholic or born-again Christian cross-bench groups. Brazil is, after all, a country where stable unions and the rights of children outside matrimony have long been recognized (Htun, 2003: 88), and where those of sexual minorities are being gradually advanced.[20]

In consequence, the women's movement has not faced much organized, party-centred and value-based opposition in Congress. Feminists were able to block an attempt to include a constitutional clause protecting life 'from conception' during the drafting and subsequent revision of the constitution, although a bill that would have obliged all state hospitals to provide legal abortion was stopped in its tracks by a Papal visit in 1997. Nonetheless, the following year the Ministry of Health issued internal guidelines instructing state hospitals to provide legal abortion to rape victims as part of a wider government initiative on gender violence; this elicited remarkably little reaction. Similarly, when Brazil moved to sign the Optional Protocol to the CEDAW and the National Council of Bishops dutifully invoked the Vatican line that this represented an 'assault on national sovereignty', this view found no political constituency.[21]

Electoral system

The level of women's representation in elected office was very low before and during the military dictatorship, never rising above 0.6 per cent,[22] except in 1966 when four women MDB deputies were elected in place of husbands who had been stripped of their political rights. They in turn lost their rights and only one woman, from the pro-government party, remained until three feminist *MDBistas* were elected (Costa, 1998: 105). The lag between the political amnesty and party system reorganization of 1979 and the first democratic legislative elections in 1986 obviated the restorationist dynamics of the more sudden transitions in the Southern Cone. The foundational transition elections of 1982 produced a record eight women deputies, which leapt to 26 (5.3 per cent) in the 1986 Constitutional Assembly elections, as Table 2.1 shows. Nevertheless, in the 1990s numbers levelled off at around the 6 per cent mark, despite the introduction of the quota law. A rise to 8.2 per cent in 2002 elections suggested that the number of women elected was beginning to reflect the increase in candidates, although it was also a consequence of the PT's sweeping victory.

Table 2.1 Brazil: women's representation in municipal, state and national elected office, 1982–2004

Year	Municipal		Year	State		National	
	Councillor	*Mayor*		*State deputy*	*Governor*	*Federal deputy*	*Senator*
1982	—	1.9	1982	3.0	0	1.7	0
1988	—	2.0	1986	3.3	0	5.3	0
1992	7.4	3.4	1990	5.5	0	5.6	2.5
1996	11.1	5.5	1994	7.8	3.7	6.2	4.9
2000	11.6	5.7	1998	10.0	3.7	5.6	3.7
2004	12.7	7.3	2002	12.6	7.4	8.2	12.3

Sources: Miguel (2000) and Araújo (2001).

Gender quotas

In 1993, a PSDB deputy mooted the first proposal for a statutory quota for women candidates in proportional elections (the posts of federal deputy, state deputy and city councillor), but the bill disappeared without trace as the women's movement's attention was directed elsewhere (Miguel, 2000: 24). By 1996, the cumulative impact of the Beijing recommendations, the success of the Argentine quota law, and a 1995 women's conference in the São Paulo-based Latin American Parliament made it a priority, and the women's caucus (*bancada feminina*) supported a bill in each chamber. PT deputy Marta Suplicy, who spearheaded the bill in the lower house, had also been swayed by the positive effects of her own party's internal quota. Both bills were passed without major polemic. The 1996 law stipulated that parties should run a minimum of 20 per cent women candidates in that year's municipal elections for city councillor, and the left-wing parties voted *en bloc* in favour, except for the PPS, which voted against on the principle that it 'interfered with party autonomy', whilst the centre and right-wing parties allowed a free vote. All parties, except the PMDB, voted in favour of a 1997 amendment that raised the quota to a minimum 25 per cent for both sexes in the 1998 elections for federal and state deputies, and 30 per cent thereafter (Grossi and Miguel, 2001). However, the debates in parliament revealed the anxiety of the male politicians. A deal done among the party leaders resulted in an agreement that the 20 per cent quota should not be applied to the existing formula for party lists, under which each party was allowed to run as many as candidates as places available. Instead, the 1996 law increased the total number of candidates per party to 120 per cent of the places available, rising to 150 per cent (200 per cent for coalitions) for all subsequent elections. This, of course, diluted the effect of the quota, and inflicted zero cost on the parties as they were now entitled to run more *men* than before, aside from the additional women candidates.[23]

Unfortunately, the quota has had little impact due to Brazil's open-list, multi-member proportional representation electoral system,[24] in which the parties play virtually no role as gatekeeper due to the ratio of candidates to seats, a placement requirement is impossible, and district magnitude irrelevant.[25] Furthermore, the electoral courts still have no powers of sanction and did not until 1998 require candidates to register their sex, making it impossible to compile accurate statistics or monitor the parties. An early proposal that non-compliant parties should forfeit a corresponding percentage of candidate places never prospered (Miguel, 2000: 45).

Table 2.2   Brazil: effect of quota in municipal, state and national elections on percentage of women candidates and elected representatives, and on the female success index, 1992–2004

Year	Municipal			Year	State			National		
	City councillor				State deputy			Federal deputy		
	Candidates	Elected	FSI		Candidates	Elected	FSI	Candidates	Elected	FSI
1992	—	7.4	—	1990	—	—	—	—	5.8	—
1996*	10.9	11.1	—	1994	7.2	7.8	110.1	6.1	6.2	101.5
2000	19.1	11.6	55.5	1998	13.9	10.0	74.8	10.4	5.6	51.8
2004	22.1	12.7	50.9	2002	14.8	12.6	82.5	11.7	8.2	67.3

Note: *The electoral courts do not have reliable gender-disaggregated data for the 1990, 1992 and 1996 elections. Over 30 per cent of candidates in 1996 were listed as 'sex unknown' despite the introduction of the quota.

As Table 2.2 shows, the percentage of candidates has doubled, more so for city councillors, but the number of women elected has improved very modestly. Over three elections, the proportion of women city councillors rose only by 71 per cent, bringing them up to the level of state deputies and senators. Over two contests the percentage of state deputies rose by 61 per cent and that of federal deputies by 31 per cent, although in 1998 the latter actually fell. This can also be partially blamed on the open-list system in which candidates compete against members of the same party; the voter generally casts a vote for the individual rather than the party, although the party ticket vote has been used predominantly by PT supporters. Whereas, before the quota, women were elected roughly in the same proportion as their candidacies, a gap opened and thereafter women became less successful than male candidates, especially in *local* elections, as the female success index measure in Table 2.2 shows. This was due to the lack of effective backing from the parties, which were persuading women without preparation, campaign resources, commitment or electoral constituencies to run in order to 'make up the numbers'. By one measure, the cost of entry to political newcomers is very low. Incumbency is less of an obstacle, even though elected politicians have an automatic right to be included again on the party list. In Brazil, three-quarters of deputies seek re-election, but only two-thirds of those achieve this. Some seek other offices and some step down, resulting in quite a high turnover rate; at the start of any legislative term around half of the deputies are new (Samuels, 2001). However, women often lack the financial and time resources needed to build up a specific electoral constituency within a multi-member district. Campaign resources are not supplied by the state but must be procured by individual candidates or distributed by the parties, which will not prioritize these female 'filler' candidates.

The gap between the quota and the level of candidacies and women elected has actually widened, suggesting that phasing in the quota did not encourage parties to adapt themselves in the absence of compulsion or institutional incentives. Due to the poor implementation of the quota law in a non-conducive environment, political support for such measures actually declined. The 1997 amendment was harder to get through and a 1999 poll of parliamentarians showed only 63 per cent in favour of maintaining quotas for the legislature, and a majority against extension of the measure to the judiciary and executive, on which there are a number of bills pending.[26] PT women deputies suggested a number of remedies including electoral advertising to explain the quota, compulsory notification of the candidate's sex to the courts and at the polling booth, and a requirement that parties dedicate 30 per cent of the media airtime and money allocated by the national Party Fund to promoting and training women candidates. Nonetheless, within this individualistic system, certain women do perform very well at the polls, helping to elect party colleagues on their coat tails. In the 2003–6 intake, eight out of 42 women federal deputies received the highest vote of any deputy in their state (INESC, 2002: 11). Five were from the Left and all were elected in the poorer, more rural and 'under-developed' northern and northeastern regions where modernization theory would predict a lower vote for both women and left-wing candidates.

Executive posts are elected either by a majority with a run-off if necessary (in the case of president of the Republic, state governor, and mayors of cities with over 200,000 voters), or by a plurality (senators and mayors of smaller towns) and are not subject to any form of positive discrimination selection method. No women were elected to the senate in 1982 or 1986. Two were elected in 1990, three in 1994 and two in 1998. In 2002, however, there was a major increase, with eight new women senators joining the two finishing the second half of their term,[27] bringing their presence to 12.3 per cent. Seven out of the ten women senators were from the Left (mainly the PT), with only one 'politician's wife'. As the parties hold primaries to select candidates and run only as many as there are places, perhaps female candidates on the Left benefit from their parties' greater willingness to recognize and promote women with a strong local profile in the absence of competing male candidates.

Women representatives: difference and collective action

Women federal deputies[28] elected since 1978 have tended to fall into two categories. On the centre-right they are often the relatives of male politicians; some 'parachute' straight into national office with no prior experience, whilst others acquire a name through performing charitable works associated with their husband's office. On the Left, they generally ascend from posts in municipal- or state-level politics, backed by specific social sectors or grassroots movements. In 1978, all four women had feminist sympathies (Costa, 1998: 109) whilst in 1982, five progressive women were elected from the PMDB and PT, and two from the Right, with only one politician's relative, Ivete Vargas.[29] Although the 1986 intake was split between women from political dynasties (Costa, 1998: 114) and feminists,[30] since then the number of women with family connections has dropped from around 40 per cent in 1990 to under 10 per cent in 2002.[31] From the mid-1990s, many have had experience in women's issues, either through participation in the Beijing Conference, membership of state or municipal women's councils (*conselhos*), involvement in the parliamentary inquiries into maternal mortality and sterilization, legislative activity, or leadership positions within their parties.[32] This includes all of the PT women and most of the centre-left ones as well as some elected for conservative parties and through family connections.

Women tend not to belong to the other cross-party groupings in Congress,[33] and the low ideological definition of the centre-right results in these political neophytes being open to involvement in women's issues, perhaps as an extension of the traditionally welfarist role assumed by local politicians' wives. In the absence of party political conflict over gender issues, they seem happy to follow a feminist agenda set by centre-left representatives, the only ones with a strong party identification. This dual profile of female politicians is one factor explaining the relative absence of marianist discourses around political voice and representation for women. The women's movement has made claims largely on the basis of equity, fairness and rights. Feminism is a lesser taboo in Brazilian political discourse and is even appropriated by conservative politicians. Surveys of voter attitudes reveal that the Brazilian electorate regards women in government positively, rating them higher than men not just on honesty and reliability, but also on competence, responsibility, toughness and capability, normally deemed more 'masculine' attributes, with little resistance to electing women to executive positions (Inter-American Dialogue, 2001).[34]

The critical mass argument similarly does not hold, as the cross-party women's group has been highly effective despite the static level of female representation, due to the party political factors analyzed above. The *bancada feminina* was set up informally during the Constitutional Assembly (1987–8) when a women's movement campaign elected an unprecedented number of feminists with the aim of inscribing women's rights into the new Constitution. This recalled a strategy half a century earlier, in 1934, when nine women, mostly members of the suffragist Brazilian Federation for Women's Progress, were elected to state-level constitutional assemblies (Costa, 1998: 99; Schumaher and Brazil 2000).[35] Led by the centre-left, particularly the PT, the *bancada*'s agenda has been guided by the CNDM and feminist NGOs such as the Feminist Research and Advisory Centre (*Centro Feminista de Estudos e Assessoria* – CFEMEA). All female federal deputies and senators are nominally members, most back it solidly, and none opposes it. Differences of opinion tend to be personal, not party political, ideological or religious. Of those women who participate in the cross-party Catholic group, none has fixed positions on the issue of reproductive rights.[36] With most parties indifferent on gender issues, the *bancada* has been able to steer the party vote successfully on key bills such as the gender quota, reforms to the civil and penal codes,[37] maternity and paternity leave, rights of women prisoners, reproductive rights, anti-discrimination measures (race, HIV status, sexual orientation), and gender violence. In 1995, the whips of nearly all the parties instructed their members to vote *against* a constitutional amendment to protect life 'from conception', in a very unusual movement that goes against the normal pattern of a 'free' vote on such controversial issues (Htun, 2003: 161). Individual members, regardless of party, also generate gender equality and equity legislation on areas of personal interest or expertise, as do some male politicians, although their initiatives, whilst generally gender-progressive, appear uncoordinated with the priorities of the *bancada*.

Vulnerable institutions: the CNDM and the parties

In the early 1980s, the women's movement seized the opportunity offered by the return to electoral democracy, the reorganization of the party system and the PMDB's eagerness to establish its progressive credentials. The political capital that PMDB women had accumulated by supporting their party's candidates, opposing military rule and organizing for the campaign for direct presidential elections led to notable policy victories, such as the pioneering women-only police stations to deal with domestic and sexual violence, a public women's health programme and state-level *conselhos* to promote women's rights (Alvarez, 1990). These policies emerged through a dynamic tension between the women's movement and the parties, with the former attempting to take advantage of new institutional spaces yet preserve their autonomy, while the latter were seeking to expand their support base.

The National Council for Women's Rights: opportunity and co-option

Brazil was among the first countries in the region to establish a dedicated, national unit for the promotion of women's rights. The first attempt was made in 1936 by feminist pioneer Bertha Lutz who proposed a National Women's Bureau to deal with female workers, the household, public assistance to women and children, maternity and social security (Saffioti 1978: 207–9). She argued that it should have executive functions, in contrast to the US Department of Labour's Women's Bureau on which it was modelled and which had only an advisory mandate. However, her colleague in Congress, Carlota Pereira de Queiroz,[38] opposed a separate ministry for women, and the installation of the *Estado Novo* rendered the discussion moot. Nonetheless, as the military regime eased, the women MDB federal deputies proposed a Ministry for Children and the Family (Tabak, 1989: 95) and in 1984 future President-Elect Tancredo Neves agreed. However, he died just before taking office and Vice-President Sarney, who stepped into his shoes, had few dealings with the opposition or with social movements.

Despite this inauspicious genesis, the CNDM prospered under the first democratic government, albeit with hybrid characteristics.[39] On the one hand, it was constituted as a consultative body, with a twenty-member unpaid advisory board appointed by the president, composed of one-third women's movement representatives, and two-thirds government officials, resembling the many other state–civil society *conselhos* advising on various social policy areas set up in the wake of the 1988 Constitution (Draibe, 1998; Tatagiba, 2002).[40] On the other hand, in its heyday under Sarney it enjoyed political space that gave its first chief executive, Jacqueline Pitanguy (1985–9), considerable de facto executive and deliberative powers.[41] The Council possessed 'administrative and financial autonomy', a ring-fenced budget of US$3 million allocated by Congress, a technical support staff, and an executive-secretariat to carry out tasks mandated by the board. Its mission statement was wide, based on the CEDAW, 'to promote nationally policies to eliminate discrimination against women'. All of this was reversed in the 1990s, when it was reduced to a purely advisory body stripped of resources.

During these first five years, the CNDM won many legal and policy victories, particularly in the Constitutional Assembly, where it put forward more than 100 proposals to Congressional committees. By orchestrating the joint action of women legislators, independent women's groups and the state and municipal *conselhos*, over 80 per cent of these demands were incorporated into the final text. The CNDM worked with the Ministry of Education on non-sexist schoolbooks; collaborated with the Ministry of Health to promote information on reproduction and contraception, implement the Integrated Women's Health Programme and ensure provision of legal abortions; set up a Committee for Black Women; carried out studies on violence against women, debated the effectiveness of women's police stations and urged the Supreme Court to rule against the use of the 'honour defence' by men who murdered their partners; instituted sanctions against businesses that contravened labour law, got labour benefits extended to domestic workers and women rural workers, and established the right of women to hold land title (Pitanguy, 2003). It enjoyed enormous legitimacy and support from the women's movement, had strong links with social movements, worked closely with a cohort of sympathetic women legislators in Congress, and conducted regular cross-sectoral meetings with representatives from the ministries. It was staffed by experienced feminist activists skilled in public policy formulation and political lobbying, who benefited from high credibility, good currency with the PMDB and the political sympathy of the government. Its non-partisan image enabled it to work equally with politicians at municipal and regional level.

Appreciative of the capriciousness of party politics, the CNDM had taken the precaution of reserving places on its board for a range of party representatives. However, the PMDB became indifferent to the *conselhos* it had championed and the Collor/Franco government (1990–4) dramatically de-institutionalized the Council, as successive ministers of justice regarded it as simply another locus for patronage. Its chief executive and members of the board were frequently reshuffled and replaced by individuals with no movement connections, and a 1990 decree divested it of all administrative and financial autonomy. From occupying two floors in the main Ministry of Justice building it was reduced to two rooms in the annex, and its 150 staff and groups, working on the matters of Black women, health, education, culture, legislation, work, violence, childcare and events, were cut back to the chief executive, one staff member and a secretary by 1992. Although the CNDM's consultative functions and the structure of the board of advisors remained intact, for the next decade it lacked any executive capacity either to design or promote cross-sectoral gender policies.

Feminist hopes in President Cardoso, a progressive sociologist and founder of the PSDB, were soon dashed.[42] He refused their demands to upgrade the CNDM to a state secretariat, failed to restore the CNDM to its former status, and appointed as head a personal friend who was viewed as a technocrat without strong movement support. With just one staff member, the CNDM tried to carry out its limited Programme of Action, based on the Beijing Platform, in partnership with other entities better endowed with resources, such as the Ministry of Justice's Human Rights Secretariat, sectoral ministries and the Community Solidarity Fund, headed by the president's wife, the eminent anthropologist Ruth Cardoso. It was not until the final months of Cardoso's eight-year government that it regained its own executive staff, albeit still under the aegis of the Human Rights Secretariat. In September 2002, an executive decree created a National Secretariat for Women's Rights, which the incoming PT government then transformed into the Special Secretariat for Policies on Women (*Secretaria Especial de Políticas para as Mulheres* – SPM), attached to the President's Office. The secretary of state has the status of minister and a seat in the cabinet, as in Chile's SERNAM, whilst the first presidential message delivered by Luiz Inácio Lula da Silva in 2003 contained a section affirming the government's commitment to gender equality and equity.

The CNDM's mixed fortunes illustrate the impact of the foundational, organizational and ideological characteristics of the party of government. PMDB support for the Council was always highly contingent on individuals in the government, principally the president and minister of justice, and once it lost its foundational *raison d'être* – its opposition to military rule – it lost any policy orientation. For all the PSDB's alleged social democratic credentials, its caucus character (elite-dominated foundation and no mass membership) left it aloof from social movement claims and it presided over an evisceration of both the national and state women's *conselhos*, both for fiscal reasons and because the women's movement could not exert pressure on the tightly knit clique of party leaders. It has no policy on gender issues *qua* party, and feminists within it tend to act individually, not collectively.[43] By contrast, from 1994 the PT had committed itself in its election manifestos to upgrade the CNDM to an executive level Secretariat with autonomy, a substantial budget and decision-making powers, cross-sectoral access and influence.[44]

Glocalizing legislation and policymaking

Since the mid-1980s, Brazil has been increasingly alert to the prestige and legitimacy that participation in international rights regimes can confer; governments of all hues have played a proactive role as a global 'good citizen' defending the universalist principle of human rights and supporting the creation of new enforcement mechanisms such as the International Criminal Court (Hurrell, 1996; Pinheiro, 2000). The interplay between its international commitments and national legislation has been dynamic, each influencing the other, and both gave a legal mandate to the CNDM's work on areas such as labour, political and reproductive rights. Brazil ratified the CEDAW in 1984, removing all reservations in 1994, and in June 2002 the Senate approved the Optional Protocol. The Convention provided an important template for feminist demands in the Constitutional Assembly, a key conjuncture that enabled women's groups to transcend political differences in pursuit of common goals. The resulting constitution made equality between men and women explicit (including within the family), recognized stable unions, and mandated the state to take steps to prevent domestic violence. It outlawed sex discrimination in the labour market, guaranteed women four months' paid maternity leave, required the state to protect women's employment, and gave domestic workers the right to a minimum wage, a weekly day of rest, paid annual holidays, maternity leave and social security (Verucci, 1991). Brazil hosted the conference that produced the Belém do Pará Convention, sent a delegation to Beijing headed by Cardoso's wife, and was a major player in the 1993 UN Conference on Human Rights in Vienna, defending women's rights as human rights in the face of resistance from some countries pleading cultural exceptionalism. At the Cairo Conference, it also took a progressive line, insisting on reproductive rights as a human rights issue, precisely because the 1988 Constitution recognizes the rights of couples to control their fertility and requires the State to provide them with the necessary means.[45] However, the importance of the CEDAW faded in the 1990s and Brazil did not submit its first periodic implementation report until December 2002, some 17 years late (Committee on the Elimination of Discrimination against Women, 2003a, 2003b).[46] This pattern of good intentions but low state commitment or capacity also affected the constitutional provisions, which required extensive regulatory legislation to go into effect.

The process of generating legislation and lobbying political parties and opinion-formers was led by the CNDM until 1989, but devolved thereafter to decentralized and plural feminist networks that emerged partly as a by-product of the neglect of the CNDM and closure of political space in central government. This dense and territorially, ideologically, sectorally and thematically differentiated policy community stretches horizontally from the *bancada feminina* to women in government ministries, feminists in the PT, feminist NGOs, advocacy groups and thematic networks such as those working on women's health, reproductive rights, violence, and race, and reaches vertically down through sub-national structures (*conselhos*, policy units and forums) linked to the PT. A network of state and municipal *conselhos*, founded in 1984, came into its own in response not just to the CNDM's stagnation, but also to the new institutional opportunity of the greater powers that the 1988 Constitution accorded the municipalities and states. A new national women's network (*Articulação de Mulheres Brasileiras*), representing some 800 women's groups in 27 state-level Women's Forums, emerged in preparation for the Beijing Conference. They mobilized around the 25 priority areas of the Platform of Action, translating them into 'Strategies for Equality', a template for secondary gender equality legislation in the areas of women's health, reproductive rights, family and labour law, gender violence and political rights for all three levels of government.

All this required considerable co-ordination and at the heart of this policy community lay CFEMEA, one of the continent's most effective feminist advocacy groups, which rose from the ashes of the CNDM in 1989. Founded by four women who had been on government secondment to the Council, it provided knowledge-sharing for a heterogeneous women's movement in a political system with multiple access points. It formed a bridge to the political process by consulting women's groups over policy proposals, lobbying legislators and tracking the progress of a veritable snowstorm of bills through the congress (Macaulay, 2000). In the last decade, over 150 bills affecting women's status awaited consideration each year in Congress. During the 1993 constitutional revision process, 17,246 proposals and 12,614 amendments were tabled, of which 956 concerned the chapter on social rights and would have affected women in the areas of work, health, family and education.[47] The proactive approach of CFEMEA and the *bancada feminina* in relation to the party delegations also enabled the women's movement to stave off attempts by individual legislators to introduce gender-regressive legislation.

Federalism and feminism

Brazil has a federal administrative structure, deepened by the 1988 Constitution, in which political power, resources, and decision-making are devolved to the sub-national units of government – 26 states and the Federal District and 5,562 municipalities, which are full administrative units of the federation and have the power to pass their own legislation (Souza, 1997; Nickson, 1995; Montero, 2000; Samuels, 2000). As political devolution replicates electoral and administrative structures at all three levels, the federal, state government and municipal governments each have an elected executive and legislature, and an administrative structure regulated by a written constitution. These parallel arenas of power multiply the legal instruments, political processes and distributional mechanisms with which the women's movement can engage, and create a division of labour across these fields. To illustrate: Brazil, unlike other federal systems, has unitary legal codes (labour, civil, criminal, family, electoral) that apply across the national territory, so that changes to the Penal Code – for example, to criminalize gender violence – can only be promulgated centrally; hence the mobilization of women's policy networks around the Federal Congress. However, the states are responsible for the enforcement apparatus (police, prisons, prosecution services, courts). As a result, policing of gender violence and the number and effectiveness of women's police stations vary greatly from state to state. As local government has freedom to set up new administrative structures and generate public policies, some cities have taken the opportunity to innovate and develop good practice in tackling and preventing domestic violence, even whilst many do nothing. However, the downside of this high level of local autonomy is manifest in the weak transmission of national policies from the federal ministries. As is evident in the case of the CNDM, when the central government policy body has low capacity in terms of resources, political power and ability to generate national guidelines and programmes, initiative inevitably devolves to state and municipal level, for better or for worse. To what extent, then, has political and administrative decentralization produced distinctively gendered local government?

Mayors and governors: politicians by proxy

Municipal politics have long been shaped by the tradition of dominant family dynasties and the dynamics of local bossism (Carvalho, 1997). The less economically and politically developed regions of Brazil – North, North-East and Centre-West – account for half the country's municipalities, but more than two-thirds of all the women mayors and city councillors, who are disproportionately concentrated in the small towns, with the largest number elected for the conservative PFL. This reflects a residual pattern of semi-feudal family politics in the interior whereby women enter local politics as proxies for male relatives who, until 1998, were unable to run for immediate re-election (Blay, 1979; Costa, 1998). The role of 'First Lady' confers status as well as access to the resources for clientelistic politics in the form of a charitable welfare fund found in most municipalities, which enables women to establish their own patronage base. The lower rate of election in the South and South-East regions is likely due to the greater importance of the party machines as gatekeepers to women's selection and election. Under military rule, no women was appointed mayor of a major city, but female candidates' relative success since 1985 has demonstrated that the bias does not lie with the voting public, as eight state capitals (six in the North-East, one each in the South and South-East) have elected women mayors, often for more than one term. They are mainly from centre-left parties, but half had family political connections.[48] The dynastic logic also began to trickle upwards to state level from 1994 as women governors from prominent local families began to be elected.[49]

State-level and municipal women's councils

Due to the sequence of democratization, gender policy was initiated at sub-national level through the *conselhos*[50] before it trickled up to the federal level in the mid-1980s. However, following the collapse of the CNDM, initiative reverted to sub-national level during the 1990s. Over the last two decades, the *conselhos* have multiplied and by 2002 they totalled 97 (19 state and 78 municipal).

Although the early ones bore the stamp of the PMDB governments, their degree of effectiveness and legitimacy also depended on a cross-party coalition of support. In São Paulo, the government alliance was broad enough and the women's movement sufficiently mobilized to make the *conselho* an effective space for debate, but many encountered the same creeping political co-option and competition that undermined the CNDM. Minas Gerais' *conselho* had no movement backing, and was packed with deputies' wives linked to the conservative wing of the PMDB (Alvarez, 1990: 219). In Rio Grande do Sul, Santa Catarina and Paraná, the PMDB women's proposal to create state-level women's federations aroused such suspicions about their electoral purpose that it prompted parallel women's activities in the NGOs and rival parties, especially the PT and PDT (Prá, 1992: 122–4). Similarly, when the feminist mayor of Salvador, Lídice da Mata, attempted to finance the municipal *conselho*, she was blocked by political opponents, leaving it with only two staff. The *conselhos* in Paraná and its state capital Curitiba collaborated well and enjoyed good access to the state administration as all were run by the PMDB until the party of government changed, when they were left paralysed (Prá, 1992: 140).

Rio Grande do Sul's was unique in being established by a PFL government, its first chair a member of the party's women's wing, causing it to be boycotted by the local women's movement. It was relaunched in 1991 by the PDT, which viewed it as a useful space to counterbalance the rise of the PT, in control of the state capital since 1989.

Institutional neglect also took its toll. For a long time, the São Paulo state *conselho* was the best established, presiding over the Network of Councils from 1989 until 1995. Nonetheless, it suffered political isolation from 1987–9, after some of its members had supported the defeated gubernatorial candidate. Relations were strained with the new governor and with the right-wing mayor Paulo Maluf, who in 1993 dismantled the municipal Women's Co-ordinating Committee created by his PT predecessor. The 1994 elections that brought the PSDB and Cardoso to power saw party appointees installed and budgets slashed.[51] The new governor of São Paulo, Mario Covas reduced the *conselho*'s paid staff from 38 to one, despite the fact that he had received electoral support from a women's coalition in the second round and two federal deputies from his own party were former *conselho* heads.

The orientation of the *conselhos* has also reflected the ideological cast of the parties in power. Sorocaba's was set up in 1987 at the initiative of the wives of the PMDB state governor and city mayor. Both headed social solidarity funds and this associated the *conselho* with female charitable and voluntary activity rather than gender policy until it was restructured in the 1990s (Costa, 1997). Ceará's was created in 1986 on the initiative of mainly centre-left women, (PMDB, PCdoB and PT), feminists and grassroots movements, following the election of PT mayor Maria Luiza Fontenelle in the capital city, Fortaleza. Although it was initially relatively independent, it became bureaucratized and distant from local women's groups as it absorbed the technocratic orientation of the dominant party of state politics, the PSDB (Esmeraldo and Said, 2002).

In consequence, the *conselhos'* effectiveness has varied immensely. The best followed the CNDM's agenda of women's healthcare (reproductive rights, ante- and post-natal care, provision of legal abortion), anti-sexist education, childcare and social provision, violence against women (installation of women's police stations and refuges), legal assistance, labour rights and labour market participation and, more recently, gender planning and analysis. However, like the CNDM they faced bureaucratic inertia and path-dependency, and a lack of resources, political clout and institutional insertion to achieve gender main-streaming. São Paulo state's council was unable to monitor or assist the women's police stations it had pioneered in the 1980s because the Secretariat for Public Security zealously guarded its territory. The vulnerability brought by the *conselhos'* hybrid remit, fragile resource base and ill-conceived operational guidelines taught the women's movement and the PT feminists the value of institutionaliza-tion. The Network of Councils and the CNDM drafted guidelines in the 1990s suggesting that their role, status and budget be enshrined in the local constitution (for instance, the financial and administrative autonomy of Ceará's is protected under the state constitution), not merely in local law, and that they should be attached to the mayor's office, have a cross-sectoral remit and a feminist orientation, and derive legitimacy from strong ties to civil society, which should retain majority representation on the board. In keeping with this recommen-dation, in 1999 Goiás restored its state *conselho* with full executive powers, headed by a feminist.

The new state-level and municipal institutionality also allowed activ-ists to draw on national and international legal frameworks to build local gender policy. In the early 1990s, São Paulo feminists attempted to transplant the CEDAW to sub-national government via a *paulista* equi-valent, some 50 articles proposing short- and medium-term policies on education, health, violence, work and childcare to be implemented by mayors (UNIFEM, 1998), with some 80 municipalities, representing 60 per cent of the state's population, signing up. Rio de Janeiro and Paraná's *conselhos* revived the idea in the late 1990s, using the Beijing Platform for Action as a blueprint. Rio's State Convention for Women's Real Citizenship was signed by 71 out of 91 municipalities. In the 1980s, the state *conselhos* lobbied movement representatives in the national Constitutional Assembly, whilst the Network of Councils urged that the national charter's principles be incorporated into the state and municipal counterparts drafted in 1989 and 1990.[52] As a result, many sub-national constitutions detail state and municipal government's responsibility for promoting gender equity and equality through gender units and policies on reproductive rights, domestic viol-ence and the labour market (Committee on the Elimination of Discrim-ination against Women, 2003a). At the initiative of local women's organizations, they have subsequently been amended and state and municipal by-laws promulgated, some of which have trickled up to national level after being trialled locally. In 1992, the Federal District copied the São Paulo municipal ordinance prohibiting businesses from demanding from female employees either a sterilization certificate or pregnancy test and this became federal law in 1995. Likewise, provision of legal abortion by public hospitals was pioneered in Campinas, São Paulo and Rio de Janeiro in the 1980s before becoming a federal directive in 1998.[53]

Brazil's political parties have filtered feminist claims through both commission and omission, with the porous party system constituting both an opportunity and an obstacle. Their overall indifference to women as political actors has resulted in them neither actively promoting nor blocking access to political rights, whether to suffrage or to increased representation in elected office. Such under-institutionalized and unideological parties have created a political habitus that can apparently absorb a gender equality and equity agenda without much resistance, yet that support may just as easily leach away due to these very characteristics, as evidenced by the co-option and decline of the CNDM. However, democratization has created important parallel political arenas whose new institutional and associative tools have been useful to an increasingly decentralized and horizontally organized women's movement. The next chapter therefore considers how the PT differs from the main parties in its degree of porosity, ideological definition and institutionalization, the evolution of its political habitus and its relationship with both the state and civil society.

3
The Workers' Party, Gender and Feminism

On 1 January 2003, the PT's founder, Luiz Inácio Lula da Silva (known simply as 'Lula'), assumed the office of president of Brazil. He appointed to his cabinet an unprecedented number of women, including the first secretary of state for gender policies, whilst in Congress the PT achieved twice the female representation of any other party. This chapter analyzes why and how the PT has been more consistently committed to promoting gender equality and equity than its rivals in Brazil, and even its social democratic counterparts in Latin America. It begins by considering the origins, political development and internal organization of a mould-breaking party, arguing that the strong foundational presence of women affected its political habitus and consequently facilitated the integration of gender claims into its ideology, programme and policies. It considers how the profile and success of the PT's women candidates for public elected office have been both the motive force and outcome of the party's affirmative action policies, and evaluates the extent to which party feminists have succeeded in promoting a gender agenda across multiple political arenas.[1]

'The triumph of hope over fear'

Lula won the 2002 presidential elections in Brazil with a landslide victory, securing more than 60 per cent of the vote in the second round and a mandate of 53 million votes. Not only was the peaceful election of a left-wing candidate a landmark for Brazil, but it also signalled a vote of confidence in the PT itself, won through its tenacity in the social movements and legislatures of the country. The PT originated in the metalworkers' strikes in the industrial belt around Greater São Paulo in the late 1970s, fruit of the frustration that the new unions, social movements and progressive Catholic Church felt with the political system. When the military government dissolved the two-party system in 1979, these emerging political actors seized the political moment and performed the remarkable feat of legally constituting the PT under the draconian provisions of the revised party legislation (Gadotti and Pereira, 1989; Meneguello, 1989; Sader and Silverstein, 1991; Keck, 1992). In the early 1980s, the PT made little impression due to electoral rules that the military government had imposed in order to exclude the Left,[2] and to the party's own identity as an opposition *movement* that did not take seriously an electoral process still conducted under military tutelage. But, after 1985, the party began to grow exponentially, evolving into the country's most important opposition force and becoming a persistent challenger in every direct election for the Brazilian presidency. It increased its share of the first round vote steadily, from 17.2 per cent in 1989 against Collor, to 46.4 per cent in 2002 against the PSDB's José Serra, as well as its representation at all three legislative levels (Table 3.1), and has achieved a truly national reach.[3] It has governed states and state capitals in every region, whilst the 2003 intake of senators showed its continued dominance, holding two of the three seats, in two states that could not be further apart in every sense, Acre in the Western Amazon, and São Paulo, the country's economic powerhouse.[4]

For a quarter-century the PT has exerted a powerful influence over Brazilian political life. It was the first major party to form from the grassroots rather than through an elite pact or schism, to reject a rent-seeking and clientelist attitude towards political power, and to shun the corporatist status quo. It spearheaded the campaign for direct presidential elections in 1984, facilitated a high level of grassroots

Table 3.1 Brazil: percentage of PT elected representatives, 1982–2004

Year	Senator	Federal deputy	Governor	State deputy	Mayor	City councillor
1982	0	1.7	0	1.4	0.1	—
1986	0	3.3	0	4.1	0.5	—
1988					0.9	—
1990	1.2	7.0	0	7.9		
1992					1.1	—
1994	6.2	9.6	7.4	8.8		
1996					2.0	3.2
1998	9.9	11.3	11.1	8.6		
2000					3.4	4.1
2002	17.3	17.7	11.1	13.9		
2004					7.4	7.1

participation in the Constitutional Assembly (to which it was the only party to contribute a fully drafted proposal), and led the campaign to impeach President Collor in 1992. It has maintained its close organic links with the Catholic Church and social movements, established numerous Parliamentary Committees of Inquiry into corruption and forms of social injustice, and strongly backed human rights.[5] Its presence has pulled the political centre of gravity further towards social justice issues, whilst at the same time it modified its own radical image to become electable as its early oppositionist character gave way to a more pragmatic identity as a party of government grounded in its experience in local government. Worldwide, it has attracted attention for challenging the premature obituaries for the Left in Latin America and establishing in its local governments a new model of progressive, pluralist, participatory politics, exemplified by the World Social Forums[6] hosted by the party's flagship administration in Porto Alegre (RS).

The PT is also *sui generis* in ideological and organizational terms. Founded as a broad church to embrace a heterogeneous political opposition no longer comfortable within the (P)MDB or the old Left, the political inclinations of its members stretch from militantly socialist, oriented around class and anti-capitalism, to radical Catholic, with every shade of social democrat, humanist and ex-guerrilla in between. However, the glue that cements together such a diverse rainbow coalition is not just Lula's charismatic leadership. Differences are channelled through officially recognized internal factions, which are allowed to compete internally over party management posts and policy direction, but not to present sub-lists in public elections. Policy is decided collectively by local delegates at the annual conferences or by the party delegation in the legislature.[7] Strict internal discipline ensures that individual representatives adhere to the party line, under pain of sanction or expulsion.[8] The other core element of the PT's habitus is not so much a dogma as an *ethos*, centred more on process than on political ideology. Powerfully shaped by principles and practices of the grassroots Catholic Church and liberation theology, this ethic consists of transparency, a rejection of corruption and a belief in a more participatory democracy, as well as a commitment to social inclusion and a 'preferential option for the poor'.[9] So far, this ethos has been elastic enough to allow for vigorous debate and disagreements about the specifics of public policies, whilst maintaining party unity.[10]

By Brazilian standards, the PT ranks as a well-institutionalized mass party that is not defined simply by elections. Its bureaucracy includes paid personnel, think-tanks,[11] publishing, and training events. Intra-party rules for decision-making and for holding the leadership accountable are well-defined and accepted by the rank-and-file, and the party's organic organizational structure corresponds to that laid out in its statute. It has extensive base-level organization,[12] although this pales beside the social penetration of European social democratic parties,[13] with a large activist base, well-developed subculture of belonging and a relatively stable core electorate. Its societal rootedness is based on the party's strong associations with the social movements, whilst its principled stance on their autonomy has avoided subsuming them within the party apparatus, as its left-wing predecessors did. In similar vein, the PT also explicitly rejects the hierarchical, doctrinaire, cadre-run model of Leninist party organization of the orthodox Left, and the personalist clientelism of the populist Left.

Gendered genesis and justice

Whilst Panebianco is interested in the actions of 'founding *fathers*', it is the generically *mixed* political parentage of the PT,[14] seen in its heterodox origins and early influences, that has rendered the party more predisposed towards women's political agency and the agenda that emerges from their experience of the sexual division of labour. The PT started life with a dual foundation, and a vision of a pluralist coalition. An early document claimed 'Grassroots struggles have allowed industrial workers, informal sector workers, public employees, slum dwellers, the self-employed, peasants, rural workers, women, blacks, students, indians and others to organize to defend their interests...' (Partido dos Trabalhadores, 1980). On the one hand, it drew on a relatively homogeneous base of male industrial trade unionists, typical of classic Western European social democratic parties, geographically concentrated in the multinational export sector in the South East. However, the PT could not have been born, or survived in practical and electoral terms, without the midwifery of the progressive Catholic Church, whose extensive networks and personnel enabled the PT to mobilize resources very quickly around the country to meet registration requirements. The Church not only imbued the party with its key values, but also brought new constituencies of voters and activists through a highly heterogeneous, geographically dispersed base of social movements, frequently led by or composed of women, mobilized around a multitude of issues. These ranged from the spiritual and social agenda of the Catholic Base Communities, to the material concerns of neighbourhood committees, Mothers' Clubs and the childcare, healthcare and cost-of-living groups, to the identity issues of the Black and women's movements. These non-workplace-based social movements generated new demands based on the daily consumption needs of the household, social reproduction, marginality and civil rights far from traditional masculine conceptions of class interests. This social movement experience produced some of the earliest women party activists and representatives, such as Irma Passoni, one of the first PT federal deputies, who rose up through the Catholic Base Communities and the Cost of Living movement in the working-class Eastern Zone of São Paulo.[15] Others, such as her colleague Bete Mendes, an actress involved with the Amnesty Movement[16] and the São Paulo regional strike in the late 1970s, reflected these overlapping constituencies by combining trade union activism with social movement, Church and feminist activities.

Women played a key role in the party's inception precisely because they were non-traditional political actors. Of the 18 PT women elected to Congress in 2002, several had founded the party in their home town or state.[17] In Agudos, a small town in São Paulo state, the local party consisted chiefly of women from the social movements and community groups. However, some female activists became important party leaders in industrial areas, a paradox that was the result of the enduring legacy of corporatist co-option in the majority of unions. In Santos, the country's most important industrial port, the military regime stripped militant trade unionists of their political rights and elected office, so wives and daughters, such as Telma de Souza,[18] stepped into their shoes. By the time the women were organizing a local chapter of the Women's Amnesty Movement (*Movimento Feminino pela Anistia* – MFA), the local unions were dominated by conservative, pro-regime leaders, and no new unionism emerged here, despite its proximity to the São Paulo industrial belt. Thus, the local PT branch has been female-dominated in terms of members, leadership and representation since its establishment in 1980. Telma herself served three terms as the party's municipal president, and was elected city councillor, state deputy, mayor and three times federal deputy.[19] The same occurred in Betim, a major industrial centre in Minas Gerais, where half of the city's top municipal officials appointed by the PT were women.[20]

The MFA was an extremely important conduit for women's political education and activism. Its founders participated in the 1975 UN World Conference on Women in Mexico City and, early on, it adopted an explicitly feminist agenda. Once the Amnesty Law was passed in August 1979, it provided a ready-made organizational network from which many feminist founders of the PT emerged: Bete Mendes, Maria Luiza Fontenelle,[21] Helena Greco[22] and Sandra Starling (Belo Horizonte, MG),[23] Maria Laura (DF), Iara Bernardi (Sorocaba), and Clara Charf, the widow of the guerrilla leader Carlos Marighella. Their presence immediately gave the PT a distinctively gendered political sociability, more marked in certain towns.

In the PT, three key barriers to women's involvement in left-wing party politics have been much lower. Firstly, the influence of a male-dominated union movement has been diluted by the diversity of the party's support base, which embraced both formal and informal sector workers across industry, state sector and agriculture, as well as grassroots movements. Secondly, the new Trade Union Confederation (*Central Unica dos Trabalhadores* – CUT) was unusual in campaigning as actively on broader issues of consumption, social justice and citizenship as it did on wages and working conditions (Barros, 1999). The job losses in industry and the banking sector in the 1990s also led to the CUT becoming dominated by public sector and service unions, which have a much higher proportion of female membership (Samuels, 2004b: 1007). Consequently, the party espouses a more pluralist conception of social subjectivities and citizenship. Finally, the availability of a discourse of ethics as well as one of class made the party a more amenable environment for women, who are more often socialized to think of themselves as moral rather than political agents in the public sphere. It has been argued that the PT's core characteristics and values – participation, internal democracy and attention to the reproductive challenges of everyday life – converge with women's movement principles and practice (Haas, 2001), thus explaining the high degree of political sympathy between the two.

Women's voice within the party

As PT women were involved in the genesis of a *new* party, rather than in the sustenance of a pre-existing one, they managed to retain, and eventually expand upon, their presence. There is no department aimed at recruiting women or channelling their political participation, nor has the party ever regarded women as a political 'problem' or captive political constituency. Nonetheless, women party activists have still had to struggle to institutionalize their voice. They held their first meeting in January 1981 and formed a women's committee, but for some time thereafter gender questions remained ignored or ghettoized, and organization was piecemeal. The smaller states had nothing, whilst the larger states had women's organizations of two different types; either women's committees or secretariats, or else women's caucuses (*núcleos*), with some linked directly to the state or municipal directorates, others to the Secretariat for Popular Movements, which at that time held the institutional remit for women's issues. The National Women's Sub-secretariat was founded in 1988 as an offshoot of the latter by party feminists who felt that gender questions should be made more visible and mainstreamed. This later became a full Secretariat (*Secretaria Nacional de Mulheres do PT* – SNM)[24] and, in principle, every state- and municipal-level party directorate could therefore have a local equivalent, although many still do not. The heyday of the SNM was in the early 1990s, following Lula's 1989 presidential campaign which saw a notable involvement by women who took up the purple of the suffrage movement and the party's symbol in their slogan 'Eu sou uma estrela' ('I am a star'). A series of national women's meetings[25] enabled them to influence the party's election manifestos, proposals for the Constitutional Assembly and policy documents, introduce the internal quota and hold workshops on gender policy in local government. However, from the late 1990s the SNM lost its profile and clout due to factional divisions and the continuing indifference of the party's Secretariat for Institutional Affairs, which in principle exists to promote the party's policy initiatives.[26] Under the Lula government, it subsequently revived to some extent.

Internal quota

For a decade, the tiny number of women in party leadership posts bore no relationship either to the percentage elected to Congress or the proportion active in the rank-and-file. Female affiliation was around 40 per cent in 1992, not too different from that of other parties,[27] yet the percentage of women delegates to the bi-annual national conferences and Congresses never topped 25 per cent.[28] Delegates are selected via meetings at municipal and state level, but no quota has been applied to this process.

All but four of the 16 members of the PT's first ruling body, the National Provisional Committee, were union leaders, and all were men (Godinho, 2000: 37). On average, women constituted just 6.4 per cent of the members of the National Directorate (*Diretório Nacional* – DN), an elected 83-strong decision-making body, and there was only one woman among the 20 or so members of the National Executive Committee (*Comissão Executiva Nacional* – CEN) chosen by the DN to oversee the day-to-day running of the party. The profile of women leaders also differed from that of men in the party. In generational terms, 40–45 per cent of PT leaders cut their political teeth during military rule, but men were more likely to have begun their career in left-wing parties or revolutionary movements, women in social movements. Although women often headed the municipal or, less commonly, regional party directorates, they struggled to graduate to higher leadership positions. Thus, many male party cadres who have dominated the national leadership structures have never held public elected office, whereas several prominent women elected to public office on the back of a huge popular vote have never held party leadership positions (Godinho, 2000: 61).

Affirmative action for women on internal decision-making bodies was mooted in the first year of the party's existence (Sacchet, 2002: 129), but it was not until 1988 that frustration over lack of visibility inside the party led the SNM feminists to campaign for a quota of 30 per cent. The first attempt failed at the party conference in Vitória (ES) that year and it was finally approved by the first National Congress in 1991, at which the party's statutes and general orientation were debated, making the PT one of the first parties in Latin America to institute such a measure (Htun and Jones, 2002). They pointed out the disparity between the PT's rhetoric of justice and equality, and the reality of women's under-representation in party leadership structures. As later in the national legislature, they framed the quota as an issue of institutional discrimination and fairness, rather than making marianist claims based on the 'special qualities' that women might bring, their supposedly moralizing impact or the representation of 'women's interests.' Within the PT the campaign lasted only five months, suggesting that the party was highly receptive to arguments based on pluralism (Sacchet, 2002: 162). The SNM women also organized strategically to win over the different political factions and identity groups in the PT, persuading prominent party figures, such as Benedita da Silva, to use their personal influence.

The presence of institutionalized factions has both facilitated and hindered this affirmative action. The PT had opted for a zero-sum measure; women's gain in representation would be men's loss, in contrast to the solution reached in the National Congress in 1996, where the number of candidates was simply increased. Elections to the DN and CEN must respect the gender quota and give proportionate representation to the different tendencies, which can achieve a win–win outcome if they promote female candidates. However, several smaller factions attempted to sabotage implementation by drawing up non-compliant lists and horse-trading with their rivals over male and female candidates (Sacchet, 2002: 178).[29]

The party's respect for its own statutory provisions, combined with the SNM's insistence on the strict application of the quota, increased the percentage of women on the DN from 6.1 per cent in 1990 to 30.1 per cent in 1995 (Godinho, 1996: 151), and likewise at all other levels of the party bureaucracy. The quota highlighted the sexual division of labour within the party, with women doing the menial work,[30] and has been regarded as a positive move, even by those, including women leaders, who initially opposed it.[31] However, full compliance became bureaucratic and divorced from its original spirit, with the quota being regarded as a ceiling not a floor, thereby stifling further debate about gender and leadership issues in the party (Godinho, 2000: 71). Women leaders continue to be excluded from the *informal* circuits of power and influence. The PT's headquarters in São Paulo makes it much easier for those based locally to influence daily events, and the female DN members more often represent distant regions (North, North East and Centre West) (Godinho, 2000: 53). Male DN members also tend to serve for several mandates, accumulating more experience whilst all the other structural barriers, such as socialization and the double burden, remain untouched. Women on the DN are less likely to be married, and frequently complain about the macho conduct of meetings, despite other positive changes such as the provision of childcare facilities and better scheduling of meetings.

It does not appear that the internal quota brought about an increase in female candidacies for public office as women were more likely to win DN or CEN seats after they had been elected. Nonetheless, the PT's move did provoke a number of contagion effects, the first horizontal as other centre-left political parties followed suit,[32] although the other parties still have under 10 per cent women leaders (Godinho, 2000: 17; Araújo, 2001). The national university and secondary student unions and all four major trade union organizations[33] also adopted a 30 per cent quota (Sacchet, 2002: fn 162). The CUT was the first to do so, as so many of its women members were members of the PT and had followed the quota debate with interest. However, despite changes in its rank-and-file, the CUT is still a more masculinized space than the party and it took two years to approve the quota (Sacchet, 2002: 131). One *petista* commented, 'Women in the PT don't have much visibility but they do become great advisors and parliamentary assistants. They are everywhere. In the CUT, you don't see women leaders or backroom workers.'[34]

Vertical contagion occurred in 1996 when the PT spearheaded the bill introducing the nationwide statutory gender quota for proportional elections.[35] In 1999, the PT government of Rio Grande do Sul[36] also approved a 30 per cent quota for the state administration, with similar under discussion in Paraíba. However, the PT has not applied the principle to national executive posts – Lula's female ministerial appointments amounted to just 10 per cent – although in 2001 and 2003, PT legislators proposed changes to house rules to ensure 30 per cent quota representation of women on the steering committees of both chambers.

Groundbreakers: PT women representatives

Proportional positions

Overall, the PT's record on electing women candidates to the proportional positions of federal deputy, state deputy and city councillor has often been much better than that of the other major parties (see Tables 3.2, 3.3, 3.4 and 3.5). However, given that the selection process in a system with an excess of candidates is hardly controlled by the party, the election of women does not so much reflect party support as the political capital (that is, the social movement leadership and electoral appeal) that these candidates bring.[37] In the 1982 and 1986 elections, the party committed itself to supporting all candidates equally but, as the party grew, this was abandoned and individual candidates now campaign as best they can. Certain PT women, such as Maria Laura, Benedita da Silva, Luci Choinacki (SC) and two newcomers to the PT ranks in Congress in

Table 3.2 Brazil: percentage of women candidates for federal deputy, percentage elected and female success index, by party, 1994–2002

Party	1994			1998			2002		
	Candidates	Elected	FSI	Candidates	Elected	FSI	Candidates	Elected	FSI
PPB	4.1	4.7	95.7	7.5	0.0	0.0	5.0	2.0	39.6
PTB	1.6	0.0	0.0	9.0	0.0	0.0	12.9	7.7	56.1
PFL	2.6	2.5	87.0	8.1	4.8	57.0	10.4	7.1	66.2
PMDB	6.1	7.5	125.3	12.2	9.6	76.7	10.8	5.4	47.3
PSDB	6.3	7.9	128.8	9.1	7.1	75.8	13.0	8.5	61.9
PDT	4.3	5.9	139.9	9.5	4.0	39.6	11.2	4.8	—
PT	10.2	14.0	143.5	12.2	8.5	66.4	14.2	15.4	110.0
National average	6.2	6.7	101.5	10.4	5.7	51.8	11.7	8.2	67.3

Notes: Data for Tables 3.2 and 3.3 are derived from the CFEMEA website www.cfemea.org.br. A party is included only if it has won a minimum 5 per cent of the seats in the Chamber of Deputies or state assemblies in two or more elections. PPB figures include data for the PPR and PP in 1994.

Table 3.3 Brazil: percentage of women candidates for state deputy, percentage elected and female success index, by party, 1994–2002

Party	1994			1998			2002		
	Candidates	Elected	FSI	Candidates	Elected	FSI	Candidates	Elected	FSI
PPB	7.5	4.8	62.1	12.1	8.4	66.8	12.6	7.5	56.4
PTB	4.8	4.2	86.2	11.0	4.9	42.0	16.2	8.2	46.2
PFL	4.3	5.1	119.3	12.0	8.8	71.1	15.4	7.5	44.7
PMDB	5.0	5.8	108.2	14.5	10.8	71.3	14.8	15.7	107.1
PSDB	5.9	8.6	142.4	13.3	10.5	76.2	15.1	15.8	105.7
PDT	6.6	9.3	146.0	12.0	8.3	67.0	12.0	9.7	78.3
PT	13.6	17.4	134.3	14.8	20.0	144.3	14.4	19.7	146.1
National average	7.2	7.8	110.1	12.9	10.0	74.8	14.8	12.6	82.5

2002, Fátima Bezerra (RN) and Francisca Trindade (PI), have been extremely popular at the polls and boost the party's overall showing. In 2000, Ana Júlia Carepa, one of the PT founders in Pará, ran for city councillor after a term as deputy mayor of Belém and won the largest number of votes. In consequence, the PT polled 19 per cent, well ahead of its nearest competitor with 8.8 per cent, and elected a record seven out of 33 councillors (Guidry and Petit, 2003: 73).

That said, in proportional terms since 1994 the PT has nearly always run the highest percentage of women on its party lists. However, in response to

Table 3.4 Brazil: percentage of women candidates for mayor and city councillor, percentage elected and female success index, by party, 2000

Party	Mayor			City councillor		
	Candidates	Elected	FSI	Candidates	Elected	FSI
PPB	5.7	5.2	89.5	18.7	11.9	58.6
PTB	7.7	6.3	80.1	18.8	11.7	57.1
PFL	7.4	7.3	98.1	18.9	12.1	59.1
PL	6.0	3.8	63.2	18.3	11.1	55.9
PMDB	6.9	4.8	68.0	18.9	11.7	56.8
PSDB	7.1	5.9	81.2	18.8	11.8	57.8
PDT	5.4	2.1	37.0	18.8	9.9	47.3
PSB	8.7	9.8	113.5	19.3	11.3	53.2
PPS	8.4	6.7	78.0	19.2	11.1	52.4
PT	12.2	4.8	36.3	20.2	14.1	64.7
National average	7.6	5.7	73.9	19.1	11.6	55.5

Source: Calculations based on National Electoral Court data.

Table 3.5 Brazil: percentage of women candidates for mayor and city councillor, percentage elected and female success index, by party, 2004

Party	Mayor			City councillor		
	Candidates	Elected	FSI	Candidates	Elected	FSI
PP	8.3	6.2	73.2	21.2	13.0	55.6
PTB	9.9	9.4	96.6	21.8	12.5	51.2
PFL	9.3	8.1	87.0	21.5	13.0	54.3
PL	9.7	10.5	109.6	21.5	10.9	44.6
PMDB	8.7	7.4	84.7	21.9	13.0	53.5
PSDB	8.9	6.1	68.6	21.8	13.1	53.9
PDT	8.5	5.6	63.0	21.4	10.8	44.3
PSB	10.0	8.5	85.3	22.2	12.3	49.3
PPS	8.5	6.2	72.3	22.2	11.4	45.1
PT	11.3	6.3	53.7	23.3	15.2	59.0
National average	9.5	7.3	76.0	22.1	12.7	50.9

Source: Calculations based on National Electoral Court data.

the quota law other parties have upped their numbers of female candidates, some equalizing or outstripping the PT, whereas the latter's numbers have risen only slightly because it departed from a higher baseline. Nonetheless, despite the PT's rigorous application of its own internal quota, as its competitors it has not adhered to the statutory quota, and the SNM has not pressed the party to change its statutes or 'set a good example'. Given the candidate-centred nature of the open-list system, it is more relevant to examine how many women the party actually elects and how they perform in relation to their male counterparts.

Between 1994 and 2002, the PT elected nearly double the national average of women state and federal deputies, and the highest percentage of women city councillors in 2000 and 2004, generally outperforming the other major parties (Tables 3.4 and 3.5).[38]

Since 1986, the proportion of PT women representatives has averaged 12.9 per cent in the lower house, and 16.9 per cent in the state assemblies, as demonstrated in columns (a) of Table 3.6. Although the female success index (FSI) deteriorated overall after the introduction of the quota, the third columns in Tables 3.2–3.5 show that the PT had the highest FSI for federal deputy in 1994 and 2002, for state deputy in 1998 and 2002, and for city councillor in 2000 and 2004. These data suggest that those elected have capitalized on their social movement electoral constituencies, rather than benefited from a voter preference for female candidates, or exceptional levels of party support.

Table 3.6 Brazil: PT female legislative representatives, total number and percentage of (a) PT representation and (b) female representation, 1982–2002

Year	Senator			Federal deputy			State deputy		
	No.	(a) %	(b) %	No.	(a) %	(b) %	No.	(a) %	(b) %
1982	0	0	0	2	25.0	25.0	1	7.7	3.6
1986	0	0	0	2	12.5	8.0	6	15.4	19.3
1990	0	0	0	5	14.3	17.8	10	12.0	17.2
1994	2	40.0	50.0	7	14.0	21.9	16	17.4	19.5
1998	3	37.5	60.0	5	8.5	17.2	18	20.0	17.0
2002	6	42.9	60.0	14	15.4	33.3	29	19.7	21.8

Source: As for Table 3.5.

Majoritarian positions

By contrast, for the majoritarian posts of president, governor, mayor and senator, candidates are selected either by the appropriate level of party committee or by a primary election.[39] Where nominations are controlled by officials, there is a marked tendency to reward cadres (predominantly men) for their work in the party bureaucracy, whereas the party rank-and-file exhibit a preference for candidates with a strong electoral base (often women involved in social movements). In 1988, the latter chose Luiza Erundina, a working-class northeastern migrant and social worker supported by the progressive Church and grassroots housing movements, to contest the mayoralty of São Paulo against the preferences of the party leadership (Macaulay, 1996). Factional rivalries also play an important role and the most prominent women, such as Marta Suplicy and Benedita da Silva, are notably less engaged with such in-fighting than their male counterparts. This can be a double-edged sword, giving them wider electoral appeal, but less clout within the party. Erundina was not supported by the party machine either when she ran for mayor, or subsequently for senator; in frustration, she left the party.[40] Telma de Souza was passed over as candidate for governor in favour of a party grandee, José Dirceu, despite her profile as the former mayor of Santos.[41] In the face of such internal politics, the SNM has been unable to push its 'own' candidates within the party, although many of the women elected sympathize with its agenda.

Nonetheless, women have constituted well over one-third of PT senators since 1994, when Benedita da Silva and Marina da Silva (AC) topped their respective state lists. In 2002, the PT ran eight women candidates (30 per cent of the total) and five were elected, giving the women a

62.5 per cent success rate, compared to the male candidates' 27.8 per cent. Some regard the Senate as a consolation prize, peopled by former governors or governors-in-waiting, because it is perceived that the real power and resources lie in state government, around which party politics revolve at a regional level. The party has run relatively few women for governor and elected only three female deputy governors, the latter assuming power for a few months when the incumbents ran for (re)election.[42] Its most serious candidates were Marta Suplicy (São Paulo, 1998), who finished third close behind the incumbent Covas (PSDB), and Benedita da Silva, who in 2002 was unexpectedly defeated in Rio in the first round by the previous governor's wife in a triumph of old-fashioned clientelistic politics. However, that year two *petistas* (Dalva Figueiredo, AP and Maria do Carmo, PA) both reached the second round, a reflection of the rising number and quality of female gubernatorial candidates.

For the post of mayor, the PT's performance has been mixed; it ran an above-average number of women candidates, but elected a below-average proportion in both 2000 and 2004. This is partly due to the skewed distribution of women mayors, with many members of local dynasties elected through clientelistic vehicles. As Tables 3.4 and 3.5 show, the centre-right parties have the higher FSI and the PT by far the lowest. The PT, on the other hand, does best in the major conurbations and, although it has elected numerically few women,[43] it has put women in the chief executive's seat in several major cities and industrial centres.[44] The megalopolis São Paulo, with a population larger than several Latin American republics, has had two women PT mayors – Luiza Erundina (1989–92), and Marta Suplicy (2001–4).

Women's political career paths

The career paths of PT politicians also differ notably from those of their counterparts. No other party has been represented by individuals from such a range of unorthodox political origins, many of whom are remarkable stories of social mobility.[45] They include rural workers such as Luci Choinacki and Dorcelina Folador, a disabled, landless peasant leader elected mayor of Mundo Novo (MS), whilst Erundina would begin her speeches with a litany of identities 'I am a woman, a northeasterner, a *petista...*' (Macaulay, 1996). Marina da Silva, of Afro-Indian origin, was born the daughter of impoverished rubbertappers. First educated at the age of 16, she became involved in the local Christian Base Communities, and helped found the local union movement alongside the legendary rural union leader Chico Mendes. She represented the PT first as city councillor in Acre's state capital Rio Branco, then as state deputy and as senator since 1994 (Branford and Kucinski, 1995: 17). Benedita da Silva's life story is emblematic of the triple oppressions of race, poverty and gender, and she still lives in the shantytown in Rio de Janeiro where she brought up her children (Benjamin and Mendonça, 1998). Like Marina, she had to work as a maid until her involvement in social struggles and the Pentecostal church offered escape.[46]

An examination of the professional training of the 31 PT women elected in 2002 reveals a preponderance of teachers (from primary to university), followed by medics (doctors, nurses, psychologists) and social workers, often involved in related union activity.[47] These are highly feminized professions, particularly in the lower echelons, but also constitute major categories of public sector workers, a backbone of PT support. However, a number have led unions in masculine areas such as the oil industry, petrochemicals, manufacturing and banking.[48] The majority are feminist sympathizers whilst, unsurprisingly, those least willing to associate themselves with a feminist agenda, such as Irma Passoni and Angela Guadagnin, come from a Church background.

Women in the centre-right parties may share similar professional backgrounds, but they are much less likely to have had union experience or to be of working-class origin, and are more likely to have risen through family connections, something no PT woman has done. Even Marta Suplicy, a *soignée*, upper-class feminist whose former husband was a long-serving PT senator, had a high public profile as a media sexologist before she ran for federal deputy in 1994. All six of the PT women senators elected in 2002 worked their way up from the rank-and-file; two had served as city councillors, four as state deputies, one as federal deputy and two as deputy mayors. The ten new deputies who arrived in 2003 had served between them seven terms as city councillor and ten as state deputy, whilst others had served as municipal or state secretaries. Only Senator Fátima Cleide (RO) had held no elected office, but had been president of the party's regional directorate for two terms. They are also relatively successful at retaining their seats and moving on to higher or executive offices. In the Chamber of Deputies, three PT women have served three terms in office,[49] and six have served two. Of the five elected for only one mandate before 2002, Ana Júlia Carepa went on to become deputy mayor of Belém and senator, and Marta Suplicy became mayor of São Paulo.

Pluralism and gender policy

What impact do the characteristics of the party and its representatives have on the formulation of gender-related legislation? The PT's understanding of gender questions has evolved through internal debates about the relevance of gender as a fundamental factor in structuring social power relations, the relationship between class, race and gender, and the relative importance of practical and strategic gender interests. Broadly, it has been influenced by three distinct discourses on gender policy emanating from traditional class-based socialism, feminism and, latterly, a gender and development perspective adopted by feminist state officials. The first sees women's independence and emancipation as a function of female integration into the workforce and state provision of the reproductive services that women normally carry out. The social facilities and income-generating programmes that would benefit women in the poorer social classes have been advocated mainly by the party's popular movements and trade union departments, which initially regarded the SNM with suspicion and hostility, dismissing the feminists as 'middle class'.[50]

The second has put questions of sexual citizenship and reproductive rights on the agenda, inevitably generating some tension with the Church-based elements in the party, although this should not be overstated. The PT has never adopted party policy in favour of decriminalization of abortion for fear that it might be turned into a *cause célèbre* by its opponents and lose them not only the progressive Catholic but also the evangelical vote, which is far more fickle. Nonetheless, its legislators have strongly supported the legal abortion movement,[51] framing it as a public health rather than a reproductive rights issue, and internal discipline ensures that members with a personal religious objection to abortion are not allowed to contradict the party line in public.[52] The PT has also contributed to Brazil's relatively tolerant sexual culture. Since the homosexual movement's support for the metalworkers' strikes 1979–80 (MacRae, 1992; Green, 1994), the party has been openly supportive of sexual citizenship rights.[53] The party has had a gay and lesbian group since 1992, and ran ten openly gay candidates in major cities in 1996. Its 1994 election manifesto detailed policies to eliminate discrimination on the grounds of sexual orientation,[54] which over 80 municipalities and seven states have banned in their constitutions and by-laws. Marta Suplicy sponsored a same-sex civil partnership bill in Congress, and as mayor of São Paulo hosted the country's largest ever gay pride rally. PT administrations in Recife (PE) and Porto Alegre unilaterally extended pension rights to the homosexual partners of state employees, all of which set the scene for the Cardoso government's decree of equal legal status and inheritance rights for same sex couples in 2000. The Lula government went further in its first months in office, submitting a motion to the UN Commission on Human Rights calling on all countries 'to promote and protect the human rights of all persons regardless of their sexual orientation'.

In the early days, the class-based view (prioritizing practical gender interests) predominated over the feminist view (privileging strategic gender interests). The party initially clung to the foundational myth of the party's workerist origins; the founding document of the PT, the two-page manifesto signed in the Colégio Sion on 10 February 1980, employed the term 'worker' no less than 19 times, focusing on a critique of the corporatist system of labour relations. The party's early election slogans urged 'Vote PT – The rest is bourgeois' ('Vote no três – o resto é burguês') and 'Workers vote for workers' ('Trabalhador vota em trabalhador') until it became clear that what the PT considered its natural electoral constituency most certainly did not want to vote for 'people like themselves'. A pamphlet on women's issues for the 1988 municipal elections sported headings such as 'What about women's oppression under capitalism?' and 'The women's movement and the construction of socialism', a class-based discourse that later disappeared. Nonetheless, this was a new pluralist Left and the party's first programme, from June 1980, declares 'The PT considers that forms of discrimination are not secondary issues, as the problem of the woman worker segregated in the factory, farm and, often, in the home, is not secondary...The party will struggle to overcome these problems just as much as it will fight any other form of oppression' (Partido dos Trabalhadores, 1998).

Through the efforts of the SNM, the 1994 election manifesto's language and approach were more clearly informed by a feminist notion of gender as a constructed social category, and by an emphasis on equality-in-difference (Partido dos Trabalhadores, 1994). In the late 1990s, a gender and development discourse was incipient in the party's literature, as the SNM held seminars on gender planning and PT municipal administrations won recognition for their innovative gender policies. However, Brazil has never had any comprehensive anti-poverty programme, whether based on universal entitlement or on targeting, and programmes have been piecemeal and incoherent. Consequently, the issues of gender equality and equity and poverty have been debated quite separately. With the Lula government's promise to prioritize poverty reduction, party women began to examine more systematically questions such as the feminization of poverty and the gendered impact of the social security reforms, debates that have been far more advanced in Chile (Macaulay, 2004).

Legislating gender

The PT has been very active in the legislative sphere and, in 2002, despite being then only the fifth largest party in term of representation, it sponsored more bills than any other.[55] Even in opposition and in a legislative environment dominated by the executive, the PT also converted more bills into law than any other party,[56] and exercised recognized leadership in the two houses.[57] In the area of social policy, PT politicians have legislated notably on human rights issues (slave labour, racism, sexual orientation, land reform, the elderly), health (generic medicines, free drugs for AIDS sufferers, mental asylums), corruption and nepotism, reform of the judiciary, citizen security, poverty reduction and food security. Whilst progressive gender legislation has been proposed by lawmakers across the political spectrum, the PT's representatives have played a critical role in translating into legislation the gender policies mandated by the party rank-and-file and the women's movement. In the Constitutional Assembly the PT group, led by then federal deputy Lula, pushed through the constitutional provisions on maternity and paternity leave, and later PMDB and PSDB apathy on gender issues allowed *petistas* such as Marta Suplicy, and later Iara Bernardi, to become key players in the *bancada feminina*.[58] Although the PMDB dominated the women's caucus in the 1980s,[59] between 1991 and 2002 representation was more evenly distributed, with the centre-left electing half the women deputies in 1990,[60] 1994[61] and 1998,[62] and two-thirds in 2002, with most of those from the PT, as the columns (b) in Table 3.6 demonstrate.[63] Individually, PT legislators have pursued personal interests within this broader agenda. Benedita da Silva succeeded in extending social security rights to domestic workers,[64] whilst Luci Choinacki did the same with maternity rights for women rural workers. The 1992 parliamentary inquiry into violence against women was set up at the behest of Sandra Starling, and Marta Suplicy spearheaded debates on sexuality, discrimination, affirmative action and sexual harassment. Iara Bernardi has also pressed for non-sexist language in all official documents, a ban on the use of sexual images of women in advertising, better treatment for victims and automatic prosecutions in cases of sexual assault, and removal of discriminatory provisions from the penal code.

Special Secretariat for Policies on Women

The Lula administration quickly signalled its commitment to women in government by appointing three female ministers (Benedita da Silva (Social Welfare), Marina da Silva (Environment) and Dilma Roussef

(Mines and Energy)) and two secretaries of state (Matilde Ribeiro (head of a newly established Special Secretariat to Promote Racial Equality)[65] and Emilia Fernandes (SPM)), nearly all of them long-time party activists who had held other elected and government posts for the party.[66] After the election, the party put together a transition team in which for the first time gender concerns were represented by two feminists, Vera Soares and Matilde Ribeiro, who were determined to press for gender sensitivity in all areas of the incoming government. The party's gender policies at sub-national level bore visible fruit. As Soares commented, 'the technical advisors in the transition team no longer make a face when we talk about public policies for women. Many of them had already encountered this issue when they worked in [PT-run] municipal government, that is, they had to deal with women in their region'.[67]

The SPM was finally ratified by the Senate in May 2003 with a remit to advise the president on the drafting, co-ordination and implementation of gender policies, discrimination awareness campaigns, and gender planning mechanisms for all government levels, as well as to co-operate with national and international organizations and oversee the enforcement of agreements, conventions, and action plans on gender equality agreed by the federal government.[68] Structurally, it comprised a cabinet and three sub-departments (for institutional networking, monitoring of thematic programmes, and gender planning). A 'Women's Charter' was debated through a nationwide consultation exercise, with meetings at municipal and state level culminating in a National Conference on Policies for Women in July 2004. The resultant National Plan for Policies on Women was launched the following December, at the end of the National Women's Year designated by the PT government, and focused on discrimination in the labour market, non-sexist education, gender violence, women's health and strategies for mainstreaming. In the same month the president also signalled his intention to tackle more controversial areas when he announced a special commission, composed of representatives of the executive, legislature and civil society, to draft legislation to decriminalize abortion and extend the definition to include foetal abnormalities. The Women's Committee in Congress created working groups for the themes of social welfare and security, work, housing rights and violence, and both the upper and lower houses established special parliamentary committees to systematize the various gender-related bills. However, one of the immediate constraints on the Secretariat has been a budgetary one. The previous government had allocated 10.9 million *reais*, increased to 24 million at the beginning of 2003, but in a round of sweeping budget cuts designed to balance the books and placate international lenders, the SPM's budget was cut to just over 4 million. The first priority was to secure a large operational budget for the unit, with a view to achieving 20 million *reais* in the financial year 2004–05. Regardless of the institutional changes, the new Secretariat can only carry out effective mainstreaming work with sufficient resources, as the experiences of the CNDM and SERNAM show.

The PT's distinctive political habitus, based on an ethics of pluralism and rejection of traditional political culture and practice in Brazil, resulted from the specific circumstances of its genesis in the late 1970s. These same circumstances gave it a dual base in which women were unusually active participants, which in turn produced a gendered political sociability that was less inimical to women's political agency. The PT's internal organizational structure, along two separate but complementary axes, has facilitated the spread and institutionalization of a feminist agenda. The *horizontal* axis, expressed through its internal secretariats and close ties to social movements, enabled different social groups to press their claims within the party.

Such porosity, political pluralism and openness to a plurality of social subjects was absent in the older left-wing parties in Brazil. However, this permeability is one-way; new claims can be absorbed into the party's agenda but, unlike in other parties where they are adopted only as a function of political opportunism, the PT's *vertical* aspect as a routinized, bureaucratic and ideological party enabled it to 'fix' commitment to these claims in its party programmes, as evidenced by its revamping of the CNDM. The next chapter examines how the party has put its principled commitment to women's rights into practice in sub-national arenas of government.

4
O *Modo Petista*: Local-Level Gender Policy

This chapter turns to the PT's municipal and state administrations, the only arenas in which the party had governed up to 2003, in order to examine how it implemented its policy positions on gender equity and equality. The first half analyzes how it used the institutional space and representational frameworks available in sub-national government to balance its commitment to promoting grassroots participation with gender mainstreaming. The chapter then considers the level of political backing that local party representatives, bureaucrats and activists accorded gender issues and the extent to which feminists inside and outside the party were able to influence *petista* local governments, whose gender policies are examined in the final section.

O modo petista de governar

The PT's foundational membership of trade unionists and community activists saw the party grow electorally from a local base, from two municipal administrations in 1982 to 411 in 2004. By 2005, it had governed ten of the 26 state capitals and been re-elected in nine, winning more votes than any other party in the major metropolitan centres in the 1996 and 2000 municipal elections. In 1994, the PT won its first two governorships (Federal District and Espírito Santo), expanded to three in 1998 (Rio Grande do Sul, Acre and Mato Grosso do Sul), and in 2002 re-elected two, lost Rio Grande do Sul and acquired the northeastern state of Piauí. This generally steady increase in geographical spread and local government experience has enabled the PT to build up a repertoire of governance practices based on its core principles, including gender equality.

The plethora of individual case studies on local PT administrations[1] demonstrates the interest in the party's very particular approach, which it systematized in the so-called *modo petista de governar* ('PT way of governing'), attempting to identify and replicate good practice through its Secretariat for Institutional Affairs (Bittar, 1992). PT municipal administrations have served, variously, as a platform for national office, a locus of opposition to state and national government, and as a laboratory and showcase. The party's hallmark has been a two-pronged approach consisting of grassroots participation and an 'inversion of priorities'; that is, a preferential option for the poor that aspired to redirect public resources towards the most marginalized sectors. The 'participatory budget' (PB) process practised in most PT-run local governments, and now adopted by non-PT administrations and even overseas, is the most refined expression of the first, whilst its minimum family income programme exemplifies the second. Its administrations have attracted plaudits for their innovative policies, winning prizes from national and international bodies in public policy areas as diverse as sustainable agriculture, microcredit, urbanization, low-cost housing, recycling, income generation, food security, physical and mental healthcare (especially the family doctor programme), infant mortality reduction, child protection and reduction of child labour, education and literacy, public transportation, good government in terms of participation, transparency, decentralization, modernization and fiscal responsibility, and, not least, gender equality and equity.[2] Changes made to the Municipal Organic Law (MOL) under PT administrations saw Campinas (SP) stipulate that the city's school curriculum must contain elements of women's history and sex education, Santos earmark public funds for a women's shelter and Belo Horizonte require the city to provide non-sexist education, a shelter, a women's legal support centre, cheap canteens and public laundries. A competition run by the Ford Foundation and the Brazilian Institute of Municipal Administration (IBAM) to recognize best practice in tackling gender violence awarded all five prizes to PT administrations – Londrina (PR), Porto Alegre, Santos, Diadema (SP), and Rio Branco – whilst in 2002 Santo André's programme 'Gender and Citizenship' received a top UN prize, among other plaudits. What approaches, then, oriented the PT's notable performance in this area?

Local state, mixed strategies

A survey of PT administrations reveals a wide range of experiences and approaches to gender equity and equality, ranging from the small towns of the interior, where gender policy is subsumed within social policy and the domain of the mayor's wife, to a fully dedicated unit situated within the executive branch, from ad hoc policies to bold attempts at mainstreaming gender perspectives into city planning. Likewise, the political conditions affecting women's participation and ability to influence policy vary enormously, and include the political will of the mayor, the size and resources of the municipality, the organizational capacity of local women's movements and the presence of feminists in the local administrative apparatus. However, despite the differences, a number of common strands and strategies emerge.

Participation, consultation, policymaking

From its inception, PT feminists rejected two existing models of targeting women. Traditional patronage-oriented politicians employed welfarist programmes or foundations through which the mayor's wife would deliver charity to poor women and their families in exchange for votes.[3] These maintained the social quo, did not increase citizenship and offered only a marginal response to some practical gender needs. They were equally scathing about the way opposition parties had instrumentalized and colonized the women's movement during the transition to democracy, regarding the PMDB and PCdoB's 'women federations' as party-electoral tools, mobilizing women only to co-opt them. It viewed the largely PMDB-sponsored municipal and state-level women's *conselhos* as fertile ground for clientelism, given that the mayor or governor generally had power to appoint its members and local women's movements were often poorly organized or non-existent.

The PT women also criticized the hybrid character of the *conselhos*, which, with one foot inside and one outside the state, they saw as neither fish nor fowl.[4] Did these councils represent women to the state or vice versa, and how 'representative' could they really be? They blurred different functions (participation, representation, deliberation, execution of decision-making) that were all necessary, but none alone sufficient, and which needed to be allocated to separate but interlinked entities. The party therefore began to experiment with institutional formats that would best combine grassroots participation, democratic representation and executive powers to achieve the optimal relationship between party, government and civil society, and to pursue more effective and progressive gender policies. The model that each PT administration chose was in large part the product of timing, of the mayor or governor's perception of the issue, and of the foresight and organizational capacity of women in the party and in the local women's movement.

Executive gender units

In several of the cities where the PT first came to power, it either ignored or dismantled the *conselho*, which was often closely identified with the party or person of the previous incumbent.[5] Party women lobbied instead for a space *inside* the administration, through which a gender perspective could be mainstreamed. The discussion started in Fortaleza in 1986, where the local women's movement found itself divided over what mechanisms to demand from the new PT administration. Communist-affiliated groups advocated a *conselho* in order to preserve movement autonomy, whilst PT-linked women wanted a full-blown municipal department (*secretaria*), with autonomy, resources and powers to execute programmes (Esmeraldo and Said, 2002), in a debate later repeated in São Paulo, Porto Alegre and elsewhere. However, given the fiscal constraints affecting the earliest PT administrations, women agreed to settle, as a temporary measure, for smaller units with less status (Nogueira *et al.*, 2000: 12). Only after much lobbying were these stopgaps upgraded, in some cases, with those in Londrina, Campinas and Acre promoted to *secretarias*.

Of lower status is a Women's Co-ordinating Committee (*Coordenadoria Especial da Mulher* – CEM) attached to the mayor's or governor's office, with a remit to oversee and advise on gender-related work programmes in other departments, and a more modest budget and staff. In both PT administrations in São Paulo, party women lobbied for a *secretaria* but ended up with a CEM, as did the cities of Santos, São Paulo, Diadema, Mauá and Piracicaba (SP), Angra dos Reis (RJ), Belo Horizonte, Dourados (MS), Recife and Caxias do Sul (RS). However, the CEM suffered problems of identity and mandate; it had neither the representative nor advisory remit of a *conselho*, nor sufficient powers as a low-level executive body with little profile and few resources. In consequence, it became marginalized from both the support base of the women's movement and the city administration.[6] Learning from this experience, women in Goiânia (GO) and Porto Alegre argued, but in vain, for an institutionally bolstered CEM.

Some towns, such as Diadema, Santo André, Porto Alegre and Maringá (PR), opted for a Women's Advisory Unit (*Assessoria dos Direitos da Mulher* – ADM), which had even fewer resources and powers, and was often subordinated either to the mayor's office or to a social welfare or human rights department, functioning alongside bodies for other special policies or vulnerable groups. The mayor's office in Niterói (RJ) had a special executive co-ordinating committee for policies for the elderly but no gender unit, and Londrina's Municipal Secretariat for

Women was followed by a similar one for the elderly, whilst in both Porto Alegre and Santo André, the ADM shared office space with cognate bodies for blacks, youth and the disabled. This suggests that gender was conflated with issues of minority rights or with poverty reduction measures. Many municipalities have made their priority children and, more recently, the elderly, potentially downgrading gender issues or subsuming them within the family. Those cities without a dedicated unit tend to target women within their community development or social welfare programmes.

Conselhos revisited

The PT has had to face a central dilemma as a party that grew out of the social movements and transformed itself from a mass movement into a party of government. On the one hand, the party encouraged its members to be active in the rich array of participatory mechanisms enshrined in the 1988 Constitution, which, in turn, have fostered the civil society organizations that the party wished to represent in its policies and priorities. On the other hand, the party also pioneered *new* forms of local participation as part of its project of channelling popular demands and stimulating greater density in civil society. It has been a challenge for the women activists in the new units to find the right balance, to avoid the dangers of becoming femocrats distanced from the women's movement and of politically co-opting the grassroots groups to which the state apparatus or party had effectively acted as midwife.[7]

During the first PT administrations the need became clear for viable channels for feedback and civil society oversight as well as support and legitimacy from the local women's movement. In the absence of pre-existing representative bodies or networks, PT women's units would often set up so-called women's forums, periodic consultation events that were open to all-comers but were not stable forms of consultation.[8] Thus, despite the PT's initial scepticism about the *conselhos*[9] and some element of party political competition to sponsor initiatives for women, it came to appreciate that they could perform an invaluable representative role and intermediary function if they were made more democratic, with more effective links to the executive. The ADM in Maringá called its first city-wide women's consultation in 2001 and concluded that the existing *conselho* needed to be reactivated and democratized. The second PT government in Porto Alegre set up a new one composed of one-third government and two-thirds non-governmental representatives, with the latter elected by the local women's movement, rather than appointed by the mayor. Others have set up *conselhos* by another name.

Although the city of Santos had a CEM, the PT also installed a 'Women's Forum' composed of 30 government and civil society representatives. The first PT government (1993–6) in Belo Horizonte also established a 'mixed committee' composed of representatives of civil society and key secretariats to co-ordinate policy, chiefly on gender violence.[10] In towns without a strong women's movement or feminist voice within the party or local government, a *conselho* represented both the minimum institutional form that a women's mechanism could take and an invaluable tool for awareness-raising.[11] In Betim, gender issues were initially addressed through the Secretariat for Social Affairs. However, tactically Mayor Maria do Carmo Lara aimed to set up a *conselho* that could then encourage local women's groups to exert pressure on the municipal government for an executive body, as she recognized the need for both.[12] The PT's only woman councillor in Ribeirão Preto (SP) gave an almost identical account of the party's reluctance to move too far ahead of the pace of civil society, while simultaneously feeling the need to take necessary initiatives.[13]

'Paperclips and passion'

Establishing these units was far from straightforward. Party officials often perceived gender equity as a zero-sum, special interest claim, competing with others: 'If you create a women's secretariat, they'll all want one', was the view of one mayor. The demotion of the hoped-for unit was also due to political and fiscal factors as newly elected PT mayors had to deal with the populist overspending of their predecessors from other parties. After the PT won Goiânia in 1992, a committee set up to restructure the *conselho* recommended a CEM with the status of a *secretaria*, as in Londrina, to be linked to a participatory forum for consultation with local women. The mayor refused to include this proposal in the party's plan for government, partly because he wanted to carry out a full administrative reform, but also because it was a manifesto pledge of the PCdoB, the PT's rivals on the Left.[14] A year later he established an ADM that started life with little more than 'paperclips and passion'.[15]

As some PT administrations entered their third or fourth mandates, these units were able to stabilize and make the case for more resources through the PB or the municipal legislature. This gradual institutionalization was the result of a number of factors. The award-winning performance of specific projects helped the party as a whole to recognize the legitimacy of gender issues. Over time, women in the party analyzed and built on the party's experiences with local gender policies, diffusing them through the SNM's publications, and regional and national training events. These also fostered important policy and issue networks of party feminists, bureaucrats and elected officials, (Borba *et al.*, 1998). On the other hand, the party's national Secretariat for Institutional Affairs never evinced any interest in gender issues, so the party failed at gender mainstreaming within its own institutional structure.

During the 1980s, feminists were still struggling to find a voice in the national party apparatus and, in the local administrations, energies were taken up with tackling basic infrastructure and charting turbulent political waters. In 1989, the CNDM began its decline, but that year also saw the inauguration of the PT's first significant municipal governments. The election of Luiza Erundina enabled an active local women's movement and a mayor committed to gender policies to make serious strides. The CEM, for all its deficiencies, became a model for later PT governments, and her administration also funded a refuge for victims of domestic violence, made contraception freely and widely available in health clinics, increased childcare provision and offered legal support for women workers claiming sexual harassment or discrimination. The public hospital in Jabaquara was obliged to provide legal abortions and the city imposed sanctions on companies that required new female employees to undergo pregnancy tests or provide proof that they had been sterilized (Macaulay, 1996: 217). In nearby Santos, Telma de Souza also installed a CEM, ran women's literacy courses, increased tenfold the number of childcare centres, especially for public employees, opened a support unit for victims of violence, provided social and rehabilitation services to the women's prison, and set up care and prevention programmes (including free condoms and needle exchanges) for sex workers and drug users. Not for nothing did party activists refer affectionately to these two unorthodox politicians as their 'Thelma and Louise'.

These advances notwithstanding, other PT governments – in Porto Alegre, Vitória, Campinas, Diadema, Piracicaba and São Bernardo do Campo (SP) – were particularly unresponsive to gender claims, due partly to the indifference of the PT mayors, but also to disunity among women in the local movement and within the party. The electoral victory had caught *petistas* unawares and they had not organized to have gender proposals inserted into the party manifesto or government action plan. The SNM responded to this missed opportunity by stepping up its lobbying inside the party. As a result, the party's First National Congress in 1991 affirmed 'All our municipal governments, present and future, will adopt public policies to combat discrimination [against women], as a matter of priority' whilst the party's blueprint for local government included a whole chapter on women (Bittar, 1992).[16] By the 1992 elections, PT women appreciated that they needed to mobilize earlier and be clearer about their priorities and the kind of relationship they wanted between the state, as the executor of gender policies, and the women's movement. Thereafter, the party's local work on gender questions improved and consolidated.

Nonetheless, the first state administrations were disappointing. The governor of the Federal District admitted that gender questions had been relatively low on his agenda;[17] the Programme of Government referred only to women's healthcare, emphasizing family planning and ante-natal care, and after the election the *conselho* limited itself to domestic violence (Governo do Distrito Federal, 1995).[18] Espírito Santo's state government was in such disarray, facing huge debts and internecine fighting, that women's issues, along with other social policies, barely got a look in. The state governments elected in 1998 and 2002 delivered much more, because party and movement women had been insistent about local candidates' pledges; Mato Grosso do Sul and then Rio Grande do Sul set up CEMs linked to the governor's office. Acre's gender work was initially concentrated in a local NGO and a support centre for women sex workers, founded when the governor had been mayor of the capital. After re-election, it upgraded to a special secretariat, alongside similar for youth, indigenous peoples and sport. Even the impoverished northeastern state of Piauí managed a gender unit within the Secretariat for Social Welfare.

Strategizing for space

The institutionalization of gender policies in PT administrations often depended upon the actions of individuals (mayors, women's unit co-ordinators, city councillors), as well as upon the effective strategizing of women inside and outside the party. The cases of Porto Alegre, Santo André and Londrina, all towns with a strong PT presence, are instructive of a number of different variables.

In Porto Alegre, despite its advances in other areas of participation, notably the PB, internal movement divisions and a lack of commitment by successive mayors prevented women from securing their preferred form of institutional representation until the *fourth* PT mandate. A gender unit was neither offered nor demanded during Olivio Dutra's term (1989–92), which focused on administrative and fiscal reform. Lesson learnt, PT feminists persuaded the party to insert into the 1992 Programme of Government a commitment to the establishment of a

Forum of Municipal Secretaries and a high-powered CEM that would consult with an open-access Women's Forum. Disappointingly, this was ignored by the incoming mayor, Tarso Genro (1993–6), who also blamed spending constraints. The two forums were scrapped, the CEM downgraded to an ADM with no budget, little autonomy and a skeleton staff. In frustration, the PT women added an amendment for a CEM to a PSDB-sponsored bill for a *conselho*. The city council approved the bill, the mayor vetoed it, the legislators overturned the veto and the issue ended up, farcically, in court. This breakdown of communication was further exacerbated by confusion about the functions of the different types of women's entities. The ADM co-ordinator set up a new Women's Forum that promptly declared itself autonomous and split the movement, which ended in two competing celebrations on International Women's Day, both sponsored by the mayor's office. Matters improved little under Raul Pont (1997–2000), when the ADM was subordinated to a new *coordenadoria* for human rights and another tussle over appointments ensued within the movement. However, when Dutra was elected governor in 1998, the combination of assiduous lobbying by feminists prior to the election, the track record of the ADM and the SNM's arguments persuaded him, on this occasion, to set up a CEM linked to his cabinet.[19]

The case of Santo André, a large industrial city in the São Paulo metropolitan region, illustrates how commitment to integrating gender issues into local government is not necessarily a linear process. It was governed for three terms (1989–92, 1997–2004) by the same PT mayor, Celso Daniel, who immediately established an ADM with relatively high autonomy. He also invited a feminist geographer from the university to look at the feasibility of mainstreaming a gender perspective into the city's master plan,[20] which was collectively drafted by a 'women's axis', an informal network of sympathetic officers and technical staff in the city hall. Disappointingly, the entire plan was blocked by political stonewalling in the Municipal Chamber and never implemented, despite Daniel's support.[21] He lost the following elections and, when he returned in 1997, inexplicably downgraded women's space in the administration. The ADM was moved from the mayor's office to the department of social welfare in the Secretariat for Participation and Citizenship, alongside units for the elderly, children and the disabled, and then after 2000 housed in the human rights department of the same.

With all these changes, institutional memory and continuity was lost, the cross-sectoral work done by the women's axis ceased and gender was conflated with 'social inclusion'. However, the previous capacity-building work done by the ADM and the women's axis had left a lasting legacy in the shape of a newly confident women's movement. When the ADM began publicizing its first services for the victims of domestic violence and wanted to consult over the city's 'gendered' master plan, the staff realized that no appropriate structures existed. They drew up a register of every women's group in the city, mainly church and neighbourhood groups, which bore fruit in a two-day women's forum with more than 600 participants. There followed training workshops for leaders provided by 19 city departments, and city-wide activities for International Women's Day. During the first PT government, initiative on gender policy came from the state, principally the ADM and the women's axis, but in the second and third this shifted to NGOs, the local movement and sympathetic civil servants dispersed through the administration, in much the same way as occurred with the CNDM nationally. For example, a local NGO, the Centre for Health Education, continued to pioneer work on domestic violence prevention, offering group therapy both to victims and the male aggressors. The positive cumulative effect was to put gender issues, especially women's health and domestic violence, politically if not literally on the map (IBAM/ISER, 2002).[22]

Londrina, which established the country's first fully-fledged executive gender unit in 1997, presents a converse case, where the pre-existing strength of the local women's movement proved more important than specific party political orientation. 'Little London' mushroomed from a planned settlement of small farmers into a city of half a million inhabitants in western Paraná state. By the 1970s, it had also developed into a pole of left-wing counter-culture, becoming the cradle of feminism (Brazil's first 'second-wave' feminist periodical, *Brasil Mulher*, was published there) and of the pro-amnesty and democracy movements. Since 1989, it has been a stronghold of the PDT and PT (which has governed it three times, 1993–6 and 2001–8) and the movement has been united enough to bargain for space and state resources with both. In November 1992, a PDT woman city councillor, inspired by the PT's policies, replaced the moribund *conselho* with a CEM, to which the movement persuaded the PT mayor-elect to accord autonomy and an executive, rather than advisory, function. He appointed as co-ordinator an activist with over two decades' experience in the women's and social movements.[23] The following PDT administration actually upgraded the CEM in 1997 to a *secretaria*, increasing its powers and staffing, and appointed as head a PT city councillor.[24] A surprise win by the PT in 2000 ensured the continuity and strength of its work.

Political intermediaries

Of the various political actors who are pivotal to this process – mayors, councillors and government officials – it is not necessarily the sex of the agents or their number that matter, but rather their feminist sympathies and ability to act as an interface between the party, state apparatus and local women's organizations. Several of the PT women mayors, such as Luiza Erundina, Marta Suplicy, Telma de Souza, Maria do Carmo Lara and Maria Luiza Fontenelle, were explicitly supportive of the women's movement agenda and opened up space in their administrations (Barreira, 1993). Dorcelina Folador regulated land title and pressed for pensions for women rural workers, promoted family agro-industry, school scholarships, women's adult literacy, assistance for women market traders and free childcare, funded an ante- and post-natal care centre for young rural women and procured for the local hospital mamograph and ultrasound equipment normally found only in larger cities. Others, such as Angela Guadagnin, subsumed women's rights within action for families or poverty-reduction measures.[25] Some male mayors, such as Celso Daniel and Luiz Cheida in Londrina, were highly receptive to gender claims, some were hostile and indifferent, and a few cynics pledged total support for gender policies prior to the elections, only to plead budget constraints once the votes were counted (Nogueira *et al.*, 2000: 26). Political and administrative pressures inevitably combined with the mayor's personal style and views. Despite – or, perhaps, because of – Marta Suplicy's personal feminist profile, women gained less space in her administration than under the more working-class Erundina. Although the CEM was revived, it remained marginal to a city government highly centralized around the mayor's office. Its staff, feminists long involved in the SNM, came from a left-wing faction in the party, and were ignored by the mainstream group in power.[26]

The mayor's wife has historically run charitable funds associated with political patronage and clientelism, and in principle the PT has opposed the figure of First Lady. However, in small towns she is likely to be a PT militant and social movement activist, and often assumes a key unpaid role in an otherwise understaffed and underfinanced municipality, so most PT administrations have attempted to recast the local charity as a social justice fund. Typical was Monte Alto (SP), a micro-municipality, where women's issues were handled by the mayor's wife, who was also in charge of the local Social Solidarity Fund. The informal character of this remit for women and children, inevitably focused on immediate, practical gender needs, sometimes led to competition and conflict with women in the local party, organized groups, city council and gender unit, who felt that gender inequality merited a strategic and long-term social policy approach, rather than personal discretion.[27] On the other hand, leverage within the administration could open new doors; Mato Grosso do Sul's CEM was set up by the governor's wife, before being handed over to a professional staff, whilst that in Dourados, the second largest city in that state, was headed by the mayor's wife.

Where the mayor was indifferent or hostile to gender issues, PT women councillors have played a pivotal role, often single-handedly, in translating women's demands into local legislation and policy. They have helped local women's groups use the new municipal institutions by introducing legislation or altering the MOL to incorporate many of the gender rights enshrined in the national and state constitutions, regulate the *conselho*s or women's units, specify the city's responsibility for gender policies, and allocate public resources. During the first PT mandate in Porto Alegre, when the party had no active women city councillors, Helena Bonumá, a party activist, collated amendments to the MOL and co-ordinated mobilization around the city's master plan.[28] In Goiânia, Marina Sant'Anna put through a clause requiring men and women to take joint responsibility for household labour, and presented bills obliging the municipality to provide childcare, a shelter and legal abortion.[29]

However, although Rio de Janeiro state deputy Rose Souza persuaded the other ten women in the legislature to back her bills on domestic violence and legal abortion, independently of their party's position,[30] cross-bench women's action has been rare because of the higher level of direct clientelism in sub-national politics and the low numbers of elected representatives. In 2001–4, the PT had only one councillor in 872 towns; in 11 per cent of cases this was a woman.[31] These lone PT women have exercised multiple leadership roles in the local party, as founder, local branch secretary, head of the local party women's section, city councillor, head of the PT delegation in the municipal chamber, and active participant in the local women's movement. Their effectiveness as change agents suggests that critical mass is far less important than party political commitment to gender policies and their multiple linkages with the local and national women's policy networks, inside and outside the party.

PT feminists also realized that a feminist caucus within the executive branch, whether informal or institutionalized, could greatly ease integrated, mainstreamed gender policy within the executive branch, and provide a valuable bridge to local women's groups (*conselho*s, forums and party women). The case of Santo André shows how successfully gender policy initiatives can be generated from inside local government, if political support and institutional space are available to feminist bureaucrats, who were able to open up new arenas for participation, managing to support rather than co-opt these local women's networks. In Porto Alegre (1989–92), women working at the Social and Community Education Fund set up women's programmes, and began to liaise with colleagues in other departments doing likewise. Before the 1996 elections, PT women identified allies, proposing them for strategic government posts, resulting in a working group whose 1999 seminar on gender policies produced a number of important cross-sectoral programmes, such as the integrated approach to gender violence (Nogueira *et al.*, 2000: 18). Other cities with such a gender policy forum – Campinas, Recife, Angra dos Reis and Piracicaba – have found the gender studies departments of provincial universities an important source of expertise for policy formulation.

For such a caucus to exist, women need to be appointed to senior executive positions in municipal and state government. Erundina's cabinet was one-quarter female, while Cozete Barbosa (Campina Grande, PB) and Maria do Carmo Lara placed women in nearly half of the top posts, due both to their feminist sympathies and to the preponderance of female PT activists in certain locations. However, the PT has not applied a quota for these jobs, and only Goiânia's mayor agreed, in 2001, to a self-imposed quota of 30 per cent, with appointees drawn from a list prepared by the Women's Forum and the PT women's group. Although their favoured candidate for the key post of secretary of health did not get the job, the campaign developed invaluable networks among health professionals and among grassroots groups.[32] A survey of 22 of the PT's 1989–92 administrations revealed that women occupied over 15 per cent of top posts,[33] a situation that had improved, patchily, by 2001 when Aracajú (SE) had 36.6 per cent female appointees, São Paulo 22 per cent, but Belo Horizonte zero. Whilst some headed departments of public works, housing, planning, extractivism, labour, policing, prison affairs, legal affairs, information technology and finance, most were concentrated in the 'feminized' social sectors, with education/culture/sport, health and social welfare accounting for around half of them. This may partly reflect the professional backgrounds of women party activists, drawn overwhelmingly from education and healthcare, and partly a persistently gendered view of public administration only partially challenged by the PT.

In conclusion, institutional learning has led several PT administrations to adopt a four-legged model that combines entities with separate but complementary functions: an executive-deliberative body such as a CEM or secretariat with powers and resources to oversee policy; a caucus of feminist bureaucrats to push sectoral policies; a representative-consultative *conselho* with mixed government–civil society composition; and an open-access, participatory Women's Forum. Each offers a different state interface with civil society – the first two have none, the third is closed and the fourth open – but all show the influence of the PT. Even where elements are missing, the party's receptivity to gender issues can open up policy channels. In Angra dos Reis, in the absence of feminist groups, the local Church-linked Mothers' Clubs worked with the PT administration and local health professionals to pass an amendment guaranteeing sex education, health services and workplace protection.[34] Santo André shows that strong political backing and a women's axis can set the pace of gender policy even in the initial absence of a structured local women's movement, whilst Londrina and Porto Alegre underscore the importance of well-organized – or at least united – feminist groups in negotiating gender policy with the parties. The latter case also illustrates the dangers of confusing grassroots bodies with representative and executive ones, but it eventually ended up with a very effective local policy community, combining all of them.[35] We now turn to examine the content of the gender policies that this institutional matrix was developed to support.

Policy influences and participation

The core gender policies promoted by PT administrations reflect the influences of a class- and poverty-focused popular women's movement, international feminism, and gender and development thinking. The policy mix has been heavily rights-based and includes women's labour market participation, via childcare provision, literacy or occupational training; poverty reduction via income generation and income transfers; gender violence; health provision and reproductive rights; anti-sexist education; and gender mainstreaming in city planning and budgeting. Many of these measures have been copied horizontally by other PT (and a few non-PT) city councils, or have trickled up, being replicated subsequently in state and/or national legislation and policy. Following the example of São Paulo, Campinas's mayor decreed that the city would warn, fine or revoke the licence of firms that violated the rights of women workers; Benedita da Silva subsequently sponsored a federal law prohibiting employers from requiring a certificate of sterilization or a pregnancy test. The success of São Paulo's local ordinance on provision of legal abortion prompted at least 13 hospitals in seven states to follow suit by 1999. A bill submitted by two PT federal deputies[36] in 1991 to make this policy national foundered in Congress, but in 1998 the Ministry of Health issued guidelines to this effect, principally when there was evidence of rape.[37]

Poverty reduction

The PT's core social justice policy is poverty reduction, through a combination of income transfers and employment policy. Its hallmark policies for income redistribution are the 'minimum income' (*renda mínima*) and the 'school stipend' (*bolsa escola*) (Caccia Bava, 1998; Lavinas, 1999; Lavinas and Barbosa, 2000; Rocha, 2001), both means-tested schemes that act like a reverse income tax, taking very low-income families up to a predetermined poverty line. The second targets families with school-age children in order to address the issues of child labour and low educational attainment, with the parents receiving a monthly allowance conditional on their child's school attendance. First implemented by the PT in the Federal District, the policy was adopted nationally by the Cardoso government, becoming the Family Stipend under the Lula government. Some three million women received these payments, yet the gender impact of these schemes has been little discussed within the party. Many variants of the scheme make payments either specifically to the mother or to the nominated head of household, which in the majority of cases is a woman, due to the preponderance of households headed by women (even if not single-parent or single-adult) and to perceptions that women are more 'available' to meet the requirements and more likely to use the funds for the benefit of the whole household (Silveira, 2001).[38] Some see the programme as boosting the mothers' financial autonomy and control over household resources (Buarque, 1999: 63), recognizing and remunerating their role as producers of human capital, whilst others object that this is a means of 'making women administer poverty', targeting women instrumentally, and reinforcing existing gender roles. Impact studies show broadly positive results, principally in meeting practical gender needs, with mothers reporting less family sickness, less anxiety around food security and more time to spend with the children, helping them fulfil their social roles as mothers. They were encouraged or required to attend literacy classes themselves and experienced decreased social 'shame' due to their access to credit and a bank account, improving their employment prospects (Castro, 2002).

Women's assets and autonomy have also been boosted through urban and rural land titles. Female-headed households are a priority in low-cost housing policy, and in Recife women constituted 75 per cent of participants in self-build projects. Income generation is most commonly offered in the form of microcredit and occupational training, now a keystone of a globalized women and development agenda. Santo André established a 'people's bank' as part of its Integrated Programme for Social Inclusion and, within six months, 43 per cent of its clientele were women. Support and training is also offered to set up women's co-operatives, although the leadership is still too often assumed by men if membership is mixed (Soares, 2001). The Mato Grosso do Sul state government responded to rural women's demands for training in muscovado sugar production (traditionally a male skill) and helped indigenous women establish collectives to buy handicraft materials and market their goods. Although Londrina offered training courses that reinforced the gender division of labour, such as domestic services, sewing, cooking, making gift-wrapping and growing medicinal plants, this was accompanied by small business training and talks on women's rights, labour law, health and gender relations, akin to SERNAM's Female Heads of Household programme.

Public services and personnel

The *modo petista* includes an old-fashioned municipal socialist stress on physical infrastructure such as sewerage systems, clean water and transport, which not only constitute important elements of a social wage, but are also valued by women for lessening the time and financial burden of reproductive labour. The social provision of 'women's services' through laundries, canteens and childcare also meets practical gender needs. Maringá provided communal laundries for both rural and urban populations,[39] whilst Belo Horizonte ran a 'People's restaurant', serving 5,500 meals a day costing only a few cents, assisted local growers in selling their products in the capital through subsidized neighbourhood markets, ran a retail and wholesale market, and helped schools and communities set up kitchen gardens. Childcare was one of the earliest demands made by party women, and Ribeirão Preto built nine childcare centres in a year, compared to just 11 over the previous 30 years. In Franco da Rocha, a low-income dormitory city for São Paulo, childcare was the only gender-related policy implemented, due to popular demand. A Mothers' Committee selected the beneficiaries based on the head of household, income level and number of children. However, despite tripling the number of places available they could meet only 5 per cent of the demand. Nonetheless, the relative expense of day-care facilities has resulted in this being downgraded in the list of social priorities. In Goiânia, as elsewhere, childcare was provided predominantly by local charitable bodies, thus avoiding a strain on state resources. Some went further in supporting the family; Mato Grosso do Sul set up Family Support Centres in 77 towns to provide occupational training, adult literacy, toy libraries and paternity testing.

PT governments have also addressed the needs of the underpaid and undervalued female public sector workers providing much of this social infrastructure and on whom the party has often relied for mobilization in defence of its municipal policies. They have moved to professionalize not only the health and education service employees, but also the lower ranks. In Goiânia street cleaners, transport workers and school cooks were encouraged to unionize and given access to adult literacy, healthcare, job training and education on issues of gender and public space.[40] In Santos, instead of having male foremen overseeing, and often harassing, the 400 female street sweepers, the women began running their own work teams and set up a recycling programme working with local schools, community and municipal bodies (RHUDO-SA and USAID, 1993: 95).[41] The Diadema CEM worked with the wives of manual labourers employed in the Department of Works, tackling issues of domestic violence, alcoholism and incest, while Santo André instituted an equal opportunities programme for its female staff as part of its programme of increasing equality, efficiency and accountability in public services (Bento and Polycarpo, 2001).

The consumers of municipal services are also largely female, low-income, and suffer from discrimination; although the mothers in the *bolsa escola* scheme became enthusiastic about education, they also frequently felt humiliated by school officials (Castro, 2002). The São Paulo government under Erundina attempted to extend the hours of provision of childcare and health services so that they would correspond better with women's working hours, but they encountered opposition from public sector unions. It did, however, manage to oblige the (mainly male) bus drivers and ticket collectors to negotiate with (mainly female) bus user representatives over wage rises and consequent ticket price hikes. This underscores a tension inherent within the PT's electoral and social base, arising from its foundational membership. The party claims to represent the interests of both workers and low-income consumers, of those socially incorporated to some extent by the old corporatist labour framework and, simultaneously, those excluded from entitlements. This is a strongly gendered – although by no means binary – component to the way in which PT administrations allocate state resources and negotiate competing claims.

Violence, health and reproductive rights

PT local administrations have carried out some of their most consistent and award-winning work around the issue of gender violence. The women's movement laid the groundwork in the 1980s, resulting in Brazil becoming a regional pioneer in services for victims; by 2003, it had over 300 specialized women's police stations and 75 shelters. This created a high level of social consensus on the issue, reducing opposition to municipal initiatives. One PT city councillor commented on her bill to set up a shelter for victims:

> There was resistance at first, largely because the men in the municipal chamber were so right-wing and macho...But they were also embarrassed and wrong footed by the proposal...They finally voted in favour because they thought it would look bad if they didn't. Some, of course, had their eyes on women's votes; it was just clientelism to them, nothing to do with defending women's rights and citizenship.[42]

In Rio Branco, national press coverage of teenage prostitution and the trafficking of women in the region raised the profile of gender issues, especially when the Casa Rosa Mulher, founded to assist prostitutes, street children and victims of domestic violence, won US$10,000 in the Ford Foundation/IBAM competition. This legitimized its work in the eyes of both the local populace, which had referred to it 'the whorehouse', and of the PT municipal authorities, which began to be more receptive to gender issues.[43]

Responsibility for tackling domestic violence straddles the three levels of government. The penal code is national, whilst the day-to-day operation of the criminal justice system lies with the state authorities, whose secretariat for public security has the powers to set up women's police stations and regulate policing. Mato Grosso do Sul's state CEM made gender violence its priority,[44] focusing on improving how police treat victims in places like Porto Murtinho, a border town with high levels of sexual violence, but too small to have a dedicated women's police station. In general, municipal powers are restricted to prevention and provision of social services to victims. Most PT-run cities stick to prevention work, such as educational material distributed in schools and public places, and provision of social services, such as a shelter and access to lawyers, social workers and psychologists. In some cases these are funded specifically through a clause in the MOL, and may be run by a local NGO or the city council. Rio Branco, São Paulo, Camaragibe (PE), Dourados and Campo Grande (MS) also have referral centres to provide advice and legal aid for prosecution, whilst first Porto Alegre, then São Paulo, pushed for a joined-up response by several government departments to provide medical assistance, housing and employment.[45] Other projects, such as that in Rio Branco, aim to protect young girls. Camaragibe's government helped 140 adolescent girls at risk of abuse in the home. Londrina, Santos and Santo André have also offered workshops on masculinity and gender relations to offenders.

Towns with a Municipal Guard also began to use it more proactively to make public spaces safer for women. The first PT mayor of Piracicaba set up a women's unit in the local guard and the CEM co-ordinator reported a decade later that it did excellent, if undervalued, work on gender violence.[46] Under Telma de Souza, Santos disarmed its guard and ran a six-month gender training programme with 600 officers, of which 40 per cent were women (RHUDO-SA and USAID, 1993: 89); São Paulo now has a 30 per cent minimum quota for female municipal police officers.[47]Administrative territorialism has also been challenged. Activists in Angra dos Reis, Volta Redonda (RJ) and Santo André noticed that many domestic violence cases crossed municipal boundaries, and joined forces to set up an inter-city network to help neighbouring towns establish police stations and regional shelters.[48] Likewise, women in life-threatening situations in Piracicaba can be transferred to other towns in São Paulo state. In Mato Grosso do Sul, the state-run refuge works in partnership with the municipality of Dourados.

The broader agenda for women's healthcare was developed in the 1980s, when the women's movement won a specialized health service and liberalized provision of contraception from national government. The 1988 Constitution municipalized provision and the progressive healthcare movement promoted a gender agenda in towns such as Angra dos Reis, Santo André, Volta Redonda, and Belo Horizonte. The PT took its lead and rejected expensive, curative healthcare provision for a more universal, preventive approach. Camaragibe achieved near-total coverage through a primary family-centred service, delivered via outreach agents, home visits and community participation. By the late 1990s, 90 per cent of pregnant women received ante-natal care, 60 per cent of babies were breastfed exclusively for up to four months and 90 per cent of children under one had been vaccinated, causing a dramatic drop in infant mortality – from 49.3 per 1,000 live births (1994) to 5.6 (2003), the lowest in the North East – due to 85 per cent of families using homemade rehydration solution.[49] Municipalities such as Diadema, Santos, Guarulhos and Jaboticabal (SP) offered ante- and post-natal care via Maternity Houses that gave vulnerable mothers access to healthcare, social services and occupational training. Others have prioritized breast and cervical cancer detection. Nor have PT cities shied away from more controversial issues; several developed policies to tackle sexual abuse of girls, give assistance to sex workers, and prevent unwanted pregnancies and HIV infection. These the party has defined as public health and rights matters, rather than moral questions. Even Erundina, who was very close to the progressive Catholic Church, authorized a city hospital to provide legal abortions, and other activists that I interviewed noted the tensions between their feminist stance on this issue and their electoral base in Church-linked social movements.

Gender mainstreaming: planning and budgeting

PT feminists were determined to go beyond sectoral policies to mainstream gender into the party's local governments through instruments such as the MOL, the master plan and the PB. Crucially, the key problem areas of urban management such as transport, the social services and the spatial division of the city were recognized as presenting gendered characteristics:

> The way in which the city is structured directly affects women's time; the location of home, services and work is vital in determining women's movements around the city. As the main administrator of the family's everyday life, women are perpetually running against the clock, trying to combine and reconcile employment with domestic tasks, with the school day, bills to pay, having to take a sick relative to the doctor and so on. Their right to enjoy and use the city as a citizen is directly linked to their social role. (Prefeitura Municipal Santo André, 1992: 3)

Although the Santo André vision of gender-sensitive city planning was never implemented, the SNM continues to promote it as a model of 'good practice' through periodic conferences.[50] In Porto Alegre, a city-wide consultation resulted in the launching of the 'Women and Citizenship Project' in 1993, included in the party programme, although the mayor later vetoed it on the grounds of cost. In Volta Redonda, the women's movement utilized every institutional space available; activists inserted into the MOL clauses on sex equality, health, workplace discrimination, and a municipal women's secretariat, drew up a Municipal Plan for Women's Rights and helped to gender-sensitize the master plan around housing, environment and safety. Mato Grosso do Sul incorporated gender issues into the training curriculum for public administrators. But, more often, lack of gender-disaggregated data and a technocratic approach has prevented democratization of the process.[51] Even though women composed 40 per cent of delegates on the Budget Council in Santos and were present in significant numbers in meetings on the master plan and civil defence plans, they spoke much less than men, possibly due to the perceived 'technical' character of the latter issue.

PT city administrations are most fêted for the PB, now enacted in over 100 municipalities, but has this enabled women to make effective claims on public resources? The local population is invited annually to debate the spending priorities for the city's social and infrastructural investment, generally conducted through a series of open, neighbourhood and, sometimes, thematic forums. These in turn elect delegates to take forward local or sectoral demands in meetings with the city's executive. Finally, representatives are elected to a Budget Council to work with the city authorities in overseeing the implementation of the final allocation of resources. Studies in Betim, Belo Horizonte, Santo André, Ribeirão Pires (SP), Porto Alegre and Campinas put women's participation in the assemblies between 39 and 47 per cent (Abers, 2000: 46; Carvalho and Felgueiras, 2000: 43; Nylen, 2003b: 63), showing an increase over time and improved representation on the higher-level representative bodies. In Porto Alegre, women's membership of the top representational layer, the Budget Council, had risen to 50 per cent in 2000 (Sugiyama, 2002: 14; Baiocchi, 2003a: 53).

Initially, PB consultation was organized on a territorial basis, and when thematic and sectoral assemblies were initiated – for example, in Santo André and Diadema – gender issues were omitted. Gradually, local women's movements began to see the PB as a strategic institutional arena, allowing them to circumvent the resistance of elected representatives, secure popular legitimacy for their demands and safeguard budget allocations. During the PT's first administration in Goiânia (1993–6), female PB delegates won funding for a women's shelter, despite the mayor's attempt to veto it, and in Angra dos Reis and Diadema they secured childcare funding. The second PT administration in Campinas (2001–4) initially set up CEMs only for youth and the black community, so women had to fight for theirs by popular vote in the PB,[52] just as Londrina's CEM ensured its ring-fenced funding of one per cent of the city budget. Where the PB included women's thematic meetings, gender issues were easier to highlight. In Recife, 531 women attended their own thematic consultation in 2001, voted for three gender priorities (poverty reduction, education policy and domestic violence), and elected 53 women to monitor the implementation of these policies. Each city secretariat also earmarked a budget for gender equity. In the PT's second mandate in Goiânia (2001–4), the ADM and local Women's Forum ran a budgetary assembly just for women, whilst Angra dos Reis and Barra Mansa (RJ) incorporated women as a priority within the long-term budget planning process, particularly in the areas of health and income generation.[53] In short, although initially the PT's internal debates and practices on gender policy and representation and on participatory approaches to governance proceeded along parallel tracks, they have now begun to converge, as a result both of the party's provision of new political arenas and of the determination of party feminists to occupy them in order to push forward a gender equity agenda.

The PT is unusual among Brazilian parties in having grown up from the grassroots, from its community and municipal bases. As its core values concern political *process* more than policy *doctrine*, the party has long valued the potential that decentralized political spaces hold for greater participation by social sectors normally alienated from political activity. In consequence, its most distinctive contribution to gender equity and equality has been the refinement of the intermediary mechanisms (sectoral and thematic citizen councils, grassroots consultations) that have offered the women's movement tools with which to influence the local state and minimize political co-option or isolation. Party and movement women have also seized on other municipal institutional instruments for mainstreaming and funding gender equity policies. They have thus contributed to local institution-building, just as the PT has been developing alternative models of popular participation and social justice since the 1980s.

The case studies in this chapter have demonstrated the complex interactions between political actors at the local level – principally the women in the party, feminist sympathizers within the administration or in elected office – and local women's groups, reflecting the horizontal and pluralist interface of the party with social movements at all levels of government. Local women's policy networks have been able to use the PT's programmatic and vertically institutionalized backing of women's rights to push sometime lukewarm party representatives into firmer commitments. Even if the PT's local government performance on gender policies still often falls far short of the party's own stated commitments and of the expectations of feminists in the party, its achievement nonetheless demonstrates the very positive difference a party *can* make.

Part II
Chile

5
In Their Place: The Political Uses of Women

The capacity of Chile's National Women's Ministry (*Servicio Nacional de la Mujer* – SERNAM) to design and deliver social policy for gender equity and equality has been conditioned in various ways by the party political and institutional environment in which it operates. This chapter begins by outlining the contours of past and current Chilean party and electoral systems, and the contingent and limited character of women's entry into those systems. It highlights how intense electoral competition has produced parties whose ideologies and political habitus are clearly differentiated in gender terms. The second section examines the character of SERNAM's institutional predecessors and their subordination to broader political projects and party interests. The chapter concludes by analyzing the party influences on representation and policy in the municipal arena, long constructed discursively in Chile as being a specifically 'feminized' political field.

Transition and restoration

In 1989, Chile emerged from nearly 17 years of military rule via a short but controlled transition, precipitated by the unexpected defeat of the Pinochet government in the 1988 plebiscite, when he asked the Chilean people for an extension of his authoritarian mandate. The military regime ensured that it left political-institutional arrangements *bien atado* ('tied up'), according the incoming democratic government little room for manoeuvre either on substantive issues, such as economic management and the human rights question, or on institutional arrangements, such as the electoral system, the 1980 Constitution and the presence of nine pro-military unelected senators (Angell, 1993). The regrouping of opposition political parties in the Coalition for

Democracy (*Concertación por la Democracia*, hereafter referred to as the Concertación) around the 'No' vote and the 1989 presidential and congressional elections following the return of senior politicians from exile restored a party system and pattern of political allegiances that the military regime had endeavoured to obliterate. The women's movement had campaigned in myriad ways for a return to democracy and expectations ran high that the new centre-left government would vigorously promote gender rights (Valenzuela, 1991; Chuchryck, 1994). These hopes were partially met with the establishment of SERNAM. However, in the arena of political representation, women actually lost ground initially, and have made relatively slow progress ever since, as shown in Table 5.1. Only 5.8 per cent of deputies elected to the restored democracy were women, a drop of over one third from 1973 levels. This must be attributed to three key factors: the gendered terms under which individual parties have historically incorporated and given political voice to women, the party system, and the post-1989 electoral system.

Gendered party politics

The Chilean party system is notable for its longevity, relative stability and clarity of its ideological divisions.[1] One can trace a line on the right from the Liberal and Conservative parties, founded in 1857, which dominated political life in the nineteenth and the first half of the twentieth centuries, through their fusion into the National Party in 1966, to rebirth into National Renovation (*Renovación Nacional* – RN) and the Independent Democratic Union (*Unión Democrática Independiente* – UDI) in the late 1980s. The centre ground was held in the middle decades of

Table 5.1 Chile: women's representation in municipal and national elected office, 1963–2005

Municipal			National	
Year	Councillor	Mayor	Year	Deputy
1963	5.9	—		
1969	7.8	—	1969	6.0
1971	7.6	—	1973	9.3
1989–92*	—	19.7	1989	5.8
1992	11.7	7.4	1993	7.5
1996	12.1	9.4	1997	10.8
2000	13.7	12.3	2001	12.5
2004	—	12.2	2005	15.8

Note: * Mayors appointed by military regime.

the twentieth century by the Radical Party (*Partido Radical* – PR), until it was displaced by the Christian Democrats (*Partido Demócrata Cristiano* – known as the DC) in the 1960s. Finally, the Left emerged with the Communist Party (PC), founded in 1922, and the Socialist Party (*Partido Socialista* – PS), founded in 1933. Both survived the dictatorship, although the former is much weakened, and were joined by a more centrist partner, the PPD. The electoral system inflicted by the outgoing military regime superimposed on this multiparty system a bipolar electoral and governing logic based on the opposing sides in the plebiscite. The Concertación, composed chiefly of the Christian Democrats, PPD, Socialists, and remnants of the Radicals, has governed since 1989, with the centre-right alliance of RN and UDI in opposition.[2] Nonetheless, the number of effective parties remains broadly the same as before 1973 and, although the ideological distance between them is now much narrower, they continue to represent distinct positions in relation to the three cross-cutting cleavages of the Chilean system (Siavelis, 2000): long-run secular–religious divisions, a class-based politics not completely erased by military rule, and the authoritarian–democratic axis. The parties remain highly competitive, with still distinct electoral bases, while the broad 'three thirds' distribution of electoral preferences across right-wing, centre and left-wing options has persisted despite changes in party names and political agendas, and a dilution of party identification under the authoritarian interregnum. Thus, we can classify parties by their spatial position on the left (PPD and PS), centre (PR and DC) and right (UDI and RN), or by other variables, such as adherence to Catholic doctrine (UDI and DC) or secularism (RN, PPD, PS and Radicals), or by degree of ideological intensity (DC, UDI and PS) or weakness (RN and PPD), all of which have a bearing on their gender orientation.[3]

Contingent and gendered citizenship

The historically competitive character of party politics shaped the very earliest integration of women as political agents. From the late nineteenth century onwards, women began to demand a voice in the national polity. However, as elsewhere in the region, suffrage was finally granted on the basis not of women's equal entitlement to the rights and duties of a citizen but rather of their allegedly special feminine qualities, and as a means of shifting the balance of power in favour of certain political actors. Male voters of all classes were gradually incorporated into the electoral system through the latter half of the nineteenth century, leaving women as the single largest unenfranchised group by the early twentieth century (Valenzuela, 1985). The Chilean system's early institutionalization around clear cleavages rendered it sensitive to the entry of new players, and the motive force behind according women the vote came from the Catholic Church,[4] with the pro-clerical Conservative Party presenting a suffrage bill as early as 1917. In the early twentieth century, Chilean political life was being transformed by the emergence of socialist parties based on organized labour. The Liberal and Conservative parties watched their vote drop from 66 per cent in 1920 to 35 per cent in 1932, the year that a ten-day 'socialist republic' was attempted. In the face of this political threat from the anti-clerical Centre and Left, the Right had an instrumental interest in women's franchise to bolster its electoral fortunes. The Radical Party, with its almost obsessively anti-clerical agenda, realized that it, the PC and PS would be significantly disadvantaged by the women's vote, even though these parties were committed in principle to universal suffrage and women's emancipation. President Arturo Alessandri's government therefore restricted Chilean women to voting and running as candidates in municipal elections – a position which lasted from 1935 to 1947. This spatial segregation was intended as much to prevent women from contaminating the national polity with their electoral preferences, as to protect the nation's mothers from being sullied by the dirty masculine business of *politiquería* ('politicking').[5] It would also provide an intermediary stage in which women could be socialized into responsible political citizenship through state education and legal emancipation, and freed from the tyranny of Church and husbands.

Electoral gender gap

This segregation is still symbolically visible today in the continued use of separate ballot boxes for men and women, providing Chile with a unique dataset with which to quantify, over a long time series, women's evolving voting preferences by candidate, party and ideological orientation, and the extent to which their ballots did affect the balance of power. I have calculated a 'gender gap' by generating a coefficient, derived by dividing the proportion of women's votes for a given party or candidate by the proportion of men's votes for the same. For example, 47.3 per cent of all the women who cast valid votes in the municipal election of 1935 opted for the Conservative Party, whilst only 21.7 per cent of male voters did so. The coefficient of 2.185 shows that the proportion of women who voted Conservative was more than double the proportion of men who did so. Table 5.2 demonstrates that the Conservatives, a pro-clerical party, were the primary beneficiaries of

Table 5.2 Chile: gender gap in elections for city councillor, by party, 1935–47

Party	Year				
	1935	*1938*	*1941*	*1944*	*1947*
Conservative	2.185	2.054	1.796	1.611	1.691
Liberal	0.881	0.908	1.244	1.151	1.070
PR	0.629	0.645	0.783	0.805	0.817
PS		0.453	0.700	0.690	0.943
Democratic	0.359		0.543	0.676	
PC		0.381		0.643	0.666

Notes: Calculations based on data in Maza Valenzuela (1995).
In Tables 5.2, 5.3 and 5.6 a figure of more than 1.00 indicates a positive gender gap, that is, that proportionately more women than men preferred a given party. A figure of less than 1.000 indicates the opposite.

the women's vote. By contrast, the Liberal Party, which was right-wing but moderately anti-clerical, was initially disadvantaged.

However, the Conservatives' gender gap advantage diminished over time, whilst it improved for the two anti-clerical parties. The Radicals were sufficiently encouraged by the expansion in their female vote, and alarmed by the growth in the Communist vote, to expedite women's national suffrage in 1949, aided by the Conservatives who once more anticipated an electoral boost (Maza Valenzuela, 1995: 42).[6] Table 5.3 shows that the

Table 5.3 Chile: gender gap in elections for deputy, by party, 1961–2001

Party	Year							
	1961	*1965*	*1969*	*1973*	*1989*	*1993*	*1997*	*2001*
Conservative	1.300	1.111	—		—	—	—	—
Liberal	1.094	1.054	—		—	—	—	—
PN	—	—	1.141		—	—	—	—
UDI	—	—	—		1.244	1.157	1.165	1.132
RN	—	—	—		1.176	1.097	1.107	1.091
CODE coalition	—	—	—	1.191	—	—	—	—
DC	1.168	1.206	1.224		0.951	1.014	1.008	0.975
PR	1.025	0.923	0.960		0.834	0.853	—	—
PPD	—	—	—		0.878	0.972	0.999	0.973
PS	0.742	0.738	0.829			0.912	0.926	0.910
PRSD	—	—	—		—	—	0.933	0.923
PC	0.673	0.729	0.748		—	—	—	—
UP coalition	—	—	—	0.804	—	—	—	—

Note: Calculation based on data from the electoral service. Data for the elections 1949–57 are lost or destroyed.

latter's gender advantage soon shifted to the Christian Democrats, a more socially engaged Catholic activist offshoot of the Conservatives.

When both registration and voting were made compulsory in 1962, the percentage of eligible women registered to vote rose by 260 per cent from the 1958 levels, so that in the 1964 presidential elections women's turnout (47.6 per cent) was nearly equal to that of men. The impact of this influx of new voters on national politics earned women a reputation as *hacedoras de presidentes* ('president-makers').

Marginal differences in voting preferences became critical from 1958 to 1973, a period notable for its increased ideological polarization, three-way division of votes and election of presidents by plurality with no run-off to produce a majority. In 1958, Jorge Alessandri was elected with only 18.4 per cent of the votes and, as many commentators have noted, if voting in 1958 had been confined to men, or if women had voted identically to men, then Salvador Allende would have been elected instead.[7] Yet the reverse also holds true; had only women voted or had men voted like women, then Alessandri would have been elected in 1970 and Lavín would have won with an absolute majority in the first round of the 1999 elections.

The gender gap advantage for the Christian Democrats peaked at 1.266 with the election of Frei in 1964, as Table 5.4 shows, but disappeared as the DC moved into the centre-left coalition after 1989. The gender gap disadvantage for the Socialists has also diminished, from 0.651 for Allende in 1958 to 0.897 for Ricardo Lagos in 1999, which last was the first presidential contest to go to a second round[8] and to pit a socialist against a single, right-wing candidate. However, the gender gap advantage of 1.147 that Joaquín Lavín, the former UDI mayor of Las Condes, enjoyed in the first round was not enough to win once the governing alliance made a concerted effort to target women voters.

Over the period 1935–2000, we can see a steady convergence of male and female voting patterns. The numerical distance between the parties with the highest and lowest gender gap coefficients was 1.826 in 1935, but this had almost disappeared by the 2004 municipal elections, when it stood at 0.145.[9] The distance remains a little higher for congressional elections (0.152) and highest in presidential contests (0.226 in the 2000 run-off), probably due to the latter's bipolar and plebiscitary character. In both the presidential and legislative elections, the gender gap advantage has benefited primarily Church-affiliated parties, shifting over time from the Conservatives, to the Christian Democrats and latterly to UDI, although it has not assisted their secular allies on the same points of the political spectrum (Liberals, Radicals and RN). This

Table 5.4 Chile: gender gap in presidential elections by candidate, 1952–2006

	Right	Centre	Left
1952	1.222	1.019	0.831
	0.887		
1958	1.064	0.999	0.651
	1.044	1.190	
1964	0.918	1.266	0.707
1970	1.221	1.156	0.736
1988	('Yes' vote)		('No' vote)
Plebiscite	1.178		0.880
1989	1.251	0.874	
	1.061		
1993	1.149	0.983	0.904
	0.967		
1999	1.147		0.892
2000	1.123		0.897
2006	1.008		0.993

Note: Data refer to the following candidates:
Right: Matte Larraín and Ibáñez (1952); (Jorge) Alessandri and Zamorano (1958); Durán (1964); (Jorge) Alessandri (1970); Büchi and Errázuriz (1989); (Arturo) Alessandri and Piñera (1993); Lavín (1999/2000); Piñera (2006). Centre: Alfonso (1952); Bossay Leiva and Frei (senior) (1958); Frei (senior) (1964); Tomic (1970); Aylwin (1989); Eduardo Frei (son) (1993). Left: Allende (1952, 1958, 1964, 1970); Max-Neef and Pizarro Poblete (1993); Lagos (1999/2000); Bachelet (2006).

underscores the salience of the religious rather than the class cleavage in relation to the political preferences of older, less educated, female homemakers, whose votes create this gender gap. As more women start to work outside the home, the gender gap may disappear completely, even if the Catholic Church's continued political power and UDI's aggressive political campaigning keep the religious cleavage alive.

Outside in: women and the party structures

Within the political parties, Chilean women have long occupied an ambiguous position. Suffragists responded to the lack of support for their cause by setting up their own parties, the *Partido Cívico Femenino* (1922) and the *Partido Femenino de Chile* (1946). However, their aims were narrow and they disintegrated once the full franchise was granted. Although this issue had united women across the political spectrum, the Videla government's swing to the right enabled party rivalries to divide the movement (Antezana-Pernet, 1994), and activists were absorbed back into the party women's bureaux, established in the 1930s and 1940s to capture municipal votes (Maza Valenzuela, 1995: 29).

With the return to democracy, the Concertación parties tried to move away from the old organizational model, where women were invisible and used for electoral recruitment and propagandizing, towards units that would promote gender issues and women's leadership. PPD feminists secured a Women's Technical Commission and then a General Secretariat, established in 2004, whilst the Socialist Party appointed a women's vice-president and abolished its women's wing. The Radicals and Christian Democrats, however, feared losing or alienating the loyalties of an older generation of female supporters,[10] so the DC set up a more 'modern' Women's Technical commission parallel to its women's section, which continued to cater for members active in the Mothers' Centres.[11]

The presence of women on the parties' national executive councils is still far from reflecting the distribution of party membership.[12] In 1991, women filled on average only 16.2 per cent of senior posts, with the PPD and PS scoring highest, and UDI lowest, a pattern that has persisted. The left-wing women of the Concertación, inspired by their European counterparts, demanded affirmative action policies, and both the PPD and PS reserved first 20 then 40 per cent of internal leadership positions for women as well as a similar quota for candidate lists for legislative elections. However, this higher target has not yet been reached in either case.[13] In 1996, the Christian Democrats, after much debate,[14] finally introduced a 20 per cent quota, but only for internal positions (Franceschet, 2001: 221). Meanwhile the Right remains ideologically opposed to affirmative action policies. RN has a spokeswoman on women and the family, but little rank-and-file organizational structure, and UDI has only a Family Issues department. The mission of UDI's original Women's Committee, set up in the early 1980s, was to 'combat Marxism, defend the home ... fight the vices of the socializing State and the totalitarian menace, and defend the 1980 Constitution as a means of living according to our ... historical tradition' (Soto Gamboa, 2001). However, unlike the other functional groupings (youth, professionals, workers) and territorial representatives, it received no representation on the party's General Council.[15] It has since disappeared and UDI has developed other ways of courting women's votes.

Party origins and gendered political sociabilities

Gendered patterns of political recruitment and electoral preference are largely a function of the way that party origins and histories have generated distinct and gendered subcultures and modes of political sociability. Chile's six main parties have 'distinct platforms, historical identities and constituencies' (Siavelis, 1997: 668), as well as varying styles of leadership, decision-making and association. The Radical Party's sociability was centred on highly masculine spaces – the fire brigade, the Reform Club, the Masonic lodge, the lycée and university (Lomnitz and Melnick, 1998; Maza Valenzuela, 1998) – just as the Socialist Party's socialization was traditionally rooted in the trade unions. However, the Communist Party's base was more diverse, encompassing the *poblaciones* (shantytowns), whilst the Christian Democrats' also centred on more feminized spaces where women have greater presence – the family, the Catholic Church, and neighbourhood organizations.[16] UDI emerged from the *gremialista*[17] movement founded in the Catholic University's law faculty by Jaime Guzmán after the collapse of the Right in the 1965 elections. Since then it has remained controlled by a small male cabal of young neo-liberal economists, technocrats and lawyers who cut their teeth in the military government (Garretón, 2000; Huneeus, 2000, 2001; Joignant and Navia, 2003). Three of these parties (PR, PS, and UDI) have subcultures underpinned by strong notions of *fraternity* (Pateman, 1989) and have ended up promoting fewest women leaders, and running and electing the fewest female representatives (PR and PS 1963–73, and UDI after 1989), because women were quite simply absent from the parties' core arenas of leadership and candidate recruitment (Navia, 2004).

The most resistant to promoting women's leadership have been the two semi-confessional parties, DC and UDI, whose internal organizational structures mirror those of the Catholic Church. These are cadre parties, with stringent conditions of entry and an evangelizing mission, their leadership initially formed of a male secular–political priesthood and supported at the base by a largely female rank-and-file. This is most marked in UDI, which was formally constituted as a party in 1983 not just to support the military regime, but also to ensure that it would become the standardbearer of the legacy of radical authoritarianism after any transition (Huneeus, 2000). Like its spiritual inspiration, Opus Dei, the exclusionary fundamentalist and masculine Catholic sect, UDI's structure is hierarchical, centralized, hermetic and internally disciplined, its leaders united through religious, generational, educational and cultural homogeneity to form a self-appointed 'moral aristocracy'. Women provide a majority of its votes, members (60 per cent) and activists, but very few party leaders or national representatives.[18]

By contrast, the DC is much more heterogeneous, with clan and generation-based factional divisions.[19] In the 1960s, the party's organicist philosophy of social integration and a Third Way between capitalism and Marxism – a fusion of social justice with social harmony – culminated in its strategy of *promoción popular*,[20] which both mobilized politically marginal social sectors, and brought them into the DC's corporatist structure as electoral bases. Thus, in 1962 the party established a Women's Department, as it did for the peasantry, urban labour, shantytown dwellers and youth. Although this social Catholicism makes the DC less hierarchical than UDI, women still account for only 13 per cent of its leaders.

The two new parties of the secular centre-right and centre-left, RN and the PPD, have the weakest forms of sociability because they lack a mass base and are dominated by notables; RN is composed of politicians with strong individual local bases, the PPD of high-profile media-friendly national leaders. The former was founded in 1987 within a right-wing coalition as a post-Pinochet successor to the National Party. Despite those continued links it has promoted itself as a pro-democratic, business-oriented, modern conservative party, willing to negotiate with the opposition, and is more heterogeneous than UDI from which it split in 1988. The PPD formed before the plebiscite as a flag of convenience for the Left when Marxist parties were still banned. Both therefore originated as umbrella organizations, which has produced 'catch-all' characteristics as regards ideological profile and electoral strategies as well as a heterogeneous leadership. Their more permeable elite structure and electoral-professional character have given them the highest success rates in electing women candidates. Like UDI, the PPD is electorally very efficient but it differs, in terms of national elections at least, in selecting a much higher number of women candidates due to its self-imposed quota and achieving the highest female success rate, as Table 5.6 shows.

The Socialist Party now runs the highest percentage of female candidates as its quota has managed to override the ideological orientation and cultural weight of its long tradition. The restorationist logic was powerful in a party forcibly ripped from office in 1973, its militants and leaders sent into exile. It remains a highly competitive environment, with ideologically-based factions[21] and a large pool of seasoned party activists on which to draw for leadership or electoral positions. Plumb (1998) argues that many younger activists preferred to stay in the PPD rather than move to the PS when the two parties separated in 1992 because of the much greater upward mobility in the former, but this has begun to change. When President-Elect Frei personally requested nominations of women for ministerial posts from the Concertación parties, the Socialist Party executive failed to pass on the list drawn up by party women.[22] However, President Lagos appointed women to five out of 16 ministerial posts in line with his party's own quota and the feminist demand made back in 1988.[23] One of his campaign slogans was 'Lagos winning, women governing', and in 2005 the Socialists chose a woman, Michelle Bachelet, as their presidential candidate. She went on to win the second round of presidential elections in 2006, becoming Chile's first woman head of state.

Thus, it seems that the more weakly institutionalized parties are more open to supporting women's candidacies than those mass-based, institutionalized parties that have stronger subcultures of political community. However, the latter have been shifting towards a more electoral-professional profile. Deracinated by the military regime, the centre-left parties have struggled to regain their pre-1973 level of penetration into organized civil society and have found themselves competing with UDI's new right-wing populism. It is argued that the Chilean populace has become depoliticized, oriented towards consumerism and individual choice rather than wider political debates (Moulian, 1998; Paley, 2001), with policy responsibility delegated from the electorate and parties to distant technocrats (Posner, 1999; Schild, 2000; Silva, 2001, 2004). This process is paralleled by a decline in the activity levels of the social movements (Oxhorn, 1994), although this was perhaps a symptom of a shift from partycratic co-option to a more genuine autonomy (Schneider, 1995). Parties remain the backbone of the political system, but their relationship with state and society has been reconfigured.

Electoral system

The electoral system provides further structural disincentives for women's representation and voice. As in Brazil, Chile's electoral system employs open-list proportional representation with the D'Hondt method for allocating seats. By 1973, Chile had 28 electoral constituencies for the Chamber of Deputies, with a district magnitude varying between two and 18.[24] However, the military government reorganized these into 60 districts, each electing only *two* representatives.[25] Voters must choose one of no more than two candidates presented by each party or coalition; there is no 'party vote' as in Brazil. The system was designed to encourage bipolar, centripetal electoral competition to replace the polarized dynamics of the Allende period (1970–3), and to bolster the right-wing parties, which had seen a decline in their share of the vote over several decades.[26] The first-placed party list must receive twice the number of votes (66.7 per cent of the total) as the second-placed in order to win both seats. This very high threshold rewards the two main coalitions with a disproportionate number of seats relative to votes,[27] and denies a foothold to minor parties, preventing them from growing incrementally from low levels of representation, as the PT managed to do in Brazil.

The system also hinders the entry of non-traditional political actors because the very low district magnitude – one remove from a first-past-the-post system – creates fierce internal competition for selection. Within both coalitions, candidacies are distributed first by sub-coalition, by party and then party faction (Magar *et al.*, 1998; Siavelis, 2002: 423), creating multiple layers that women aspirants have to negotiate.[28] Although some parties are democratizing and decentralizing the selection process, it remains heavily dominated by the central elites.[29] In some cases, women have been deselected[30] or had their political achievements ignored in order to accommodate new male cadres. In 1993, María Antonieta Saa was almost denied selection as the PPD's congressional candidate for Conchalí, which she had governed very successfully as mayor, in favour of an unknown male candidate in favour with the leadership.[31] The 40 per cent quota of the PPD and PS adds an additional selection criterion and, as in the PT, is the last to be met; both parties ran under 20 per cent female candidates in 2001. Concertación women have also grumbled that they end up competing against one another for the same constituency, reducing the pool of electable women still further. The binominal system creates a perverse 'rival partners game' (Magar *et al.*, 1998: 718), as both coalition candidates know that only one of them is likely to win.[32] Once selected, female candidates must then battle for party and coalition resources to support their campaign. Today, the cost of running for Senate in large urban constituencies is over one million dollars (Angell, 2003: 104) with business donations targeted at individual candidates rather than parties. Here too, women have to compete with male-dominated networks of influence. In 1993, three women running for re-election found themselves pushed into second and third place as their male running-mate received more backing;[33] women's re-election rate (33.3 per cent) was half of men's (59.2 per cent).[34]

This is a very difficult electoral system to which to apply positive discrimination measures. In 1997, women parliamentarians from the Concertación submitted the first statutory quota bill, for a 40 per cent minimum for candidates of either sex,[35] but it lay dormant until 2002, when a socialist deputy submitted a bill with a 30 per cent floor. If implemented, the open-list system would not automatically convert the proportion of female candidates into an equivalent level of representation, but with a capped number of candidates and a high success rate for the

Table 5.5 Chile: percentage of women candidates for deputy, percentage elected and female success index, by party, 1969 and 1973

Party	1969			1973		
	Candidates	Elected	FSI	Candidates	Elected	FSI
PN	5.3	3.0	56.3			
DC	6.8	7.1	104.6			
PR	2.6	0.0	0.0			
CODE coalition				4.0	4.6	114.9
PS	3.4	13.3	430.8*			
PC	9.5	9.1	95.0			
UP coalition				11.3	15.9	147.4
National average	5.3	6.0	115.1	6.8	9.3	140.4

Note: * The FSI for the Socialists is skewed in 1969 as they elected two of only three women candidates.

parties of the two main blocks, the effect would nonetheless be more noticeable than in Brazil. This would, however, imply a zero-sum game for male deputies of all political stripes. As the electoral system is enshrined in the 1980 Constitution, any modification requires a two thirds majority, contingent on the collaboration of the right-wing opposition, which has a vested interest in the continuation of the current system as well as an objection to positive discrimination measures. It is also hard to imagine centre-left male politicians agreeing to a measure that would deprive them of their virtually guaranteed seats.

The percentage of women candidates for deputy has risen steadily, from 5.3 per cent in 1969 to 14.4 per cent in 2001, even though the percentage of women elected fell in 1989. Tables 5.5 and 5.6 show that,

Table 5.6 Chile: average percentage of women candidates for deputy, percentage elected and female success index, by party, over four elections, 1989–2001

Party	Candidates	Elected	FSI
UDI	8.1	2.7	31.4
RN	9.8	11.1	115.0
DC	6.4	4.4	67.1
PPD	13.6	17.9	138.7
PS	14.0	11.5	80.1

Note: Averages for PPD and PS include data for PPD only in 1989 elections.

in terms of ideological orientation, the Left has fielded and elected more women candidates, followed by the Right, with the centre parties trailing in third place.[36] The tables also show the female success index (FSI). It is notable that in the period 1969–73, women candidates performed better than men; in 1973, women's success rate was 140 per cent that of men's. However, after 1989 women's electability lagged behind men's due to intensified intra-coalition and intra-party competition for nominations combined with the masculine party cultures. Again, left-wing women candidates have the highest FSI, the centre parties the worst. At the level of the individual party, the best performers are the two newest and most electoral-professional parties, RN and PPD, the worst are the two most religiously oriented and socially conservative parties, UDI and DC,[37] for the reasons noted above. The gendered characteristics of competition within the party system and of individual parties not only explain these finer differences in women's representation, but have also influenced the formation of state-led gender policy for several decades.

Engendering the good society: state women's units

The latest wave of historiography on twentieth-century Chilean state- and nation-building has explored the diverse ways in which different areas of state policy, such as agrarian reform (Tinsman, 2002) and the modernization of the mining sector (Klubock, 1996), either explicitly or inadvertently reshaped gender relations. Individual political parties, governing alliances such as the Popular Front coalitions of 1936–48 (Rosemblatt, 2000), dominant social institutions such as the trade unions and Catholic Church, and various state welfare bodies all promoted what Tinsman calls 'gender mutualism', a socially conservative vision that tended to reinforce women's domestic role. Women's organizations had also been making their own claims for social and political rights since the nineteenth century, and engaged in a wide range of philanthropic, welfare, educational, cultural and political activities (Gaviola *et al.*, 1986, 1994; Frohman and Valdés, 1993; Valdés and Weinstein, 1993; Maza Valenzuela, 1995). However, after activist women had been absorbed by the political parties in the 1950s (Antezana-Pernet, 1994), successive governments began to establish dedicated national state institutions that both targeted women for social welfare purposes and rallied them in support of the political regime and project of the day. These two objectives were inextricably linked due to the highly party politicized nature of Chilean society and the strategic importance of women as an electoral group in such a finely balanced party system. Each administration sought to leave its ideological imprimatur upon these bodies, believing that mobilizing women was crucial to its own interpretation of the Good Society, of which the Good Family represented both the microcosm and core.

The first type of state-sponsored women's organization consisted of semi-autonomous charitable bodies, such as the Housewives Association (under Videla) and the People's Clothing Foundation (under Ibáñez), providing handouts and some limited income generation, and presided over by the First Lady. They were the precursors of the first Mothers' Centres (*Centros de Madres* – CEMA) set up in this period and later institutionalized under the Christian Democrats.[38] This kind of organization was concerned with the material, moral and spiritual welfare of poor families, issues that engaged not just the Catholic Church,[39] Christian Democrats and right-wing parties, but also the Socialists and Radicals in their pursuit of social hygiene. As these bodies operated at local community level, they also formed a key part of the parties' strategy of electoral penetration into civil society. For that reason, successive administrations rebranded them in their own image; CEMA was renamed COCEMA (*Coordinadora de los Centros de Madres*) under the Allende government and CEMA-Chile under the military regime.

The same occurred with the second category, the executive branch bodies, of which SERNAM is the latest variant. The first National Women's Office (*Oficina Nacional de la Mujer*) was launched in 1951 by the Videla government (1946–52), reformed under the same name by Eduardo Frei's Christian Democrat administration (1964–70), and reconstituted as the National Women's Secretariat (*Secretaría Nacional de la Mujer* – SNM) in 1972 under Allende's socialist coalition government. Under the Pinochet regime, the name was retained but the institutional location altered. The changes of name and structure of this government department under four consecutive administrations, in dramatically diverse political contexts – Third Way reformism, socialist revolution, right-wing authoritarian military rule, and democratization – reinforced the view that it was a partisan instrument.

The Frei government was the first to target women as a political constituency, and the *Centros de Madres* became keystones of the DC's grassroots work, electoral fortunes[40] and political project of eliminating class struggle and the threat of the Left (Power, 2002: 107–8). Women, defined as apolitical defenders of home and hearth, were to be educated as good housewives and community managers, responsible for the social reproduction of both family and community. The centres, some

6,000 of which were formed in this period (Valdés and Weinstein, 1993: 59), belonged to the community section of the party's Council for Popular Promotion[41] as functional, neighbourhood-based organizations, thus combining both sectoral and territorial penetration.

During Allende's Popular Unity (*Unidad Popular* – UP) government, parties across the spectrum competed for women's support as polarization deepened and debates about the nation's future assumed an increasingly gendered character. The Mothers' Centres continued to proliferate, rising to 20,000 with around one million members by 1973, and were also viewed by the UP as a potentially captive constituency. Although it won over a number, many remained loyal to the Christian Democrats, others were internally divided and some worked actively with the opposition in protest activities, mirroring national political disintegration. Nonetheless, this extensive organization of women at neighbourhood level, engaged in a wide range of activities, from urbanization, food distribution, health clinics, daycare centres, literacy and work training, was clearly the precursor and often the origin of the *pobladora* groups that re-emerged under authoritarian rule, even if their affiliations were divided sharply along party political and ideological lines.

Allende's government framed women's interests and social role within a socialist rubric; that is, in economic and reproductive terms. Its policies prioritized women's labour force integration via the socialization of domestic work (communal laundries and canteens) and involvement in the new food distribution organizations. However, it failed to appreciate that distributive policies viewed as emancipatory for a male working-class public could have unintended and negative consequences on women because of their different inscription in gender roles. The political climate of rapid revolutionary change, combined with the shortages provoked by both economic mismanagement and sabotage, not only made many women fearful, but also increased their domestic workload. The UP recognized that it had lost women's support by making practical gender needs more difficult to meet whilst failing to address any strategic ones, but the SNM, established in 1972, came too late and reached too few women.[42] Encouraged – but not instigated – by the right-wing opposition, anti-Allende groups such as Women's Power (*Poder Femenino*) took to the streets protesting at the shortages and price rises, and urging the military to intervene (Power, 2002). As Power notes, throughout the twentieth century the political Right has often been better than its competitors at speaking to the life experiences and value systems of women and at capitalizing on women's continuing exclusion from the male world of party politics and government

(Baldez, 2002). Although *Poder Femenino* used the non-partisanship of their members both as a political strategy and collective identity, the main opposition parties monitored its impact and lent valuable political and organizational resources (Power, 2002: 170–4). It also functioned as an important locus for unifying the opposition parties, and the National Party and the Christian Democrats came to regard women not just as a source of votes, but also as a means of toppling the government itself.

General Pinochet's speeches lauded women for saving the fatherland, and called for their active support. The military regime, like the DC and the Church, regarded the nation's mothers as pivotal to its foundational anti-Communist project by exercising a special role in transmitting traditional 'Chilean' values within the home. The regime invoked an image of social relations as an unchanging hierarchy, the military's paternalistic model of government mirroring the natural order of father, mother and child. Pinochet claimed 'Women and the Armed Forces are inextricably united through a spiritual bond that allows them to generate, maintain and promote the Great Chilean Family' (Munizaga, 1988: 32). It also sought to boost these supposedly innate feminine qualities via three structures: the CEMA-Chile network, the SNM and the 10,000-strong female volunteer force, all supervised by the First Lady, the symbolic mother of the nation in the authoritarian-patriarchal schema.

Also run entirely by volunteers, the SNM's goals were to integrate women into the social, cultural and economic development of the country via organized voluntary work, and to foster healthy moral living and public service. Its explicitly propagandistic function was reflected in its regional structure where local leadership was assumed by the wives of appointed military regional governors. Nationally, it fell under the auspices of the General Secretariat of the government, as a subsection of the Civil Organizations Division, which also oversaw the sectoral organizations for youth, guilds (*gremios*) and culture. This Division was heavily influenced by Jaime Guzmán, who advocated a corporatist-integralist model of social organization that would depoliticize civil society by replacing class-based organizations (trade unions and political parties) with cross-class ones under the control of central government.[43] In the absence of parties,[44] UDI was able to operate first as a movement and then as a party through these state institutions (Pollack, 1999: 130) whose upper-class activists were receptive to its message, enabling it to reach a substantial working-class audience.

In 1975, CEMA-Chile was also restructured as a political instrument. Although nominally a private, non-governmental body,[45] its leadership structure echoed the SNM's, with regional, provincial and town vice-presidents who were generally military wives and worked under the authority of the regional government. It quickly became part of the military government's welfare apparatus, plugging the gaps in increasingly threadbare state welfare provision. The poorhouse benefits it offered tended to reinforce the most discriminatory features of women's employment – home working, low earnings, occupational training in feminized skills such as sewing and handicrafts, non-unionization, isolation and dependence on the organization for materials and benefits. However, its members were neither brainwashed nor uncritical, and they often complained about the arrogance of the outreach workers, favouritism, the irrelevance of the training courses, and the rising costs charged for inadequate services (Levy and Lechner, 1986). The number of centres actually dropped abruptly after the coup – from 20,000 in 1974 to 9,837 in 1988. CEMA-Chile was not dismantled after 1989, but allowed to continue in moribund form as a private entity, headed by the wife of the head of the army, not of the president, after the statutes were changed in 1991. This forced the Christian Democrats to find other means of reaching low-income women, one of their core constituencies.

Although these state-sponsored organizations were intended to discipline women within a conservative conception of gender relations, the regime's policies produced the opposite effect. As their families suffered hardships and human rights abuses, women felt empowered to act in the public arena in the absence of men (Baldez, 2002). Pinochet's project of atomization and privatization, of transforming the macro, public sphere into a mirror of the patriarchal, micro sphere of the family, was inverted in the 1980s as Chilean feminists produced their own version of 'the personal is political' in their slogan *¡Democracia en la casa y en el país!* ('Democracy at home and in the country'). This in turn generated demand by women in the recently reconstituted centre-left parties for a new kind of state institution that would be free of party political interference and work within the international gender rights framework, rather than within a political ideology.

Centralized power, local government

Any analysis of the space available at the local level for women to exercise political agency and enact gender policy must take into account Chile's historic centralism and recent half-hearted decentralization. Urbanization occurred relatively early, along with the consolidation of the primate capital Santiago, home to the political and economic elite that controlled both the rural and the industrial sectors, as well as to the political parties and state bureaucracy. A rentier economy, in which wealth accumulated in the political and geographical centre of the country, produced a strongly centripetal polity and political parties with national penetration. Consequently, shifts in the political balance of power came from centrally generated decisions to integrate further classes or categories of electors, such as the two-stage extension of suffrage to women.

In this unitary state, the municipalities were mere administrative agents for central government and conduits for brokering favours between the central party machines and the particularistic demands of the local populace. This form of electoral clientelism differed from Brazilian *coronelismo* insofar as the intermediaries were not powerful individuals and their cronies, but institutionalized parties and their representatives. This model combined top-down control with extensive grassroots penetration and outside the parties there was little organized group activity aimed at influencing municipal authorities (Valenzuela, 1977). Although electoral competition was fierce at local level, ideological differences were less important than access to the power and resources distributed by the central authorities.

After 1973, the Pinochet regime reorganized local government as part of its political project of dismantling the populist, developmentalist state. All sub-national units of government were brought into a new hierarchy; the president appointed the governors (*Intendentes*) of the newly created regions, as well as their subordinates, the provincial governors, who in turn oversaw the mayors.[46] Municipalities remained nominally under civilian tutelage, but within a system of authoritarian centralism. The Junta immediately dismissed all the elected mayors, reinstated most of the National Party and Christian Democrat ones, and replaced the rest with military officers and selected sympathetic civilians via a complex appointment system involving the Regional Development Council, the *Intendente* and even the president of the republic. The 1980 Constitution later instituted a system of indirect representation consisting of Local Development Councils (*Consejos de Desarrollo Comunal* – CODECOs), corporative bodies that represented local business and professional interests. Having rid all governmental structures of party political penetration, the military government embarked on a programme of rationalization, privatization and deconcentration of certain ministries so that social services, notably education, would be delivered by the municipalities, the lowest link in a centralized chain of command.

Since 1989, regional democratization has been minimal, even though direct election of the *Intendentes* and regional councillors was debated as far back as 1991 and the latter promised, but not delivered, by Lagos. The intermediary layers of government are not endowed with equivalent powers or autonomy, although the regional structures mirror those of national government (see Table 7.1). The *Intendente* presides over the regional cabinet, composed of the regional branches of each ministry, as the president of the republic does nationally. The cabinet debates priorities and the governor prepares the budget and plan for government for the approval of the regional councillors (*consejeros regionales*), who are themselves indirectly elected by the region's city councillors (*concejales*). The provincial level of government is of minor political or administrative importance, and the provincial governors act merely as the representatives of the *Intendentes*.[47] It has no deliberative structure, only advisory bodies. Without arenas for political representation, the regions and provinces function as deconcentrated branches of national government, somewhat disconnected from the municipalities.

However, one of the first constitutional reforms proposed by the Aylwin government was municipal democratization. The Right's political support for decentralization was overridden both by its reluctance to fund state expansion and by its electoral self-interest (Angell *et al.*, 2001: 89). It blocked the municipal reforms and insisted instead on the creation of regional governments where they hoped to gain ascendancy in a political field otherwise dominated by the Concertación (Bland, 2003; Eaton, 2004a, 2004b). The latter's ever more centralized parties had little incentive to accelerate either reform, confirming O'Neill's (2003) argument that the pace of decentralization in Latin America has been driven primarily by political parties whose chances of winning national power are low. It was not until November 1991 that the Concertación endowed local government with legal autonomy and passed a new municipal code providing for the direct election of city councillors, whilst the military-appointed mayors and CODECOs remained in office until the June 1992 elections. The 1925–73 electoral system was restored, with councillors elected on party/coalition slates using the D'Hondt distributor, although with a greater district magnitude than in congressional elections.[48] It also restored the traditional system of indirect election of mayors. In 1992, candidates won executive office outright if they belonged to the list with the most votes and received a plurality of at least 35 per cent of the valid votes. Otherwise, they were chosen by their fellow councillors via a system of inter-party 'quota' agreements, resulting in 29.3 per cent of all contests ending in a split mandate of only two years. The threshold was lowered to 30 per cent for the 1996 and 2000 elections, encouraging parties to concentrate their campaigning efforts on 'mayoral' candidates, at which UDI has been notably successful. The introduction in 2004 of a separate slate and direct election of mayor by simple plurality reinforced this trend.

Municipal maternalism

From early on, the Chilean municipality was discursively constructed as an extension of hearth and home. In this semi-privatized public sphere, women's transgression could be recast as a form of political mothering as they performed the role of municipal housekeepers. Women's electoral contribution was also noted by the sponsor of the suffrage bill, the Conservative Party, which in 1935 ran one third of all the 65 female candidates and elected two thirds of all female councillors, as the party had called on women voters to cast their ballots specifically for their Conservative sisters (Valenzuela, 1995). Tables 5.7 and 5.8 show the varying degrees to which political parties promoted their female candidates in the period 1963–2000. The percentage of women running for city councillor doubled, as did the number elected. Whereas, prior to 1973, the Communists ran the largest number of female candidates, after 1989 the conservative opposition ran more (just over 20 per cent), with which the Concertación caught up only in 2004. Since 1989, UDI has led the field, contrary to its record in the national legislature. In the centre, the Radical Party was again one of the worst performers, whereas the DC peaked in the late 1960s.

Table 5.7 Chile: percentage of women candidates for city councillor, percentage elected and female success index, by party, 1963–71

Party	1963			1967			1971		
	Candidates	*Elected*	*FSI*	*Candidates*	*Elected*	*FSI*	*Candidates*	*Elected*	*FSI*
United Conservative	13.8	8.8	60.3						
Liberal	10.0	7.7	74.7						
PN				11.1	6.8	57.9	14.2	10.8	73.4
DC	10.9	7.6	67.4	14.2	11.7	80.1	11.8	3.8	29.4
PR	7.1	2.8	37.9	9.5	3.1	30.2	9.2	3.6	36.6
PS	4.6	2.2	45.4	7.1	2.0	26.9	10.0	5.4	52.2
PC	11.0	7.1	61.4	14.4	8.8	57.3	14.6	8.5	54.4
National average	9.3	5.9	61.4	11.0	7.8	68.2	11.9	7.6	60.7

Table 5.8 Chile: percentage of women candidates for city councillor, percentage elected and female success index, by party, 1992–2000

Party	1992			1996			2000		
	Candidates	Elected	FSI	Candidates	Elected	FSI	Candidates	Elected	FSI
UDI	22.1	19.6	51.3	19.7	—	—	23.9	22.7	93.5
RN	19.7	14.8	71.0	17.9	—	—	18.6	16.8	88.2
Coalition	20.3	15.9	72.5	18.7	—	—	23.0	13.3	78.8
DC	12.6	9.7	74.1	14.0	—	—	16.6	14.7	86.8
PR	8.1	7.0	85.9						
PPD	16.6	14.6	87.1	14.0	—	—	18.8	16.5	85.7
PS	14.1	8.6	57.7	18.9	—	—	17.0	14.6	83.2
PRSD				9.0	—	—	14.7	13.7	90.7
Coalition	13.4	10.0	72.3	12.9	—	—	17.3	13.8	84.2
National average	16.6	11.7	66.9	17.7	12.1	78.2	18.9	13.7	84.0

However, at no time did women's success rate in any party outstrip that of men, leading to the conclusion that there is actually no elective or electoral affinity between women and the municipal *casa grande*. This is perhaps surprising, as running for a local legislative post is regarded as pointless by most aspiring politicians. Lily Pérez, in 1995 the only city councillor among the mayors on the board of the Association of Chilean Municipalities, met resistance from within her own party, RN, when she wanted to run for councillor in La Florida, a municipality that the party thought it would never control.[49] She was later elected deputy for that district, making her a rare example (along with María Antonieta Saa) of a woman who made the transition from municipal to national politics. Quotas for candidates in municipal elections have not even been suggested, although the larger district magnitude would mitigate the zero-sum logic of congressional elections.

There are no gender-disaggregated data on mayors before the coup, but the proportion of women is unlikely to have been higher than that of city councillors, given the competition for the patronage goods that the post offered. It is therefore startling that women constituted nearly 20 per cent of the mayors appointed by the outgoing military regime (Ministerio del Interior, 1992).[50] The presence in local government of many professionally well-qualified women, often lawyers linked to *gremialismo* and Guzmán's UDI group at the Catholic University, resulted from three converging factors: Pinochet's aggressive project of depoliticization of polity, society and economy, by which the reins of state power were handed over to technocrats and managers rather than politicians; a long-run discourse of municipal marianism; and the Chilean tradition of the municipality as an administrative, not political, unit. They were placed *in loco parentis* of a temporarily infantilized local populace, forming part of a nexus of public maternalism that encompassed the CEMA-Chile network, voluntary groups and SNM, a counterpart to Pinochet's authoritarian paternalism. María Angélica Cristi, mayor of Peñalolén, commented 'Women mayors have done their job very well. The municipality is like a big household, it's like running a big family.'[51] Public opinion on their performance was favourable, as they were seen as competent and not partisan or corrupt, qualities associated with the traditional image of the municipality as a site for masculine, patronage-oriented party politics. Thus, the municipality became feminized in contradictory ways, both as the locus for an authoritarian project to target working-class women, and as the arena of grassroots oppositional struggles over collective consumption issues and women's defence of family and community.

Re-gendering municipal politics

In 1992, the proportion of women mayors dropped to 9.6 per cent, in a localized echo of the remasculinization of national politics, remaining around this level until it rose slightly to 12.3 per cent in 2000. Women's more restricted access to intra- and inter-party circuits of informal negotiations left them persistently disadvantaged in the allocation of the mayoral office (during indirect elections)[52] and of mayoral candidacies (in the direct elections of 2004).[53] Some of the many women CODECOs, administrators and appointed mayors attempted to convert their local political experience into an electoral base. Just under half (180) of the incumbent mayors (55 per cent of men and 47 per cent of women) ran for election, mostly for UDI. Although 21 of these women were elected councillor or mayor, many had found themselves facing unexpectedly stiff internal party competition for seats in the prize Santiago municipalities. The indirect electoral system resulted in these women candidates having to compete against their male party colleagues, whereas a direct contest would have allowed them to capitalize on their local government record. They were also ambivalent about the need to join a political party. María Olivia Gazmuri, former mayor of La Reina, needed the party's logistical support. However, she sensed that her chances were actually greater as an independent candidate as party affiliation undermined the perception of the city hall as a non-political arena in which women mayors were respected managers. She lamented 'I lost votes when I joined RN'.[54] They were forced to become *políticas* after years of regarding party politics as a dirty business:

> We women view municipal administration as a technical matter. It was very hard for us to get into party political work as we enjoyed the non-political running of the municipality. Men mayors were much quicker to join the parties and most of those who are now deputies got involved with UDI or RN much earlier than we did.[55]

She also noted, as in the Costa Rican congress, a gendered approach to the office: 'When men are mayor, they keep their professional interests going. Women mayors do only that one job, one hundred per cent.'

UDI has also developed into a lean, mean electoral machine, overtaking RN through its highly utilitarian approach to candidate selection.[56] Its female candidates felt that they were denied institutional backing due to their alienation from the informal and extremely male-dominated circuits of power within the party apparatus, which also prevented them from reaching higher office.[57] Most of that party's male legislators had an apprenticeship as mayor; Lavín was able to launch a political career that nearly took him to the presidency from Las Condes, where his UDI running mates agreed to conduct 'non-campaigns' so that the party's vote would be concentrated in his candidacy.[58] María de la Luz Herrera, who had been the military-appointed mayor, had to content herself with polling under 2 per cent of the vote until 2004, when she could finally campaign freely on her own behalf and came second with 20 per cent.[59]

Although women incumbents still suffer party discrimination,[60] UDI's electoral pragmatism has made it cognisant of the electoral capital they represent and it is now much more likely than other major parties to run women for re-election.[61] Women offer a double attraction to voters, combining the practical, technocratic, anti-politics image that UDI projects with a maternalist appeal to the positive characteristics associated with women in public life. In 2004, UDI adopted the same strategy as the Conservative Party back in the 1930s and trumpeted its high percentage of women candidates – 20.3 per cent for mayor, and 21.7 per cent for city councillor – almost double that of the Christian Democrats. It paid off; UDI elected 22.4 per cent women mayors (the DC managed only 7.1 per cent) and 22.1 per cent women councillors, demonstrating that the Right has been much more adept historically at manipulating gendered representations of political agency.[62]

Incubated in the local and national government bureaucracy of the military regime, UDI began life drumming up support in the shanty-towns and competing directly with the DC, whose work with slum dwellers began in the 1950s and 1960s (Scully, 1992), and with the Communists, who had maintained a clandestine structure under the military regime through protest activities in poor areas (Oxhorn, 1995; Schneider, 1995; Paley, 2001). The latter's organizational model proved instructive to UDI's expansionary strategy (it is even dubbed 'the Communist Party of the Right') as it targeted low-income neighbour-hoods with negligible social capital where there was little presence of these two parties, the Catholic Church or even minimal state welfare provision (Oxhorn, 1994). A cornerstone of this strategy has been the recruitment and charitable work of women activists; in 1984, UDI's Women's Committee launched a campaign to collect food for the shantytowns and women comprised nearly half the party's first slum committee (Soto Gamboa, 2001). This helped the party to become the primary operator of municipal clientelism whilst the centre-left parties have became more centralized and distant, partly a function of their long exclusion from the administrative structure of local government. Such was the reward that, in July 2003, it officially registered itself under the slogan 'la UDI, el Partido Popular' ('UDI, the People's Party').

It also increased its share of the municipal vote from 10.2 per cent in 1992 to 19 per cent in 2004. In the Metropolitan Region, where UDI has concentrated its organizing efforts, the DC's vote has dropped by one third since 1992, whilst UDI's has practically doubled. Table 5.9, which shows the gender gap in municipal elections by party, demonstrates the migration of a significant number of women's votes from the DC to

Table 5.9 Chile: gender gap in municipal elections, by party, 1971–2004

Party	1971	1992	1996	2000	2004	
	Councillors and mayors (elected indirectly)				*Councillor*	*Mayor*
PN	1.256					
UDI		1.154	1.152	1.118	1.079	1.096
RN		1.106	0.988	1.046	1.052	1.063
DC	1.267	1.010	1.032	1.003	1.039	0.997
PR	0.843	0.898				
PPD		0.975	0.984	0.975	0.991	0.953
PS	0.822	0.838	0.924	0.935	0.939	0.969
PRSD			0.906	0.925	0.933	0.951
PC	0.804	0.845	0.793	—	—	—

UDI. Moreover, its selection of female candidates may be bringing extra dividends. Over the ten elections since 1989, the average gender gap advantage for UDI has been 1.166, dropping to 1.118 in the 2000 municipal elections. However, the three female UDI mayors elected in the Metropolitan Region all won a noticeably bigger gender gap advantage.[63] However, the party's aggressive penetration of the municipal sphere has implications for gender policy, given that its stance on gender relations is highly conservative, an aspect explored further in Chapter 7.

Political parties have long been dominant actors in Chilean social and political life, strongly and vertically institutionalized, intrusive and hegemonic in the public sphere, with a historical propensity to penetrate and permeate social structures. This chapter has demonstrated how women's access to political voice has been configured not just by party ideologies, but also by the competitiveness of the party and electoral system and by very distinctive individual party sub-cultural, genetic and organizational characteristics. Women's claims for political voice were used politically as a bulwark, first against anti-clericalism, then communism, whilst the marianist justification for women's agency persists to the present day. Chilean parties have also generated state institutions and policies aimed at promoting women's 'proper' role in society as defined by their ideological orientation in relation to two key cleavages in Chilean political life – class and religion. SERNAM has not been exempt from these periodic tussles between competing political visions, as the next chapter will show. Finally, the military regime, through its simultaneous projects of deconcentration and depoliticization, reached a peak of municipal maternalism, a gendering of local government that the most gender-conservative party, the *pinochetista* UDI, now appears to be appropriating for its own electoral ends. However, in general the town hall has not turned out to be a privileged locus of women's political engagement in a still highly centralized polity, dominated once more by parties that have returned with a new mixture of technocracy, electoral professionalism and old-style clientelism.

6
Between Ideologies: The National Women's Ministry

Chile's National Women's Ministry (*Servicio Nacional de la Mujer* – SERNAM) is the continent's most active and institutionalized national state mechanism for women, with well-established programmes and a gender mainstreaming mandate. It has enjoyed the full support of a centre-left coalition government through three terms of office (1990–2005) and a formal status unparalleled until recently.[1] Created in the midst of major political change, the agency has been inscribed by the processes of democratization, party system realignments and decentralization analyzed in the previous chapter. Some aspects of the orientation of SERNAM's gender policies and its contribution to the consolidation of democracy have been traced elsewhere (Chuchryck, 1994; Dandavati, 1996; Matear, 1996; Waylen, 1996). This study offers a more institutional analysis, focusing on how, specifically, party political processes such as ideological differentiation and electoral competition have moulded and constrained its foundations, its relationship to the international gender rights regime, and its ability to promote gender legislation and programmes in the domestic arena. Here, we see the ministry has been obliged to engage in tradeoffs and manoeuvres in navigating not only the antagonism of the political opposition, but also the internal ideological divisions within the Concertación and its constituent parties.

Party ideology and differentiation

Although the Pinochet regime made neo-liberal policy approaches so hegemonic that parties no longer offer alternative economic development models, the party system has realigned around new political dividing lines both between and within parties. Since 1989, these have tended to be moral and ethical valence issues, hinging on questions of human rights, individual freedom and responsibility, sexuality, the family, and social organization and cohesion (Londregan, 2000), derived from the persistent secular–religious cleavage. In order to compete with the initially overwhelming popularity of the Concertación and maintain a separate identity in a strongly centripetal political system, the right-wing parties have especially centred their efforts at ideological differentiation in the field of 'private' issues, all of which are suffused with competing notions of gender relations.

For instance, in the 1999 presidential contest there was little difference between the two candidates on social and economic policies (Angell and Pollack, 2000: 363) so Lavín played on his image as a family man (he is the father of seven children) and on the support of the Catholic Church, noting that Lagos was divorced and remarried. He also employed a discourse that was simultaneously anti-party and strong on moral values, highlighting his opposition to divorce and abortion, spectres that the Right has invoked since the 1989 elections (Baldez, 2002: 179), and promised a pragmatic, results-oriented approach to crime, unemployment and poverty. This depoliticizing rhetoric, mixed with a reinforcement of the religious cleavage, won over a key cohort of female voters, and put him just half a percentage point behind Lagos. Consequently, in the second round Lagos appointed Soledad Alvear, the first head of SERNAM and the most visible female government minister, as his campaign manager. His manifesto pledged an increase in state childcare facilities, legislation to outlaw discrimination in the workplace and in pension schemes, flexible working, and affirmative action to increase women's candidacies and access to public appointments at all levels of government. He had been put on the defensive on the abortion issue in particular and met with priests to assure them that he was not planning any liberalizing legislation, despite earlier declarations that he supported his own party's policy position in favour of reintroduction of therapeutic abortion.[2] This recalibration of his campaign enabled him to scrape a victory with a very slightly reduced gender gap.

This party politicization of gender issues frames the activities of SERNAM and of feminist legislators. The parties of each alliance differ in their attitudes to gender policy, distinctions laid out, sometimes in absolute terms, in their foundational documents. For instance, the DC's declaration of principles states that it will not countenance any form of divorce,[3] whilst RN's commits it to protecting life 'including that of the unborn'. However, these differences are played out in more complex and contradictory ways in the context of party competition in the electoral arena, and patterns of conflict and collaboration in the legislative arena.

RN and PPD occupy the centrist, secular space on the political spectrum; both have diffuse social bases, and are 'catch-all' in their electoral appeal, and liberal in their focus on the individual, rather than on social sectors or class. RN initially shared a highly conservative declaration of principles with UDI, stemming from their brief fusion in the late 1980s, which stated 'RN treasures the functions and virtues of women as bearers of life, the heart of the family and transmitters of moral and traditional values. RN advocates equal rights in all fields in which women work alongside men, so long as these activities are compatible with a woman's functions as mother and educator of her children'.[4] However, in practice it holds more pluralist views on social mores,[5] and does not share UDI's moral absolutism and doctrinal mysticism. Its conservatism is mainly economic so its attacks on SERNAM have centred on a criticism of state expansion. Whilst it endorses SERNAM's programmes aimed at practical gender needs, it has been internally divided on issues of sexual and reproductive citizenship. As RN has been overtaken by UDI at the polls, the liberal element on the right is in decline.

On a liberal, pluralist and feminist spectrum, it is not the PS, but rather its electoral partner, the PPD, that occupies the opposing pole to UDI, perhaps a result of its leaders' greater youthfulness. From its origins as an umbrella for the leftist opposition to Pinochet, the PPD has developed a political strategy based on quality-of-life issues, ranging through social justice, education, environment, and human, indigenous, women's, gay and consumer rights. It sells itself as 'a party of ideas not ideology', and leaders consciously position themselves politically around such emblematic issues as divorce, abortion, discrimination and AIDS (Plumb, 1998), which pivot on highly contested ideas about reproduction, family and sexuality. The PPD's mission statement advocates shared childcare, the right to reproductive choice, workplace and constitutional equality and statutory positive discrimination measures to equalize women's political participation.[6] Although the lack of an organic social base and strong institutional structure linking supporters to leadership has allowed the representatives of both RN and the PPD latitude to take individual positions on gender issues, the latter's voting patterns in Congress have been more consistent in favour of feminist policy positions.[7]

The three most ideological parties in the Chilean system are the Socialists on the left, the Christian Democrats in the centre and UDI on the right. All three have clear doctrinal foundations, with founding fathers,[8] key thinkers, and think-tanks producing policy documents based on the party philosophy.[9] Although the bulk of the Socialist Party is reconciled to neo-liberalism, it still speaks the language of poverty, class and civil liberties, which continue to trump gender or the PPD's 'post-materialist' agenda. Nonetheless, feminists within the party produced recommendations on gender relations, including a commitment to 'create a sense of collective responsibility towards childcare and domestic labour' (which the Right would dub social engineering), responsible paternity, the recognition and protection of 'various family forms, especially de facto unions', a divorce law, and the constitutional approval of affirmative action (Partido Socialista de Chile, 1995). Given the former mass and strongly institutionalized character of the party, they expected that this platform, once approved, would be promoted by the party in government and parliament, but were often disappointed as the party adopted a largely defensive position on these issues.

UDI and the DC compete on the same territory. Although neither is strictly confessional, both vie for the endorsement of the Catholic Church and they share a similar corporatist and moral integralist discourse. Women are cast as the bedrock of the family and as bearers and transmitters of the nation's values (often invoked as *chilenidad* or 'chilean-ness'), of which both parties claim to be the guardians, the DC due to its hegemonic role in Chilean politics since the 1960s, UDI through its origins in the dictatorship and stewardship of Pinochet's legacy. In consequence, both seek to mobilize women within the party and in society. However, DC modernizers and feminists advocate greater secularism and pluralism and insist that party policy on family and sexuality need not reflect that of the Church. This position, and the influence of PS and PPD in the coalition, has split the party over key valence issues such as decriminalization of adultery and sodomy, regulation of assisted fertilization, parental recognition of children, divorce, adoption for non-married couples and teenage sex education programmes (Walker, 2003: 186).

UDI, on the other hand, is much more dogmatic. It adheres uniformly to the integralist precept that Catholic moral values are based on natural law and hence are non-contestable. It therefore believes that Chile's political institutions should not be influenced by globalized cultural norms, including those on gender rights (Blofield, 2001: 40). It has made itself a mouthpiece for the views of both the Vatican and the local Church hierarchy, and has been the most hostile towards SERNAM. UDI has therefore managed to move successfully into two fields where it believed it could capture votes: the territorial arena of the municipality and the discursive arena of morality, capitalizing on the DC's internal divisions.

The politics of a new gender rights institution

SERNAM originated in the activities and debates of the women's movement of the mid-1980s. Women's organizations had become more vocal and co-ordinated, both in opposition to the military regime, and in drafting a series of demands for a future democratic government, as they moved *desde la protesta a la propuesta* ('from protesting to making policy proposals').[10] In 1986, the Civil Society Assembly (*Asamblea de la Civilidad*), whose leaders included two women later prominent in SERNAM and party political life, Maria Antonieta Saa and Soledad Larraín, issued a series of 'Women's Demands'. Two years later, Chilean feminists placed a full-page newspaper advertisement outlining a series of gender equality measures, including immediate ratification of the CEDAW, the creation of a ministerial-rank national government office for women, the elimination of sexism in education, and a requirement that 30 per cent of all government decision-making posts be held by women. The Alliance of Women for Democracy (*Concertación de Mujeres por la Democracia* – CMD), established in the wake of the victory of the 'No' vote against the Pinochet government on 5 October 1988, then published these ideas as a fully-fledged set of cross-sectoral policy proposals that would provide the basis of SERNAM's eventual mandate (Montecino and Rossetti, 1990). The authors of that document later came to constitute a feminist policy network with members dispersed in key posts throughout the new administration – in the state bureaucracy, parliament, political parties, SERNAM itself, private research centres and feminist NGOs. These 'femocrats' have played an important role in legitimizing SERNAM, lobbying for resources, providing political support, and contributing experience of international debates on gender issues acquired during exile. Their 'insider' status in relation to the Concertación parties gave them access to key decision-makers in the inner circle of the new government, yet also made it difficult for them to maintain a critical stance and prioritize their gender agenda.

Chilean feminists were also linked into the transnational gender issue network. They were inspired by Spain's Women's Institute and Equal Opportunities Plan (EOP), but also forewarned of the pitfalls in establishing a national gender unit by Jacqueline Pitanguy, the former head of Brazil's National Council on Women's Rights, who recounted how easily a weakly institutionalized body could be stripped of its feminist identity, budget, legitimacy and access to the executive when party political sands shifted. She persuaded them that they should lobby for the highest possible degree of institutionalization, an earmarked operational budget, a wide-ranging mandate, and executive, rather than advisory, status. CMD women thus exerted pressure on the centre-left party leaders and on the newly elected President Aylwin and his right-hand minister Enrique Correa, who became key allies in this project. SERNAM was officially created by law on 3 January 1991 after seven months of extensive negotiation and compromise in Congress, not only with the right-wing opposition but also within the parties of the Concertación itself.

Conservative restrictions

Whilst the ministry's future director, Soledad Alvear, conducted delicate negotiations, changes were forced in the original proposal by the conservative parties to which feminism and the international women's rights movement had become the new *bête noire*. With the end of the Cold War and the defeat of the more radical Left in Chile, the Right found a new scapegoat in Gramsci. RN asserted that, when the Left talked of gender relations, equality between the sexes and an end to discrimination, 'its real aim is to destroy all Western Christian values', in an assault on the hegemonic arenas of social and cultural values prior to the conquest of the state.[11] UDI saw in 'the weakening of marriage, the legalization of abortion and permissiveness in regard to pornography and drugs' a systematic attack on 'the family and public and private morals'.[12] Gender, then, was the new face of leftist internationalism. Conservatives expressed their ideological misgivings about the appropriateness or necessity of a state agency to carry out what the free market, along with welfare safety nets and charity, should be able to accomplish. The idea of a 'socializing state' tackling gender inequality and inequity, they regarded with as much suspicion as the economically interventionist state represented by the *Unidad Popular* years. They argued that marriage and the family simultaneously lay beyond the remit of the state, yet required its protection as the bedrock of a 'natural' social order. The issue, therefore, was not whether it was legitimate per se for the state to target policies at the private sphere, but rather what the objectives of this intervention should be; viz., the conservation or the transformation of existing gender relations. The Right's determination to contest any proposals affecting social relations led to tussles over SERNAM's status, remit and financing. In Congress, the opposition wielded a formal power of veto over legislation and constitutional amendments due to its over-representation through the Pinochet regime's institutional engineering, as well as an informal veto over certain areas of public policy that they defined as untouchable by aggressively framing the bounds of political debate.

Firstly, SERNAM was given a hybrid executive status. UDI and RN opposed full ministerial status, which would give it executive powers and a separate budget, so it was defined as a 'service' (that is, government department) that would co-ordinate and plan, but not implement, public policy.[13] However, in compensation, SERNAM's Director gained the status of minister and a guaranteed seat in the Cabinet, a standing that other agencies housed in the same ministry do not enjoy.[14] It was also placed under the aegis of the Ministry of Planning, in line with its inter-sectoral mandate,[15] and functions as a strategic unit in the government, with direct access to the president without being at his whim or identified with his person as its predecessors had been. The Right insisted on capping the number of staff that SERNAM could employ, as economic conservatism made it hostile to any proposal that might inflate the state bureaucracy. The conservatives also denied it a municipal presence, fearing that governing parties would use this for political and electoral purposes.

The Right also left its stamp on SERNAM's foundational principles, which ended up conflating women with the family and invoking biologically fixed and complementary sex-gender roles. The final phrasing defined the agency's aims as 'equality of rights and opportunities in relation to men, in the process of political, social, economic and cultural development of the country, respecting the *nature and specificity of women that derive from the natural differences between the sexes* [my emphasis], including a proper profile for family relations'. The only part of the bill not passed unanimously was an item introduced by UDI founder Senator Jaime Guzmán, which attempted to define women's role in society as primarily within the family, qualifying their equality with men.[16] SERNAM was chiefly tasked with strengthening the family (mentioned in no less than five of the objectives in its mission statement), giving greater dignity and value to domestic labour, stressing the fundamental value of maternity, and promoting women's equal access to 'the different areas of society'.

Despite the fact that much of the Right's cavilling about SERNAM's remit was ideological posturing, it had the effect of excluding from the agency's mandate crucial concepts such as women's rights (including reproductive rights) and a definition of gender relations as socially constructed and contingent. It indicated clearly which kinds of issues would be easy to legislate and promote, and which would become political flashpoints. This party politicization delimited the parameters of public debate and induced self-censorship in SERNAM, whose first two Christian Democratic heads were acutely aware of the party's religiously inclined electoral base and debt to the Catholic Church for its outspoken opposition to the military regime. They also feared presenting the opposition with an opportunity to undercut the new government's moral authority. However, right-wing attempts to hobble the new agency also led SERNAM to act in a more tactical manner to put the missing issues back on the agenda in different forms.

Divisions within the Concertación

The establishment of SERNAM, by law rather than by presidential decree, constituted an explicit attempt to break with past modes of government regulation of gender relations, in particular the electoral instrumentalization of women that had characterized previous government units. However, the Concertación parties did not initially see it this way, and some expected that their women's departments would colonize and run the ministry and make it a party political tool. The ministry's close relationship with the governing coalition, through family and party political ties, proved a double-edged sword. The insular composition of the Chilean political class has often made support for SERNAM contingent upon personal and factional, rather than programmatic or party political, backing. In the first round of appointments, the most senior posts went to the spouses of three party leaders[17] in order to reflect the balance of parties and factions within the coalition, outweighing other considerations such as their organic linkages with the women's movements, or their technical capacity in the area of gender. Whilst this increased SERNAM's authority and leverage over support and resources within the political elite, it also dented its wider credibility, enabling the Right to dismiss it as a sinecure, ironically akin to the involvement of the wives of the military top brass in the SNM under Pinochet. This criticism was misplaced, because the SERNAM Preparatory Committee had stipulated the minimum professional qualifications required for each grade of staff. Therefore, the lower-level appointments were filled with technical personnel and long-time activists from the feminist movement who had been involved in the design of the ministry. In addition, SERNAM has not turned out to be a career dead-end for women politicians. Alvear was subsequently appointed Minister of Justice under Frei and Minister of Foreign Relations under Lagos, and in 2004 emerged as a potential presidential candidate for the Concertación. Her successor, Adriana Delpiano, went on to become under-secretary of regional affairs, a key post in promoting decentralization.

The second Concertación administration saw SERNAM mature, as the government moved into a consolidation phase. The key appointments were less party political, with Frei unexpectedly nominating as the new minister Josefina Bilbao, who had headed the Commission on the Family and was a respected jurist with a good record in human rights.[18] A DC sympathizer, but not an activist, with no history in the women's movement, she was expected to push the ministry to the right, and the Socialist Party immediately registered their disapproval. However, she skilfully used her position and personal attributes to steer a course through the treacherous waters of the sexuality and morality debates, and even came to advocate a divorce law. She proved more independent than Alvear of the DC and the official Church line, possibly as she was not a career politician and therefore immune to party sanctions. The Christian Democrats continued to dominate both the Concertación and SERNAM, aided by the ambivalence of the Socialists in adhering to their commitment to promote women in public office. In the round of cabinet appointments made in early 1994, the PS not only failed to suggest any women candidates for the three major ministries it was allocated, duly doled out to representatives of the party's three main factions, but also allowed the top post in SERNAM to go to a DC sympathizer. The Women's Ministry was regarded as marginal in terms of the balance of power within the coalition,[19] so the PS was happy to trade its lip service to gender equality for more strategic gains and settled for deputy minister.[20] The frustration of socialist women at their lack of influence in SERNAM and their own party was somewhat alleviated when Lagos appointed Adriana Delpiano of the PPD, who had been Minister for Natural Resources under Frei and second-in-command of Lagos's election campaign, as the first non-Christian Democrat women's minister.[21] In addition, Lagos signalled early on his willingness to tackle thornier issues by making the passage of Chile's first divorce law a priority for his administration. However, they soon discovered that even a socialist Women's Minister faced significant political constraints.

Clear divergences quickly emerged between the Socialists and Christian Democrats over the proper functioning of SERNAM, the kinds of gender interests it should prioritize, and the self-imposed limitations of the coalition government's agenda. These faultlines first appeared in the clash between socialist Deputy Minister Soledad Larraín and Christian Democrat Minister Alvear. President Aylwin asked for the former's resignation in November 1992, following her public disagreements with the Concertación's decision not to broach taboo issues regarding the family, reproductive choice and sexuality in their first term. She spoke out in favour of a divorce law and open discussion about therapeutic abortion, sex before marriage and consensual unions.[22] The dismissal was badly handled, her position sacrificed to internal differences within the coalition, and she was unsupported by her own party. On her resignation, Larraín lamented the government's avoidance of controversial issues: 'We can do it in cases such as CODELCO [the state copper company], but when it relates to women's daily lives we are very afraid to get into a debate'.[23] Conflict between the DC and PS recurred – over the divorce issue and the report to the Beijing Conference – until the Christian Democrat grip loosened. However, even Socialist appointees have found themselves constrained by the Right's assertive agenda-setting. Delpiano, who was also not a feminist sympathizer, did not take a lead on either divorce or the 'morning after' pill, and maintained the official anti-abortion line. That notwithstanding, over the last 15 years the ministry has become more institutionalized and won a number of victories, emboldening it in these proscribed areas. Meanwhile the visible influence of the Concertación parties has faded as the appointments below that of the director of SERNAM are now predominantly technical, rotating personnel between university gender units, NGOs and research centres.

Legislation, policies and programmes

SERNAM's mandate is to promote women's economic, social and political integration by mainstreaming equal opportunities within the state apparatus, collaborating with international organizations, intervening in the domestic legislative arena, designing and implementing social policy, and promoting shifts in social values and attitudes. It has chosen to focus predominantly on economic and social rights for two reasons. Firstly, a more generalized political and social demobilization occurred in the post-transition period as parties and state agencies squeezed out organized civil society (Oxhorn, 1995; Mosovich Pont-Lezica, 1997; Silva, 2004). Secondly, the rule of the technocrats was carried over from the Pinochet regime, even if they were now also concerned with social justice (Montecinos, 2001). On the other hand, despite the hostility of the Right and the complications of party politics, the ministry has based the overall approach of its two Equal Opportunities Plans (EOPs) on the CEDAW, made *gender* a central category, and sought to attend to both inequality and inequity in women's social position.

International gender rights regime

SERNAM's architects were acutely aware of the importance of tying their work into the international gender rights regime, just as the

Aylwin government actively locked Chile into the human rights regime via the ratification of international conventions and the truth commission. However, this put the Christian Democrats in a contradictory position, as they invoked the principles of universalism in relation to civil and human rights, situating them with the internationalist Left, but not in relation to *women's* rights (Londregan, 2000). UDI and the DC's Catholic integralist elements have been wary of adopting legal norms that would allow a judicialization of gender rights through national and international courts. UDI has retreated to a defence of national values and sovereignty and Chilean particularism[24] whilst its partner, RN, has been more ambivalent, preferring to position itself as moderate, modernizing and secular. SERNAM's international remit means it has prepared the government's statements and reports for the UN summits, conferences and treaty obligations, and is included in the Foreign Ministry delegations to all regional and international events, where previously bureaucrats or the First Lady would have represented Chile. The latter's role has been discreetly diminished in a move to professionalize gender policy work and to remove the association with 'charitable works'. This leading role has boosted SERNAM's prestige both within Chile and in the region, but also unleashed the ire of the Right.

Eight days before the 1989 elections, General Pinochet ratified the CEDAW, although the military government had signed it nine years earlier. This move, intended to attract women's votes to the right-wing parties and to project an image of a modern Chile, also inadvertently opened the door to closer alignment with international norms on gender equality. The Convention formed the bedrock of the Concertación women's demands, whilst the first objective of the 1994–9 EOP was 'to speed the harmonization of national legislation with the specifications of the international treaties signed by the Chilean government'. Chile's first periodic implementation report, submitted in 1991 and considered in 1995 by the UN's treaty monitoring body, prompted the Committee on the Elimination of Discrimination against Women to criticize the lack of a divorce law, the absolute prohibition of abortion, poor statistics in the report, and a focus on de jure rather than de facto rights. When the second and third reports were considered in 1999, the Committee highlighted the low level of political participation, the high rates of teenage pregnancy, wage differentials, inequality in administration of marital property and, once more, the issues of abortion and divorce (Committee on the Elimination of Discrimination against Women, 1991, 1995, 1999). Perhaps because neither the reports nor the Committee's comments were widely disseminated in Chile,[25] political reaction was muted, although the Committee's comments doubtless gave SERNAM additional leverage with the government on the necessity to push gender policy beyond its political comfort zone.

Instead, it was the Optional Protocol, signed by the executive branch in 1999, that created political furore. The vote in Congress on ratification was split along government–opposition lines, and the government was defeated. Although the protocol has no powers to force a country to change its legislation, the Right refuses to recognize the jurisdiction of the Committee, just as it rejects that of international human rights courts. In January 2002, Cardinal Errázuriz spoke against ratification in the Senate Committee on Foreign Affairs, arguing that it 'opened the door to legalizing abortion'.[26]

The biggest flashpoint was SERNAM's report to the Beijing conference, attacked by UDI and RN representatives parroting the Vatican's objections (Blofield, 2001).[27] The word 'gender' was banned in the Chilean parliament (Oyarzún, 2000) and UDI even alleged, incorrectly, that the final document, to be signed by the Chilean delegation, 'would have the force of an international legal treaty' (Fundación Jaime Guzmán, 1995). New fissures opened within SERNAM and within the DC. Josefina Bilbao declared 'Chile's position is that of the Vatican', with which the ministry apparently agreed that certain topics discussed in Cairo, such as reproductive health and family planning, should not be revisited. She also met with Cardinal Carlos Ovieda and sent the National Report to the Episcopal Conference and the Vatican, a deference not shared by leading DC modernizers such as President Frei's wife, Senator Carmen Frei, and deputies Mariana Aylwin and Ignacio Walker.[28] In the Senate, nine of the ten Christian Democrats allied with the opposition in proposing a motion criticizing the report, after the Chamber of Deputies had approved it (Walker, 2003: 185). Their Chamber colleagues and coalition partners in both houses promptly condemned this manoeuvre, regarded as a cynical betrayal of the alliance's internal discipline, given that the report had been the fruit of intensive consultation and ministerial debate, and was based on the EOP, the Programme of Government and the Report of the National Commission on the Family. President Frei finally approved it a few weeks before the Conference.

This incident typified gender debates in Congress, with a lot of political posturing ending in eventual support for SERNAM's final position. UDI and RN have successfully split the alliance along secular–religious lines and made political capital, but do not always win the argument. SERNAM has been skilful in deploying the UN's authority and has taken a more independent stance in international arenas than at home. Chile signed the final document of the International Conference on Population and Development at Cairo without any reservations and was *not* one of the Latin American countries backing the Vatican in 1994 or 1999. In October 1994, Chile ratified the International Labour Organization's Convention 156, which aims to encourage men to share family responsibilities and, in November 1995, the Belém do Pará Convention on violence against women. In 1993, in the UN NGO Committee in New York, Chile voted in favour of the application by the International Lesbian and Gay Association to have consultative status with ECOSOC, supported inclusion of reference to 'sexual orientation' in the Beijing draft Platform for Action and gave backing to the Brazilian government's more recent proposal to the UN on human rights and sexual orientation.

Gender legislation

Domestically, SERNAM has been involved in various legal and constitutional debates related to the institutionalization of the ministry, constitutional amendments, new legislation and reforms of the legal codes, and the use of international instruments as a template for reforms.[29] As legislative activity in Chile is purely national, intra- and inter-party divergences or agreements over competing conceptions of gender relations are evident in the drafts and final texts of bills, the parliamentary debates and the voting record. In particular, the legislative process is complicated by the power of the Right in Congress, particularly in the Senate, where most of the vetoes on gender bills occur.

Chile has not engaged in the wholesale overhaul of its 1980 Constitution as the institutional legacy of the Pinochet regime made it difficult to revise a document intended to 'lock in' the political system and avert radical social policy reforms (Ensalaco, 1994; Londregan, 2000). However, in May 1999 a SERNAM-sponsored amendment introduced two changes. In Article 1, the masculine noun in the phrase 'men are born free and equal in dignity and rights' was replaced with the gender-neutral 'people', while Article 19 now reads 'men and women are equal before the law'. The latter wording had actually appeared in an early draft of the Constitution, but was omitted in the final version because it appeared to grant equality to married women, a principle that its authors, closely linked to *gremialismo* and integralism, rejected (Fries and Matus, 1999: 85). The changes had first been proposed by the Aylwin government in May 1992, but were packaged with other more controversial reforms, such as the removal of the commander-in-chief of the army, and consequently defeated (Gómez and Matus, 1994: 14). Nonetheless, SERNAM regarded this new legal norm as the basis for women to use the courts to enforce equal rights and eradicate discriminatory laws.[30] The amendment finally passed with an overwhelming majority, the only dissenters a few right-wing parliamentarians who alleged, as always, that this would pave the way for the legalization of abortion, with UDI Senator Carlos Bombal suggesting that Article 1 should read 'persons are *conceived* free and equal'.

Revision of family law and the Civil Code was a priority for SERNAM and Concertación legislators. In 1989, Chile was a more conservative society than its neighbours (Htun, 2003: 133), but 14 years later women had acquired shared authority over children and a divorce law had finally been passed after a long battle. Conversely, although married women acquired full legal capacity, the majority still lack control over marital property, with the head of household still presumed to be a man, and de facto unions are not legally recognized or granted the same inheritance rights, which means that Chile remains a conservative outlier in the region (Deere, 2004). This is one of the key areas in which the religious Right has staked out its territory and fought SERNAM's initiatives.

In 1991, the ministry submitted a bill to give married women more control over property in marriage and to abolish the existing arrangement by which the couple entered into joint ownership of property, automatically administered by the husband, who was also his wife's legal representative. It proposed alternative regimes that would allow either equal participation in acquired assets, with each retaining control over their own property until the end of the marriage when assets would be split equally, or complete separation of assets acquired before and during the marriage. However, although the Chamber of Deputies approved it unanimously, the bill was rejected in the Senate and right-wing legislators insisted on retaining the existing regime, obliging couples to consciously opt into one of the alternative regimes. Due to lack of public information about the new options, the default regime, which disadvantages women in terms of ownership, administration, possession and disposal of the couple's assets, has continued to be the norm (Fries and Matus, 1999: 116; Htun, 2003: 138).

The marital property bill, finally passed in 1994, also included a proposal to decriminalize adultery, which the criminal code defined and penalized in a sexist manner.[31] Although it had been a dead letter for decades, integralist elements in UDI, RN and the DC saw an opportunity to capture the moral high-ground. The Chamber of Deputies opted unanimously to make adultery a civil rather than a criminal issue, but a warning from the Episcopal Conference of the Catholic Church that this would implicitly condone adultery (Londregan, 2000: 200) forced the government onto the defensive. President Aylwin, SERNAM and the Senate Constitutional Committee then proposed *extending* the criminal definition of adultery, so that it would apply equally to men and women. Socialist, PPD and Radical Senators responded with an amendment to restore the lower house's position, with the Christian Democrats divided. UDI and the institutional senators supported criminalization, whilst over half the RN delegation absented themselves, indicating the party's deep discomfort on an issue where their liberal leanings dictated that marital infidelity should be a private, civil matter (Londregan, 2000: 205). In the end, adultery was made a civil offence that did not discriminate by sex.

The next Civil Code amendment was the removal of legal discrimination between three categories of children – legitimate (born in wedlock), illegitimate (conceived outside of marriage and recognized only by the mother) and 'natural' (born to unmarried parents and recognized by the father)[32] – through a bill tabled by SERNAM in 1993, after two attempts by left-wing legislators had already failed. Yet again, the lower house approved the bill unanimously with the Senate divided. Initially, conservative Christian Democrats lined up with the Right, alleging it would undermine the institution of the family and encourage out-of-wedlock births (Htun, 2003: 139). However, the bill finally passed in October 1998 as a 'family-friendly' measure, with unanimous support from the DC and majority backing from the Right because, although it gave children equal rights of inheritance and legal representation and strengthened mothers' right to demand child support, it retained the legal distinction between children born inside and outside marriage.

The 1994 law on domestic violence had also started life as a 1990 bill proposed by left-wing parliamentarians.[33] Taken over by SERNAM, it was subsequently watered down by right-wing legislators, including conservative Christian Democrats, who objected to the proposal to imprison abusive spouses (Matear, 1999). However, despite being declared 'urgent', the bill spent three years in transit (Haas, 1998: 16). The Left was obliged to agree to a more 'family-oriented' approach, in which family unity was to be paramount, while the Right also made strenuous efforts to ensure that domestic violence was not defined as potential grounds for divorce. As a result, over 65 per cent of cases resulted in 'reconciliation', with preference given to therapy, family counselling, and fines or community service as punishment (La Morada *et al.*, 1999). Although implementation of the Family Courts, created through a 1997 executive bill, was delayed for lack of funds, leaving the inexperienced civil courts to continue to deal with the issue, the law has had positive knock-on effects, raising awareness (the number of complaints has multiplied exponentially) and giving courts the power to issue protection orders to remove abusers from the family home. The government also created an Inter-Ministerial Commission for prevention of domestic abuse, SERNAM started to train legal system professionals, the police and courts established special units to register complaints, and scores of municipal centres, projects and health programmes were set up to assist victims.[34] The criminal code was finally revised in 1998 to make sexual violence (rape and assault) a crime against the person (of either sex), not against public morals. Punishment now corresponds to the gravity of the crime and not the reputation of the victim. This revision also removed the crime of sodomy, thus effectively decriminalizing homosexuality, a reform that prompted surprisingly little political reaction.

The most contentious issue raised by SERNAM has undoubtedly been divorce. After over a decade in power, the Concertación government finally rid Chile of the notoriety of being the only Latin American nation with no divorce law that allowed subsequent remarriage.[35] Until 2004, Chileans had to use a piece of specious legal trickery, annulment, which dissolved the bond as having never legally existed, and over the last two decades the ratio of annulments to marriages rocketed.[36] During the transition, Concertación feminists regarded a divorce law as a priority but delegated the topic to the subcommission on gender legislation in the Constitutional Working Group (Montecino and Rossetti, 1990). An inner circle within the coalition then determined that it would not form part of the government's first term agenda for fear of detracting attention from the other elements of the democratization agenda such as truth and reconciliation.[37] Nevertheless, two feminist politicians, from the Humanist Party and PPD, submitted the first bills in 1991, albeit as lost causes. Marriage reform first received government support from President Aylwin at the end of his mandate during the launch of the National Commission on the Family's report, but the stance of the coalition partners has been mixed.[38] In 1993, the PS women's section persuaded the party to include in the second Programme of Government a mandate for the executive to introduce divorce legislation (Partido Socialista de Chile, 1995: 31–2). However, some, like Isabel Allende, initially regarded divorce of secondary importance compared to poverty and exclusion (Hite, 2000: 79, fn 8) and so the party retreated to a commitment to 'promote a wide national debate', relegating the issue to individual conscience and to the initiative of the legislature, not the executive branch. At the coalition negotiating stage, the Christian Democrats vetoed the initiative and the Socialist interior minister simply omitted to raise it with President-Elect Frei.[39] When the PS finally launched its pro-divorce campaign in 1994, splits deepened within the coalition. While reform-minded Christian Democrats came out in favour, when the 16 women Concertación candidates for federal deputy ran under the slogan 'Women of their word' in 1997, the party leadership pressurized the five DC women to retract their pledge to support the divorce bill in Congress or their backing for the women's manifesto, both of which they refused to do.[40] The debate aligned across party boundaries, with the PPD and PS almost unanimously in favour, the DC divided between secularizers and integralists, RN regarding it as a matter of individual conscience, and UDI utterly opposed. In 1995, a new bill was submitted, this time drafted by a cross-bench group. In 1997, after several failed attempts, the Chamber of Deputies finally approved a law allowing uncontested divorce. However, it did not reach the Senate Committee on Constitution, Legislation and Justice for debate until April 2002 and, urged on by the Church, conservative senators tabled bills and amendments to make the process of divorce as unwieldy and prolonged as possible.[41] In 2004, after a decade of political debate and with public support for reform as high as 85 per cent, the Senate finally approved a new law that lowered the waiting period to one year of separation, in the case of divorce by mutual consent, and three for unilateral petitions, a reduction from the three and five years proposed in the original bill, aimed at making the couples work at reconciliation.[42]

Dynamics of legislation

Party political factors have affected the passage of legislation in different ways. Individually, the parties react to gender-related bills not just along a binary government–opposition axis, but also according to their own ideological orientation (Haas, 1998). Generally, consensus has been achieved only when bills can be framed as pro-family. The law preventing public schools from expelling pregnant teenagers could be viewed by the secular Left as upholding girls' right to education, and construed as a 'pro-life' measure by the religious centre-right (Blofield and Haas, 2005). The PS and PPD have tended to vote consistently, with the PPD pushing the feminist agenda more assertively than the PS, whose traditionalist elements have occasionally opposed initiatives such as gay civil union. This means that both the government and opposition benches have been divided, the former due to the deep schisms in the DC between its secularizing modernizers and Catholic traditionalists, between its delegations in the Chamber (liberal) and Senate (half of them conservative). In the latter case, RN is as divided as the DC in its voting, but not along clearly doctrinal lines. Its quality as a 'catch-all' party and lesser orientation around moral and value issues allows for greater dissent. UDI has consistently used its delegation to veto or stall bills, such as those on domestic violence, parental recognition of children and sexual assault, but sometimes votes in favour once a majority consensus has emerged in Congress following modifications to the bill.

For female legislators, intra-coalition unity has been easier than cross-bench collective action. For example, women Concertación deputies lobbied strenuously to set up the Family Committee (Haas, 1998), which was then colonized by feminists and succeeded in blocking the two most draconian anti-abortion bills. However, inter-coalition collaboration increased with the arrival of a more socially liberal generation of RN representatives, such as Lily Pérez, Arturo Longton, Carmen Ibáñez and Osvaldo Palma, who have adopted a feminist discourse and worked with the government on bills such as divorce, pregnant schoolgirls' rights, abandonment and family support, the right to breastfeed at work, higher penalties for offences against women and children, positive discrimination reforms to the electoral system, restoration of therapeutic abortion, distribution of the 'morning after' pill, the CEDAW Optional Protocol, outlawing sexual orientation discrimination, and gay civil union – positions no UDI representative has ever taken.

Given that executive-sponsored bills have a much higher chance of being debated and approved (Siavelis, 2000), SERNAM's role in sponsoring gender legislation has been crucial, but sometimes ambiguous. In the first administration, it chose several strategies: self-censorship, avoidance or delegation of controversial issues to the legislature, appeasement of the Right's family-conservative agenda, and a preference for meeting women's practical gender needs rather than challenging existing gender relations. Some interpret this conservatism as resulting from the Christian Democratization of the ministry, part of a deliberate project to undermine the feminist movement, its agenda and alliance with the Left (Baldez, 2001). On the other hand, it may have been a rational decision by the executive branch to promote only legislation on which it will not suffer a humiliating defeat at the hands of the right-wing alliance, a calculus compounded by SERNAM's weak ties to key legislators and opinion-formers. While the secular legislators succeeded in pushing through bills on domestic violence, daycare, pregnant students and divorce, other bills, such as those on alimony and maintenance, criminalization of sexual harassment and therapeutic abortion, have not prospered. In some cases,[43] where multiple bills exist (paternity, domestic workers, anti-discrimination), the executive-sponsored version has taken precedence, and where SERNAM has taken bills but modified their content under pressure from the Right, coalition representatives have sometimes voted against or introduced competing bills.

Legislation also appears to have lagged behind rapid changes in social attitudes, even given the conservative view of women's domestic role engendered by Chile's still comparatively low rate of female labour force participation (Lehmann, 2003). Party policy positions on abortion and divorce became radicalized and distant from public opinion for a number of reasons: the need for parties to distinguish themselves from their competitors in a centripetal system, lack of feedback and participation mechanisms within the parties and between government and populace,[44] and the growing influence of Catholic integralism on the Right, which could marshal networks, resources and a significant social base, leaving the centre-left on the back foot (Blofield, 2001: 49).

Programmes and policies

Party political influence has been relatively weak over social policy, which is generated almost entirely within the executive branch. SERNAM's cross-sectoral work depends much more on the collaboration of strategically located feminist sympathizers and on inter-ministerial committees, such as those addressing domestic violence, teenage pregnancy, and the needs of female heads of household and women seasonal agricultural workers (*temporeras*). The main obstacles have been bureaucratic inertia, producer capture and path-dependency, rather than ideology. However, despite SERNAM's technical character, its programmes fall within the social policy paradigms defined by external political actors.

Nowhere is this clearer than in the policy areas of poverty and women's labour market integration, which overwhelmingly dominated the first decade of the ministry's activities (SERNAM, 2000), due to their close affinity with the Concertación government's ideological focus on 'growth with equity'. Much of the earliest gender legislation strengthened women's labour rights, through the introduction of redundancy pay, the regulation of conditions for workers in the service, domestic and agricultural sectors, paternity leave, and leave of absence for a parent caring for a sick infant. The labour code was altered to remove prohibitions on women in particular jobs, and the practice of employers asking prospective female employees to take pregnancy tests was made an offence. Occupational training and childcare provision became the keystones of SERNAM's programmes targeted at low-income groups. The female heads of household programme has been running since 1992, and was made a priority programme for the government's anti-poverty campaign in 1997. By 1999, it operated in 80 municipalities, and benefited 35,000 women and their families. The *temporeras* programme, running since 1991 through the municipalities, provides childcare to 5,500 of the 200,000 female fruit pickers and packers, but only during the main agricultural season. Although they include education and personal empowerment components, in the main these programmes have met practical gender needs, enabling women to increase their financial autonomy within a neo-liberal logic that tends to exacerbate inequality and exploits gendered notions of work and value (Barrientos *et al.*, 1999). They also treat women primarily as vectors of development and, on this issue, party political differences are minimal.

The Right has held contradictory positions on women's waged labour, rejecting it as a key element of socialist approaches to gender inequality and as a cause of family breakdown and social decay. Thus, in 1990 UDI and RN insisted on removing from the SERNAM law the original goal of integrating women into the workforce.[45] But their moral conservatism is at odds with their support for the neo-liberal policies of both the Pinochet and Concertación governments. During the 1980s, women responded to economic crisis by taking on paid employment as a survival strategy whilst, in the 1990s, economic deregulation pushed up female employment in insecure and highly flexible fruit processing jobs in the agro-export sector (Barrientos *et al.*, 1999). Chile's transformation into a marketized society has seen welfare safety nets slashed, citizens redefined as consumers, and labour market participation help up as a touchstone of social integration and as a means of tackling poverty and fostering self-sufficiency (Montecinos, 1994; Schild, 1998a, 2000). Indeed, SERNAM's 'equal opportunities' discourse assumes the liberal approach of levelling the playing field for competition for jobs, access to education and other public goods. The Right has not objected to measures that increase the productivity, size and flexibility of the labour pool, but opposed the cross-party bill to criminalize sexual harassment. After 13 years, the Senate finally approved the bill in January 2005, but only as a modification to the Labour Code, thus restricting its remit to the workplace and leaving it as a civil offence. Lavín's 1999 manifesto advocated 'helping women combine family and work' through home-based and part-time employment in low-waged, traditionally female jobs and the employment of other women as home-based childminders. This reflects the party's emphasis on the family as the primary unit of society and leaves unchallenged the gendered division of labour and women's double burden.

Contentious policy areas

Reproductive rights have been off-limits for legislation since 1989, although they have formed one of the key valence issues for parties and politicians. Abortion in Chile was permitted 'on therapeutic grounds' from 1931 to 1989 under Article 119 of the Public Health Code, but the military regime took a predictably pro-natalist stance, whilst its integralist ideologues attempted to radicalize the issue. In 1974, Jaime Guzmán was unsuccessful in including complete prohibition of abortion in the draft text of the 1980 Constitution, whose Article 19 still states that 'the law protects the life of the unborn', but managed to insert it into the 'binding laws' of the transition. In September 1989, a legislative committee headed by Admiral Merino, a member of the junta, revoked Article 19, without consultation with the Chilean Medical College, whose own commission was debating the very subject. The legacy has been a legal and constitutional order that the incoming civilian government found hard to alter, a useful tool for the Right to invoke moral panic, and the highest abortion rate in South America, running at one termination for every three live births (Blofield, 2001: 16). Of those, one third require hospitalization, and 30 per cent of maternal mortality is attributable to botched backstreet abortions. The military regime's aggressive criminal prosecution and imprisonment of women who had procured or provided terminations (Casas and Chaimovich, 1997) continues as a result of UDI and the Church's activism on this issue (Center for Reproductive Law and Policy, 1998), and of the fear and personal convictions of medical practitioners, who are required to report these cases. Although liberal Catholics in the DC, such as Josefina Bilbao, disapprove of such persecution, the government, which has maintained a resolutely anti-choice line, has turned a blind eye.

In September 1991, five socialist deputies broke ranks and tabled a bill to restore provision for therapeutic abortion to the Public Health Code. In the face of visceral opposition from the Right and a corresponding silence from the Left (Blofield, 2001: 51), it never even made it to the parliamentary committee stage. Adriana Muñóz, spokeswoman for the group, felt at the time she had been made a scapegoat by both the opposition and an embarrassed government.[46] Despite the fact that abortion is completely illegal, the Right has attempted to keep this political capital alive by introducing four bills aimed at *toughening* the laws. The Right initially seized the initiative in terms of problem-definition and agenda-setting, assisted by the Catholic Church and its ancillary bodies, leaving the centre-left paralyzed, capable only of reaction and passive resistance. UDI even appropriated the language of human rights, insisting that abortion was a violation of foetal rights, whilst the Concertación has been very reluctant to cast this as a women's rights issue, preferring to present it as protection of the family from a greater ill. Although the Socialist Party voted in 1993 to initiate a public debate, no party representative was willing to take it on. The government barely managed to head off UDI's bill in the Senate, defeating it by only two votes in 1998 (Blofield, 2001: 20).[47] However, space for debate has not been completely foreclosed. Although the Christian Democrats controlled the executive through the 1990s and were uniformly anti-abortion, when both Presidents Aylwin and Frei convened extraordinary legislation sessions the former included the legalization bill (1991) and the latter excluded the three hyper-penalization bills (1994). Despite the politicization of this issue in the 1999 presidential elections, secular left parties began to regroup and in 2003 resubmitted another bill to restore the provisions of the Public Health Code.

SERNAM was marginal to this debate, which it only joined once the pro-reform signals from senior Christian Democrats were strong enough. At the Beijing and Beijing Plus Five conferences, ministers felt compelled to pronounce Chile 'pro-life' and opposed to the legalization of abortion or its use in family planning (Blofield, 2001: 53; Friedman *et al.*, 2001: 29). Its policies on health and reproduction have also been cautious. A woman is still required to meet certain conditions before she can be sterilized[48] and the furore around the availability of the 'morning after' pill in Chilean clinics in mid-2004 was prompted by an initiative of the Health Ministry, and was thus framed as an issue of public health, not of reproductive rights. Teenage pregnancies, a priority policy area, account for over 15 per cent of births per annum, a problem being tackled by an inter-ministerial committee. Although UDI and the Church forced SERNAM to drop a teenagers' essay competition on sexuality, since 1995 the government has run a prevention programme of 'discussion days on sexuality and feelings', which by 1999 had reached more than half the state schools in the country.

Participation and representation

SERNAM's greatest weakness has been its privileging of economic and market citizenship over sexual and political citizenship. Despite the concerns of its founders, its promises to the UN and the pledged commitment of every Concertación president, it has failed to address the structural and institutional barriers to women's political participation. It has shied away from changing the rules of the electoral demand-side through gender quotas, anticipating resistance from all political parties in such a competitive environment (Franceschet, 2001: 218). Instead, it has concentrated on the 'supply side' by running leadership training workshops and empowerment classes aimed at enabling individual women to compete better in the electoral marketplace.

The centripetal pull of a highly institutionalized party system has also given SERNAM stronger links to the political class than to the women's movement, and it consults ordinary women only as consumers of its services and programmes, which are designed and evaluated by the tightly-knit feminist policy community that moved from the CMD into academia, NGOs and government. Nonetheless, whereas the first EOP (1994–1999) was drafted by a feminist consultant, the second one (2000–10) was drawn up after a series of town hall meetings and consultations with women's groups and local authorities (Franceschet, 2003). In the mid-1990s, SERNAM also set up a Participation Programme and the demand-led Civil Society Fund to facilitate capacity-building by grassroots women's groups, which SERNAM's critics charge that it had crowded out (Baldez, 2001; Schild, 1998a, 2000). Although others argue that it has created a new institutional space and therefore strengthened the women's movement (Franceschet, 2003), in the absence of institutionalized forms of consultation, such as Brazil's councils on women's rights, this interface is likely to remain weak.

SERNAM's remit and capacity to push through gender equity and equality legislation and policy have been strongly influenced by the politics of both government and opposition, by intra- as well as inter-party ideological conflicts. Some, like Baldez (2001), see the ministry in consequence as a 'weak advocate of state feminism', the result of Christian Democratic dominance that has silenced a more feminist agenda and robbed it of sufficient resources, and of the reluctance of the Left to invest its political capital in this area.[49] Party politics have been most evident in the legislative field, delaying or diluting feminist bills, whilst the religious cleavage and inheritance of neo-liberal social policy also marked out the boundaries of SERNAM's programmes, which privileged practical, economic gender needs to the detriment of sexual or political citizenship.

Nonetheless, SERNAM *has* pushed the limits set by this highly institutionalized and competitive party political environment, even if it has done so more slowly than many would have liked. It has been able to resist much of the tradition of party co-option of state gender units partly because party cultures, with the exception of that of UDI, are shifting towards an electoral-professional model. The decision of Concertación presidents to postpone conflict along the religious dimension may have allowed the integralist Right to consolidate a powerful oppositional block, but the latter eventually lost the argument on adultery, divorce, sodomy and the status of children as the ministry and its feminist allies exploited secular–religious splits within parties such as RN and DC. SERNAM has also frequently maintained its own stance in the international arena, and insisted on importing the language of gender, reproductive rights and plural family forms into its programmes and public positions. In a still ideological party system where private sphere issues are politicized as primary party-electoral valence issues, these are no small achievements.

7
Decentralization Deficits: Delivering Policy at the Local Level

Although designed at national level, SERNAM's major social policies have been implemented at regional and municipal level. This chapter therefore considers the contradictions and problems that have arisen for a state institution defined as a 'functionally decentralized public service'[1] operating in a historically highly centralized country, and examines the ways in which the local political and bureaucratic opportunities and constraints differ from the national environment. Specifically, it analyzes the extent to which party political features such as electoral clientelism, ideology and internal institutional structures have affected, through omission or commission, SERNAM's attempts to get its gender policies to trickle down to local government.[2]

Truncated decentralization

SERNAM has a formal institutional presence at national level and regional level, but none at provincial or municipal level. Table 7.1 gives a summary of the structures of representation, participation and administration in which SERNAM has sought to gain a voice. This illustrates the complexity of penetrating different levels of government in a still vertically organized polity where political and economic resources are very unevenly distributed, due to historical factors as well as the party political horse-trading that occurred early in the transition over the parameters of both regionalization and municipalization.

As the SERNAM bill passed through Congress in 1990, the Right wielded its veto power to ensure that the new Ministry would have no formal structure or representation at communal and provincial level, which they feared both as a beachhead for the diffusion of the feminist values they so derided, and as undesirable competition and a challenge

Table 7.1 Chile: representation, participation and gender policy process at all levels of government

	National	Regional	Provincial	Municipal
Executive	President: Direct election	13 *Intendentes*: Appointed by president	51 governors: Appointed by president	341 mayors: Indirectly elected from among city councillors until direct elections in 2004
Cabinet	All national ministries, plus SERNAM	Regional line ministries plus regional SERNAM office	None	Steering Committee for Municipal Development and municipal secretaries
Legislature or representative body	Deputies and senators: Directly elected using binominal open-list PR system	Regional councillors: Indirectly elected by city councillors in each province. Main task is approval of budget	Economic and Social Council has functional composition (representatives of business, labour, academia, security forces)	Municipal Council (*Concejo Municipal*): Directly elected using multi-member open-list PR system
Channels of participation	None	None	None	CESCO
SERNAM: Status	Ministerial status as department within Ministry of Planning	13 regional offices with status of regional line ministry	None	None. Operates by agreement via OMMs
SERNAM: Main activities	Legislation and sectoral agreements with national ministries	CIDEMs and mainstreaming in Regional Development Plans and Regional Equal Opportunity Plans	None	Specific programmes (until 2001), then gender mainstreaming in Municipal Development Plans

to its own political colonization of local government. UDI wanted to preserve the base of support it had built up through control of the town halls under the military regime and worried that municipal branches of SERNAM would operate as the Mothers' Centres had done, opening up a conduit for party political clientelism that would favour electorally the Concertación, and particularly the Christian Democrats. The Right's fears were not unfounded; SERNAM noted that some centre-left deputies and senators indeed expected that it would target services at their local female constituents for precisely such ends. In consequence, there was no mention of municipalities, only of regions, in the law creating SERNAM and in the Ministry's first review of its work in the period 1991–4. During the first Concertación administration, the priority was to lay down a sound administrative and inter-sectoral basis for SERNAM at national, then at regional level. This created a dilemma. On the one hand, the founders were determined to eschew from the outset old-style welfarism and clientelism in order to maintain SERNAM's credibility as a technical service in the face of hostility from the Right and attempts at co-option by elements of the governing coalition.[3] On the other hand, the lack of representation below regional level has proven to be a significant restraint on its overall reach and effectiveness in delivering gender equity policies on the ground.

The politics of regionalization

Although SERNAM is the only national government department to enjoy de facto ministerial status and to have a regional structure included in its mandate, it was not clear at first that it would have parallel administrative powers at sub-national level. Nonetheless, after much lobbying and strategizing it did achieve a political status in the 13 administrative regions on a par with that of the regional branches of the national government ministries. With the backing of DC Interior Minister Enrique Krauss, the 1992 Organic Law on Regional Government and Administration formally recognized SERNAM as an integral part of the regional cabinet, which then became a crucial institutional space for pushing gender policy and claiming resources from the regional budgets.[4]

However, at the outset SERNAM's functional capacity at a regional level suffered severe resource constraints, despite the new government's commitment to decentralize both service delivery and the state apparatus as a whole. The ministry was top-heavy, its regional infrastructure weak and ineffectual during the first Concertación mandate. Following the transition to democracy, international funding was diverted away from local-level structures and NGOs, and channelled predominantly via the central government, with the exception of Swedish bilateral assistance, which compensated for the lack of central government support by funding the initial establishment of the regional offices and the Women's Rights Information Centres (*Centro de Información de los Derechos de la Mujer* – CIDEM), the only programme that operates at a purely regional level.[5] Out of SERNAM's 59 core administrative staff, a mere 16 were allocated to the regions (the director of each region and three centrally located staff), with the regional managers for each of the key programmes financed not by SERNAM but by the relevant ministries.[6] The staffing levels were also not proportionate to the size of population, leaving the Metropolitan Region relatively underserved.[7]

The second and third Concertación mandates saw a strengthening of the regions as part of the ongoing project of decentralization, especially with the internal restructuring of SERNAM in 2000. The decade also saw an important shift in the regional offices' remit, which had been broad and vague. In the period 1994–2001, they functioned as deconcentrated branches of the central agency and promoted the core programmes (female heads of household, *temporeras*, and domestic violence) through co-operation agreements and financial transfers to each Municipal Women's Office (*Oficina Municipal de la Mujer* – OMM) or town hall. Under the Lagos government (2000–5), the policy changed again and from 2002 they stopped delivering the programmes and focused exclusively on horizontal gender mainstreaming. The regional offices attempted to incorporate into the regional Strategic Development Plans the recommendations of the first national Equal Opportunity Plan (EOP), which itself was legitimated by forming part of the national Plan of Government and Concertación's manifesto.[8] Under the second EOP, they went a step further and drew up their own Regional Equal Opportunity Plans, in consultation first with local women, then with central and regional-level ministries, and finally with the governor and regional cabinet.[9] However, these shifts from a general to a specific remit and back again brought problems, as one regional director noted:

> We have gone from directly carrying out programmes with resources administered by SERNAM to returning to our original mandate as co-ordinators of public policy. This confuses the public and the other state services, which still think we are meant to be the main or only institution concerned with gender equity.[10]

Although there is no structure for political representation or contestation at intermediary levels of government in Chile, party political factors have not been entirely absent. The profile of SERNAM's regional directors reflected the same political quota system enacted nationally; in the period 1994–9, the distribution of directors was five DC, five PS and three PPD, and was almost identical under Lagos.[11] There was wide variation among the directors in terms of technical capacity, understanding of gender issues and degree of involvement with the women's movement, but this did not seem to be linked to party affiliation. Interaction with political parties of all stripes tended to be sporadic and insignificant, and regional directors accused the governing coalition parties of being ignorant of the Ministry's work, because they had failed to incorporate the Concertación's gender equity aims into their manifestos and activities. Any explicit political support from regional politicians stemmed from individual commitment rather than from a party political stance. Internal leadership changes within the local parties meant that 'previous talks were somewhat wasted because at regional level there is a tendency to personalize agreements and pledges of support'.[12] A couple of directors reported that they were in contact with local women party leaders who supported them by publicizing activities and raising gender issues in regional party forums, but in general exerted little influence. The right-wing opposition parties have been similarly disengaged, one regional director complaining 'They have kept their distance, declaring themselves publicly opposed to equal opportunities policies'.[13] The indifference of all the parties of the governing coalition to sub-national politics left SERNAM fighting its regional battles almost alone and on every front.

Challenges of regionalization

What, then, have been the mechanics of 'regionalizing' SERNAM's gender agenda? The regional directors highlighted a number of factors that assisted the promotion of the ministry's agenda at this level. Their presence in the regional cabinet, the goodwill of key political actors such as the *Intendente* and chief of staff, and the support of bureaucratic actors such as the Regional Social Commission, and the regional representatives of the Planning Ministry, the vocational training agency, and Labour Board, helped reduce resistance and politically validated its work. So, too, did the general commitments made by the second and third Concertación governments, and SERNAM's national technical achievements such as its department of planning and studies, and the existence of a policy blueprint, the EOP, that could be copied and adapted. Its sectoral specialists also negotiated with their counterparts in the ministries to design pilot plans, reach agreements, set targets, allocate resources and mainstream gender issues into the ministries' work.

Nonetheless, direct transmission of these accords down to the regional outposts of the ministries, was not that simple, despite the Chilean state's verticalism. Whilst the regional governments follow centrally determined priorities, the individual line ministries exercise considerable discretion over the content and funding of activities. Consequently, SERNAM has been obliged repeatedly to renegotiate its institutional leverage and status. As one regional director commented 'We have to lobby everyone'; that is, *Intendente*, ministerial representatives, councillors and mayors in the region.[14]

The directors continued to complain of the physical distance between municipalities and the regional capital, and of a shortage of human and material resources 'which makes it difficult to argue for certain policy interventions on an equal footing with the other public services'.[15] Given the mainstreaming mandate, they had to maintain representation on all kinds of regional bodies, spreading their staff very thinly. In the early years, they lacked gender-disaggregated information and time to become acquainted with the bureaucratic system in different areas. They also grumbled that regional infrastructure was often prioritized over social investment, and that gender policy was relegated to the following term of office, a tendency also noticed by Brazilian women in PT administrations. This was due to a lack both of understanding of gender issues and of autonomy in regional government, which was hostage to transfers of staff and resources for centrally planned programmes. Yet the greatest challenge has been to convince the regional, provincial and municipal authorities to 'integrate equal opportunities commitment and action into their planning process in a permanent and systematic way',[16] with middle-level civil servants cited as the most obdurate actors. The process of setting regional strategies has been slower than at national level as the relevance of gender issues to regional development constantly had to be argued and demonstrated, against a background of high staff turnover and a distinctly personalist style of government. The degree of discretion wielded by the regional chief executives reflects their direct appointment as the president's representatives, free of the constraints of a regional legislature.[17] SERNAM's task has been further complicated by having to operate on a horizontal plane, through the regional planning bodies, the line ministries and the *Intendente*'s office, as well as on a vertical plane, needing to refer upwards to national bodies (SERNAM, the Concertación, the government) for policy guidelines, yet obliged to encourage policy implementation indirectly and downwards at a lower administrative level in the municipalities.

Although regional circumstances were meant to dictate the exact balance of priorities, in reality regional EOPs did not diverge much from SERNAM's centrally generated policy menu, as agreed with the national ministries. The ministry has been accused of a 'one size fits all' approach to equal opportunities, which is centred on white middle-class women, and of paying less attention to *pobladoras* and indigenous women (Richards, 2003). At most, regions can prioritize certain programmes, such as the *temporeras* project in agro-export areas, or else discrete elements within a given programme. The degree of responsiveness to local women's demands varies greatly.[18] For example, the local offices of the Metropolitan Region and of Region IX, Araucanía, were lobbied by Mapuche women's groups. Whilst the first did not respond, the second encouraged input and participation by local indigenous women, and secured extra funding for culturally sensitive gender programmes. The third director of that region, appointed in 2002, was herself a Mapuche (Richards, 2003).

In the early years, there were no formalized participatory processes for drawing up the regional or municipal strategic development plans, and feedback and evaluation mechanisms were also weak. One director noted:

There are no serious follow-up studies. The indicators used for evaluation are generally quantitative, referring to observable and measurable dimensions. Our project of cultural change is a long-term undertaking and we need to generate proper instruments to assess these more subjective and attitudinal dimensions.[19]

Until 2001, there was no instrument for measuring the impact of regional equal opportunities; the ministry kept stock only of adherence to sectoral commitments, while user evaluation of particular programmes, such as the Family Violence Centres, occurred after each individual activity and through focus groups. Now, however, the regions carry out 'social dialogues' with public service providers and local women, Consultative Councils are attached to each SERNAM regional office, and regional, provincial and municipal committees monitor the compliance of regional ministries with the EOP using a new instrument with 15 national commitments and 38 targets introduced in 2002.[20] However, consultation has been hampered by the uneven distribution of women's groups, with very few in the more rural regions. Regional directors expressed frustration with the delay in deepening political regionalization; Lagos postponed the promised direct election of the regional councillors, which would have reduced institutional verticalism, and facilitated greater autonomy with respect to budgets and policies and more engagement with local women's concerns.

Municipalization of gender policy

Local authority activities targeted at women are not a new phenomenon in Chile; witness the history of the Mothers' Centres and state-sponsored charitable and welfare activities over the last half-century. Since the transition, a number of different organizations have been working with women at municipal level and, to some extent, competing for them as clients. In 1990, the government launched the Foundation for Promoting Women's Development (*Fundación para la Promoción y Desarrollo de la Mujer* – PRODEMU), linked to the president's office, a new charitable network of what are effectively revamped Mothers' Centres. It was intended to offer a democratic version of CEMA-Chile, which was still headed by Pinochet's wife but discredited by its association with the military regime.[21] PRODEMU provided an institutional space for women's groups and middle-class volunteers that wanted to leave CEMA-Chile or had never been members. Some Concertación women also saw it as an insurance policy in case the SERNAM bill then passing through Congress was so eviscerated as to strip the new ministry of any executive functions or ability to network with grassroots groups (Guzmán *et al.*, 1994: 40). PRODEMU also offers low-income women, particularly homemakers, social and leisure activities as well as income-generation training, mainly handicrafts, compatible with their domestic responsibilities and identity as housewives. However, the influence of the new discourses on women's rights, or what Schild (1998a: 245) terms the 'feminist curriculum', is visible in its approach, which provides self-esteem and leadership courses, uses the language of empowerment and individualism, and encourages financial independence. Some see this as 'achieving a happy marriage between women's autonomy and the market' (Schild, 1998b: 103) by contrast to the conservative, family-oriented model embodied by the old Mothers' Centres. Others, however, suggest that the Christian Democrats, denied SERNAM as a municipal instrument, quite consciously colonized institutional space at regional and municipal level that would allow them to regain the electoral support they had enjoyed among lower-class women in the days when they had an active women's department and control of the *Centros de Madres* (Baldez, 2001: 4). Thus, the transformation of an existing network of women's advice centres into the regional CIDEM offices and the creation of PRODEMU, the Family Foundation and the Integra Foundation (a network of childcare centres for low-income women), all headed by the president's wife and therefore dominated by the Christian Democrats for a decade, could be construed as a strategy to fend off competition for the same from both Left and Right. The gender gap data presented in Chapter 5 suggest, however, that this ploy did not bring the intended electoral benefits as UDI has maintained its gender gap advantage over the DC. All the same, the net result has been to cut SERNAM off from working-class women's groups and from childcare provision policy, and oblige it to compete for the same funding sources and female client pool.

SERNAM was therefore challenged to forge a new paradigm for relations between the municipal authorities and the female population that would break with the old model of welfarism, clientelism and maternalism, and place a gender analysis centrally in municipal planning and policy. It was initially reluctant to enter the local arena while the right-wing mayors and unelected city councillors appointed under the military regime continued to run most town halls, where its intervention would have been unwelcome. After the 1992 local elections, the 1993 re-election of the Concertación and the consolidation of SERNAM's institutional capacity, it turned its attention to the municipal sphere. The 1994–9 EOP was minimalist, urging only 'the creation of high-level entities in the municipalities, with the explicit aim of ensuring equal opportunities for women in municipal programmes and policies'; that is, the OMMs, which SERNAM promoted among the newly elected mayors, city councillors, and members of the Social and Economic Councils (*Consejo Económico y Social Comunal* – CESCO). In 1999, the ministry won another victory when the 1995 revision of the Municipal Organic Law (MOL) made one of the core functions of the municipality 'to promote equal opportunities between men and women', just as it had lobbied successfully to get a similar provision into the regionalization bill.

This modification had two effects. Firstly, it guaranteed an institutional space for gender issues, removing it from the personal whims of politicians and civil servants, as all municipalities are now obliged to draw up a Municipal Development Plan.[22] Secondly, it introduced the same shift that had occurred at regional level, moving from a focus on delivering specific programmes to an emphasis on gender mainstreaming. In principle, both are positive steps towards institutionalizing a gender perspective into municipal government. However, in practice the impact has been much weaker due to the specific political and administrative characteristics of the municipal sphere in Chile. Over the last decade, SERNAM's three-pronged strategy in relation to the municipality – establishment of OMMs, agreements with the municipalities to deliver its pilot programmes and integration of the EOP into the development plans – has been hampered by the Ministry's lack of formal structure, resources and mandate within municipal administration, and by the political vacuum within local government.

Municipal women's offices

At the outset, SERNAM promoted the OMMs with enthusiasm as a conduit for trickling gender equity concerns down to municipal level. By 1994, there were offices or similar in 66 municipalities (19.8 per cent of the total).[23] Furthermore, 49 towns operated some kind of programme directed at women, generally in conjunction with SERNAM or PRODEMU, whilst 14 carried out sporadic and isolated activities, with no permanence, longer-term aims or continuity. Overall, some 40 per cent of municipalities were running some form of gender-related activity, with a geographical concentration in the metropolitan areas, which represents a rapid level of start-up. However, six years later the number of offices had risen very modestly to 86 (25.2 per cent of municipalities).[24] It is striking that, in such a centralized country, SERNAM's Regional Development department holds no aggregate data on the OMMs. In 2002, regional offices were able to supply basic information, but it was clear that the degree of contact they had with the Offices varied considerably, as did their strategy. Responses suggested that the ministry had become highly ambivalent about the OMMs; some were actively promoting them, whilst others had none and had even given up on them, preferring to work through the Municipal Development Office. One reported:

> In this region at least we have not even tried to set up new OMMs. We don't believe it is the right structure for our needs, as it isolates women even more at the local level. Therefore we are concentrating more on incorporating a gender perspective into the municipal planning process as a whole.[25]

What, then, has happened to the municipalization of gender policy?

Political intermediaries

Due to its limited resources, SERNAM could not aspire to establish an OMM in every municipality. Instead, the regional offices attempted to identify key areas, with some prioritizing the largest and most important municipalities in a bias against rural areas that continued through the decade. However, in many cases the creation of the OMMs was quite ad hoc, depending on factors beyond SERNAM's control, such as the goodwill of local political and bureaucratic actors in allowing access to decision-making forums and resources, and the collaboration of third parties such as NGOs, municipal authorities, local businesses, and women's groups. As one regional director explained:

> We set up the OMMs depending on a number of different considerations, such as the type of commune (rural or urban), what sort of mayor was in post (personal/political will), the needs of women in the commune (according to an assessment done by the CIDEM), the resources of the municipality, minimal infrastructure, the right opportunity, awareness on the part of local authorities and/or the local population.[26]

The role of strategically placed change agents was often crucial. Mayors were prompted to institute OMMs or gender programmes for a number of reasons, persuaded variously by the demands of local women's groups, electoral self-interest, principled commitment, and the promise of 'fresh' funds. However, awareness of gender issues was low, with women's issues associated with welfarism, a factor one respondent blamed on low educational levels among municipal authorities.[27] In response to this, the Association of Chilean Municipalities, which represents the country's mayors, established its own Technical Committee on Women and Local Development in 1993. However, it chose to refer only to *equal opportunities* for women, rather than to *gender*, in acknowledgement of political differences among their membership, specifically the hostility of the Right to the idea of gender as social construction (Subsecretaría de Desarrollo Regional y Administrativo, 2001: 21).

The role of mayors

Of all the municipal actors, it is the city councillors who are most noticeable by their absence, a consequence of political centralism and the dominance of the mayor. In a study of OMMs established before 1994, SERNAM and the mayor were cited as the most important actors, whilst the city council 'supports the process but takes no initiative' (Valdés *et al.*, 1995: 13). However, the small number of women mayors has made little difference to gender policy. One respondent noted:

> The variable of sex does not ensure greater political will or commitment because in general 'women's issues' are associated with a reinforcement of gender roles and not with the generation of mechanisms to create gender equity.[28]

The mayor's wife has, in a few instances, pulled some weight in setting up women's units (in La Florida) or programmes (in Valparaíso). Some opened doors and possessed a strong gender consciousness, but others blocked access and held very conservative views. In Lolol, for instance, the Women's Office was headed by the mayor's wife who collected clothing and other items to distribute to needy women and helped in handicraft workshops. She viewed herself as the local SERNAM and her activities as a continuation, not a break, with her previous work as a volunteer in the military regime's women's institutions (Valdés *et al.*, 1995: 18). Other municipalities saw their role as promoting women's grassroots associations, reflecting the role of CEMA-Chile in its earlier phases and a traditional conception of the municipality. In Valparaíso, the wife of the Christian Democrat mayor ran the OMM and worked closely with women's groups and the sport and recreation office, providing the PRODEMU activity menu without a wider gender equity perspective.[29] In response to this tendency towards welfarism and the whiff of clientelism, SERNAM has discouraged the involvement of the local first lady in gender policy activities.

Opinions vary as to whether the party affiliation of the mayor matters. Sometimes the party political affinities of the mayor with the regional director facilitated initial contact but little more. Some directors felt that party affiliation alone would not necessarily make a Women's Office a priority.[30] One blamed the lack of OMMs on the fact that eight out of ten municipalities were governed by right-wing mayors 'who hold a very retrograde view of women and their contribution to regional development',[31] whilst another stated that male mayors and governing coalition mayors were actually the most resistant. That notwithstanding, the earliest OMMs in the Metropolitan Region appeared in Concertación-run municipalities, after SERNAM had laid the groundwork by persuading 37 mayors in the capital to sign a letter of commitment to the CEDAW principles.[32] The first four – Valparaíso, Concepción, Conchalí and La Florida – materialized in municipalities whose mayors had been appointed directly by President Aylwin.[33] Some gender work even predated the OMMs.[34] Under Jaime Ravinet, the highest-profile Christian Democrat appointee, Santiago set up a CIDEM and domestic violence centre in 1990, and became the first town hall to give its women's unit full departmental status in 1998. María Antonieta Saa,[35] the feminist mayor of Conchalí, a densely populated and deprived inner city area, created municipal councils for children and for the elderly and, while there was none for women, the municipality worked closely with women's groups and NGOs, which in turn assisted in running training courses (Saa, 1993). By 1994, the Women's Office founded in La Florida under Christian Democrat mayor Gonzalo Duarte was by far the most institutionalized of the early OMMs with a team of over ten and a comprehensive set of gender programmes.[36]

However, after several years of Concertación rule all three of these municipalities passed to UDI's control in the 2000 municipal elections, and party political differences over gender policy finally became visible at municipal level.[37] In La Florida, the change of government led to the gender equity programmes being replaced by a Family Centre. Conchalí and Santiago survived better; the former retained its Women's House, which offered training and assistance in cases of domestic violence, the latter its Women's Secretariat. The institutionalization of Santiago's women's unit initially guaranteed continuity; the staff were retained and the programmes continued, although the orientation shifted perceptibly away from strategic to practical gender needs. Whilst OMMs are rarely closed down with a change in government due to their institutional insertion, the legitimacy of SERNAM, and the unpopularity of such a move when women remain a key electoral constituency, their orientation may well be altered by the gender ideology of the party in power.[38] UDI's preferred organizational model for working with women is CEMA-Chile and Las Condes, an upper-class neighbourhood in the Chilean capital in UDI hands since 1989, has never had an OMM; SERNAM had hoped, mistakenly, that its family programme might provide an opening through which to introduce more strategic gender policies.[39] The party's main gender policy is the provision of childcare (both childminders and nurseries, despite its doctrinal preference for the first) to low-income working mothers. In this area it is competing with one of the cornerstone institutions of the Concertación government, the Integra Foundation, which by 2004 was running 856 kindergartens, with coverage in 90 per cent of the poorest municipalities.

While the parties are generally in agreement about the need to tackle poverty and encourage women into the labour market, reproductive rights remain the watershed. In June 2004, the Ministry of Health announced that it was providing free emergency contraception (the 'morning after' pill) for distribution through municipal health clinics. After protest from the Catholic Church, this was limited to rape victims. However, as health provision is deconcentrated in Chile, a row then broke out between mayors of different parties and the ministry. First, a group of three right-wing mayors declared they would refuse to allow distribution in their municipalities. Meanwhile, the Socialist president of the Health Committee in the lower house, the president of the PPD, and three PPD mayors called on all mayors, especially PS and PPD ones, to support the policy. They turned the language of the Right on its head, calling opponents of the policy 'pro-abortion' because it would force poor women to have illegal and dangerous terminations. This is a good example of how a deconcentrated model of government allows mayors to *react* politically to central government policy, by refusing to implement it, but does not allow the scope for pro-active policymaking that a more decentralized system would.[40]

For the last eight months of the Allende government, a public hospital in Santiago ran a pilot project providing terminations to low-income women, arguing that maternal deaths from backstreet abortions was a greater social ill. Had this experiment survived, it would have been a precursor to the 1990s 'legal abortion' movement in Brazil. However, no progressive municipal authority has attempted anything similar since 1989, due to the Left's paralysis on this issue and the lack of organized women's movement pressure on local politicians. SERNAM's attempt to reduce the very high level of teenage pregnancy through sex education days, delivered through municipal education services, has also been contentious, to the extent that Las Condes held a referendum on the topic. Both Conchalí and Las Condes provide educational services for teenage mothers, although the policy is framed very differently by left-wing and right-wing authorities, the first viewing it as a rights issue, the second as an anti-abortion, pro-family stance. With the failure of the Concertación parties to support SERNAM's policies at sub-national level, the only gender ideology being confidently articulated locally has been UDI's conservative one. However, the 2004 elections saw UDI's seemingly inexorable expansion halted, with the Concertación's share of town halls rising from 49.6 to 59.4 per cent and the right-wing coalition's dropping sharply from 48.1 to 29.9 per cent, so it remains to be seen whether its influence on municipal gender policy will grow in future.

Women's Office co-ordinators and bureaucrats

The other key protagonists are the Women's Office co-ordinators. On the one hand, they are able to orchestrate SERNAM activities; facilitate contact with local authorities representing different services; bring people together for meetings and joint action; negotiate with the municipal administration, officers, councillors and CESCO; and insert gender issues into local planning. Conversely, their capacity is often limited by lack of technical knowledge and inability to generate equal opportunities policies locally, lack of links to parties, a rapid turnover in the post, work overload, low salaries, and lack of formal recognition and clout within the municipal structure, as they are often not a member of the core municipal staff.[41] Some are employed fulltime, where the programme is most institutionalized, but often they are seconded from other departments, which accounts for the prevalence of former social workers in their ranks. Their understanding of gender equity is crucial in the implementation stage but, while most had worked with women's groups, community groups, NGOs or in SERNAM's offices, the majority had no background in gender training or studies. Indeed, the lack of technical capacity among municipal staff in general acts as a major brake on full decentralization. Municipal bureaucrats earn low salaries and control few resources, the jobs lack prestige and the level of commitment is low. They also resented the extra responsibilities allocated to the municipality under Pinochet and were resistant to new ones such as gender equality, unless they could be shown to be 'efficient' in achieving core goals.

Bureaucrats in the local branch of the Planning Ministry and in the Municipal Development Office can be crucial to mainstreaming efforts as they not only open up the administration to gender issues, but also bring technical backing to projects. For example, it was through the intervention of a sympathetic 'insider' that, in the early 1990s, the Municipality of Santiago became the site for one of the highest-profile NGO–municipal collaborations. A feminist NGO, Instituto de la Mujer, approached an activist working in the city hall who reformulated their proposal and acted as a bridge. In consequence, the mayor approved a programme of training and awareness-raising for women employees and consumers of municipal services, as well as a wide-ranging gender programme that prefigured SERNAM's own EOP.[42] Conversely, bureaucrats may constitute an obstacle. Many municipal civil servants appointed by the military regime's mayors remained in place after the transition due to job security legislation introduced under Pinochet. Getting the middle-ranking municipal staff on board is as important as at regional level, and gives the gender perspective some permanence and institutionalization given that 'the change of authorities every four years is not necessarily a time span that allows us to consolidate SERNAM's influence on municipal government'.[43] This was even worse in the period 1992–6, when many mayors held split mandates of only two years. Recognizing that 'where a gender perspective has soaked down to the middle levels of bureaucracy, it can survive a change in political leadership',[44] in 2000 UNIFEM and the Association of Chilean Municipalities ran a project to introduce gender awareness into the training programmes for town hall staff.

Mainstreaming, gender equity and welfarism

Until 1994, the role of the OMMs was not closely defined. From then until 1999 they were primarily used as conduits for delivering SERNAM programmes, with the intention that they would eventually be handed over to the municipal authorities. They were delivered by third parties (NGOs or other bodies), using SERNAM's expertise and policy blueprints, and funded either by line ministries, transfers from the regional offices or direct municipal funds. Although they generally did not impinge upon the administrative structure of the municipality, they were regarded as valuable, not just as an end in themselves, but also as a means of opening up space within the municipalities and of promoting changes in attitudes.

The switch from a general to a specific to a mainstreaming remit was completed with the 1999 revision of the MOL and, after 2002, all specific programmes have been financed purely out of the town hall coffers. The mainstreaming blueprint, the EOP, is more global and strategic in character than the individual programmes, which tended to be addressed to more practical gender needs, but it also requires the political commitment of the elected representatives (mayor and councillors) and additional resources. In practice, municipal authorities have tended to translate 'gender' into 'women' and 'poverty alleviation', retain a welfare mentality and be very sensitive to resource issues. In a 1994 survey of municipalities, some OMMs placed emphasis on the female voluntary workers providing charity to the poor, a model with a long trajectory from the League of Chilean Ladies, to the *Promoción Popular* of the DC, the women's volunteer corps of the military regime, CEMA-Chile, and the current activities of PRODEMU and UDI. As one regional co-ordinator noted scathingly:

> In general they maintain the traditional role of women and only work on training and leisure activities. They have been a great excuse for local authorities to say that they invest in women. Actually, they fill up women's free time with workshops.[45]

The programmes delivered by the municipality tend to reinforce a 'welfarist logic' in so far as they involve practical, measurable solutions to identifiable and quantifiable needs, through targeting specific groups. For example, identification of the beneficiary group for the Women Heads of Household programme is easy via the national system of measuring relative poverty. Indeed, channelling subsidies as part of government poverty elimination programmes has been a core responsibility of the municipality since the military regime's introduction of a deconcentrated model of service delivery for health, education and anti-poverty policies, in which the municipality acts as a mere intermediary between the ministries and target populations (Siavelis *et al.*, 2002: 285). The international policy agenda of the 1990s, which defined decentralization as a *sine qua non* for efficiency and democracy, also framed women as both the objects and instruments of poverty reduction measures.

However, most towns in the survey fell somewhere between these more traditional approaches and the more 'modern', rights-based orientation of the EOP. Whilst aspiring to develop a new model of state intervention in gender relations, it appears that SERNAM uneasily combines elements of both practical and strategic gender policy approaches, and mixes neoliberal social policy and welfarism with a more emancipatory and participatory intention.

Institutional obstacles

Beside the change in remit, the OMMs have suffered a number of other problems, such as resource constraints. The shift in policy under the Lagos government from programmes to mainstreaming undermined the enthusiasm for gender issues in the regions and municipalities. SERNAM could no longer offer pots of money, which delivered both poverty reduction and political benefit to local politicians, but rather 'intangible goods' that 'are not understood and therefore not valued'.[46] This particularly affected poorer municipalities that are loath to allocate their scarce resources to an issue they do not grasp or prioritize. For as much institutional legitimacy as SERNAM may have, the promise of extra resources has proven a bigger carrot. Resources form a bottom line, but not necessarily an insuperable barrier, in getting gender policies inserted into the municipal sphere. One director commented that much depended on the administrative capacity of each municipality, which in turn was directly related to its size, number of staff, isolation and training of staff, especially in social issues. Longavi, one of the poorest municipalities in the region, had a mayor who was very sympathetic and a director of Community Development with a high level of commitment and technical skills, which enabled the regional office to run three programmes and co-ordinate well with the CIDEM.[47] Often, other types of strategic intervention can achieve as much or more as the formation of a separate dedicated entity such as the OMM:

> The main stumbling block to agreements is the mayors' perception that in order to set up a Women's Office you need additional

resources. We have eight in the region and the strategy is to train municipal staff involved in planning or networking with the community. The intention is to enable a gender perspective to penetrate all the municipal responsibilities and become established as a key variable in municipal government.[48]

Other problems are more structural. The degree of autonomy, and the number of legal and policy instruments available to municipal governments, are both limited. As the OMMs are not explicitly included in the text of the MOL, they have never been a formally institutionalized space within the municipal structure and remain at the whim of the mayor. They lack competence within the local authority hierarchy and there is a lack of co-ordination between the OMMs and other municipal authorities. Siting them within the Municipal Development Office does not allow speedy access to the municipal planning process, and key equal opportunities resources, such as a gender-sensitive database, are absent or not used. Following the withdrawal of SERNAM from delivering specific programmes, the OMMs seem to have been cast adrift. Although most are the result of the approach of the mayor to SERNAM or vice versa, some exist outside of any formal agreement with the ministry. The latter has no central system of monitoring or data collection on the OMMs, no clear policy on the municipalities, and few funds to develop municipal gender equity policy. The OMMs in Chile are highly atomized and isolated, and their chief point of reference is the local mayor and municipal bodies, rather than SERNAM or the women's movement. There is no horizontal network, in the manner of the alliance of state and municipal *conselhos* in Brazil, through which they could share experiences and increase their collective muscle.

This disconnection is reflected in the OMMs' difficulty in promoting local women's participation in gender policy and citizenship in general, a reflection of similar problems at national and regional level. Provoste and Valdés (2000) acknowledge that, while OMMs' have played a democratizing role in general terms, increasing organizational density in the locality, women's groups are often treated instrumentally rather than empowered in relationship to state gender policy. Schild (1998a) further argues that, as SERNAM, the OMMs have also 'crowded out' local women's groups in competitions for central government project funding. Nonetheless, there are cases, such as the OMM in El Bosque, where consultation over the local EOP was genuinely participatory (Provoste and Valdés, 2000: 10). In Huechuraba, women's groups were involved in municipal planning processes and it became the first commune to include gender equity as one of the guiding principles of its local development plan (Provoste and Valdés, 2000: 12). La Florida's OMM was regarded in the mid-1990s as one of most self-reflexive and encouraged women's input into the design of the programmes. The Women's Office co-ordinator understood the need for a modern, cross-departmental and dynamic model of administration centred on women as subjects, not objects, of policy, sensitive to feedback and able to adapt its approach (Valdés *et al.*, 1995).

Part of the problem with promoting active citizenship is the lack of a wider political debate about the meanings of 'participation', which can range from election to representative bodies such as the city council, CESCO or neighbourhood council, referenda on issues predetermined by the local government or more novel forms. The Left in Chile has been unable to articulate an alternative vision for municipal government akin to the radical participatory projects of the Frente Amplio in Uruguay and the PT in Brazil. The Socialist Party never had quite the same roots in the *poblaciones* as the DC, UDI or Communists, preferring to operate through workplace-based networks, whilst the PPD lacks deep societal roots. Both hold an instrumental and de-ideologized view of the municipal sphere as a space of electoral recruitment, not as a location in which to showcase policy or encourage participatory democracy. The Pinochet government's strategies for technocratizing the municipal arena allowed the populist right, UDI, to colonize this political void, managing to pull off the trick of being at once the most doctrinaire of the parties in the Chilean system, yet presenting itself as the most 'anti-politics'. Its municipal pitch seems to offer both direct democracy and a managerial approach to running the municipality: deeds not words. UDI, for example, is known for promoting plebiscites on local policies, a tactic some regard as cheap populism in the face of a depoliticized local public (Mosovich Pont-Lezica, 1997; Posner, 1999). Its vision of the local populace as *consumers* of public services offers local women's groups no avenue for developing a more strategic gender agenda.

In the transition, women, along with civil society in general, were recast as passive beneficiaries of state transfers and SERNAM has tended to consult only the users of its services, rather than promoting more inclusionary mechanisms to enable women to challenge or engage on their own terms with the gender policies currently on offer. It restricted consultation to a small group of feminists in the NGO sector until the Lagos government, when lack of civil society participation was finally identified as a democratic deficit. Although a number of women's NGOs and municipalist entities have run events and workshops on gender policy in the municipality, these debates have been limited to the technocratic class, of more interest to feminist bureaucrats than to women city councillors or mayors, partly a result of the weakness of local legislative instruments.

Chile's parties have virtually no stance on gender policies at the local level, which is hardly surprising given that they have hardly incorporated SERNAM's agenda into their national party programmes. In addition, most of the parties, which have become increasingly verticalized and electoral-professional in character, have struggled to re-engage politically with sub-national politics, with which they had a patronage-oriented relationship prior to 1973. Women's representation in municipal politics, although rising slowly, has also made virtually no difference to local gender policies. The municipal arena has not been exempt, however, from party political skirmishes over political territory. In recent years, two new parties, the PPD and UDI, which occupy opposite ends of the political spectrum, particularly with regard to gender issues, have both been asserting their *municipalista* credentials. Although there are few real differences in relation to policies, when the Right denied SERNAM a local presence and blocked municipal democratization for reasons of electoral competition, it altered the institutional terrain, hampering the effective vertical transmission of gender policy from national to sub-national units of government. Without substantial mechanisms of debate and consultation and with a depoliticized civil society creating few horizontal networks, the local political domain has become a vacuum. The case of SERNAM illustrates how difficult it is to insert a wide-ranging equal opportunities strategy into a very underdeveloped municipal planning process, in which political parties and political actors and intermediaries are of relatively little relevance.

8
Comparisons and Conclusions

This book has traced the diverse ways in which parties in Brazil and Chile behave as gendered gatekeepers to political power and policymaking, guardians of state resources, arbiters of social relations from the most intimate and private to the most public, and a transmission belt between society and government. This chapter now compares and contrasts the two country cases, revealing the complexity of the party political variable for gender equity and equality at a time of democratization, state restructuring and party system realignment. In Brazil, gender policy and women's representation have been advanced in the last 15 years not by the central state, but primarily by one progressive political party, the PT, which has used political power and the state machinery to craft new institutions for promoting grassroots participation and a range of social rights, mainly at local government level. Conversely, the Chilean case of SERNAM showed a relatively well-endowed, centralized state bureaucracy charged with promoting gender rights, that has been caught in the midst of inter- and intra-party political conflicts that it has struggled to resist. In this way, we see the same phenomenon – the impact of parties on women's claims for representation and resources – from two complementary perspectives.

Here, I test the factors hypothesized in Chapter 1 as determining the relative porosity or impermeability of individual parties and party systems to gender issues. These are: the presence or absence of a secular–religious cleavage that crosscuts the left–right, class-based divisions; the quality (horizontal or vertical) as well as the intensity of party institutionalization; and the development of a gendered political habitus in the origins of individual parties. In this way, I seek to draw out some comparative and generalizable conclusions for a gendered analysis of political parties. This is not an attempt to quantify which country or party performs 'better' or 'worse', but rather to urge a more complex understanding of the, sometimes contradictory, gendered and gendering characteristics of parties and party systems. This can help explain how parties such as UDI can elect the most women mayors and city councillors (but the fewest deputies), whilst excluding women almost totally from the party leadership and holding highly gender-regressive policy positions. This example highlights the other key aspect of this study; namely, its attention to the spaces and places of politics – manifest in the variations in party conduct at the different levels of government.

Paragons, proxies and *petistas*

The first dependent variable examined was the degree of women's '*voz y voto*' ('voice and vote'), measured in terms of their ability to express political preferences and their representation in party leadership positions, elected office and government appointments. The early construction of women's political citizenship in the two countries reflects, on the one hand, Chile's long history of structured party political competition and, on the other, Brazil's very limited political democracy and the discontinuous and under-institutionalized character of its party system. In Chile, intense party political competition along two axes (left–right and secular–religious) and the electoral survival needs of parties of different hues led to female suffrage being consciously framed within a maternalist discourse that allowed women access to a male domain only on the basis of their alleged special feminine qualities. This resulted in the persistence of the *supermadre* conception of women's political agency only now being displaced by the language of rights and justice. In Brazil, where women's suffrage was not connected to party political ideology or competition, sympathy with the equality claims of early feminism was greater, and moral or difference-based definitions of female political agency much less prevalent.

The availability of women for political recruitment is a function of several inter-linked factors: a party's original social base, the patterns of gendered sociability and habitus that stratify the roles of different types of members and its institutional rules and culture. For example, the PT's heterogeneous genesis and relatively high degree of internal mobility have enabled it to recruit women leaders and representatives from the social movements and unions, whilst UDI's strongly hierarchical and masculine formation has restricted its women activists largely to municipal posts. We may conclude that, where a party's horizontal linkages to civil society organizations are fluid and democratic, it is easier for women to use these as a pathway into party leadership and representation. However, where these are ossified (co-opted into a corporatist structure, such as in the DC), this is much less likely. Internal factions in parties, whether informal or formally recognized, also create an additional hurdle for women political entrepreneurs to surmount.

Women are most commonly integrated into activism and leadership through the party women's departments, many of which have been transformed into technical advisory offices tasked not with recruitment but rather with promoting gender rights. The ideological position of parties of the centre-left (PT, PSDB, PS, PPD, DC) has enabled them to adopt institutional mechanisms, such as reserved seat quotas, that trump the internal patterns of male sociability. The effectiveness of such 'override mechanisms' is reflected in the PT's and PPD's greater success in electing women. However, none of these parties, not even the PT, fulfils its own or the statutory gender quota levels when it comes to recruiting for legislative elected office. Why not?

From the 1960s onwards, more women were elected to the national Chamber of Deputies in Chile than in Brazil, with the exception of 1989, the year of the transitional elections. The Chilean women's movement had not mobilized independently of the political parties during the short, pacted transition and the result was a restoration of the masculine political status quo ante. Brazil's long, election-driven transition allowed the women's movement to make gains in the 1986 elections for the Constitutional Assembly but thereafter progress stalled, despite the introduction of a statutory quota. However, one should look beyond quantitative measures to more qualitative issues to see which women get elected and why, and what their success uncovers about the personal resources they bring (money, family name, personal characteristics, a political base), the organizational characteristics of their party and cultural attitudes to women's political agency revealed in voter preference. For example, in Chile conservative Catholic discourses have cast female representatives as paragons, whereas in Brazil they have been either proxies for male relatives in caucus-led rent-seeking parties, or else have emerged from the social movement or union base of the Left, especially the *petistas*.

Party behaviour is also conditioned by the political opportunity structure, which comprises the party context (party rules on group representation both in leadership and for external posts, ideology, organizational culture, history), the political context (number of offices, level of competition, incumbency/turnover rates, electoral system), and the social context (political culture, social values and attitudes) (Norris, 2004). As both countries use open-list PR and Chile's low district magnitude (two) makes it almost a first-past-the-post system, party variables play a significant role in outcomes, but at different moments of the electoral process.

In Brazil, the cost of entry is very low due to the features of the electoral system for proportional seats (open-list and large district magnitude) and the under-institutionalized character of the parties, which neither actively recruit (as the quota law is not enforced) nor discriminate against female candidates (as they may run more candidates than seats). Even though a similar number of representatives seek re-election in both, Brazil's federal system offers more political opportunities outside the national legislature than does Chile's centralized polity, and there is greater uncertainty in electoral outcomes, making it possible for individual women with their own political resources to be elected. The PT has elected the most women in legislative elections, and achieved the highest FSI, largely due to its female activists' social movement base. In Chile, the small district magnitude and high incumbency levels result in very high competition for selection, with candidates obliged to engage in two levels of negotiation – intra-coalition and intra-party – before facing the inter- and intra-coalition electoral contest. In a system where candidacies are carefully allocated by party and coalition bosses, variation in the FSI indicates the importance of party support, which in turn reflects internal cultures and organizational practices. In Chile, prior to 1973, the Left ran and elected most women. However, in the current period, the highest FSI has been in the PPD and RN, two 'catch-all' parties formed as interim umbrellas for the Right and Left, which have weaker political sociability patterns and are less vertically organized than their coalition partners, the PS and UDI.

Party competition, ideology and policy communities

The second dependent variable of this study was the formation and implementation of state gender policy. The political parties have been one of the key gatekeepers confronting the feminist movement on its 'march into the institutions'. They mould the design of state mechanisms for women's rights, which some colonize for ideological or electoral ends, using relations of dependency and control over public services and jobs. In terms of the content, legislative success and implementation of legal reforms and gender policies, whether aimed at equality or equity concerns, progressive or regressive, parties not only construct and promote their own conceptualizations of gender relations, but also refract and filter the gender agendas propounded by other social actors such as the women's movement, the Catholic Church and transnational actors.

Before the 1980s, Brazil had never had a governmental body dedicated to gender relations, whereas in Chile the competition for marginal votes in the finely balanced party system prompted parties to target women with public policies through a succession of state agencies that inevitably bore a (party) political stamp. SERNAM was conceived as a more independent alternative but party politics (intra- and inter-coalition ideological conflicts) have still left their mark. Units need strong political support, from the parties or executive, yet such an association can result in reversal or neglect in subsequent administrations. Where influence is ideological, as in Chile, it is at least contestable. Where it is instrumental (co-option for electoral purposes), as with the CNDM in Brazil, it is more difficult for women's movements to challenge. De-activation or colonization of women's units is more likely in party systems that are weakly ideological (Brazil). However, in systems that are more polarized along a moral values axis (Chile) the women's unit becomes a hyper-ideologized battleground in party political struggles not just for women's votes and party loyalties, but also for their protagonism in building a particular vision of the Good Society.

In Brazil, party politics affected the institutional stability rather than the content of gender policy, and many women's councils at the municipal, state and national levels fell prey to the prevalent party clientelism and patrimonial politics. In the early 1980s, the PMDB's still oppositional and principled character allowed women's movement and party objectives to coincide, but as it mutated ideologically into a 'catch-all' patronage-oriented party of government, the CNDM was cast adrift. The women's movement also lacked access points for influencing the government of the PSDB, a caucus party with little rank-and-file or internal democracy. Conversely, the PT administration's commitment to upgrade the women's unit was the result of the party's strong horizontal and vertical institutionalization, able to channel women's movement demands through its internal democratic structures and convert them into party and government policy. The reverse occurred in Chile, where political support for, and opposition to, SERNAM has been relatively consistent in terms of resources, institutional status and backing for key bills and policies. A close relationship with the Concertación's political elite gave it initial visibility and leverage within the alliance and its component parties, but party political appointments soon decreased, as the women's movement knew that a technocratic and non-partisan identity would better institutionalize and legitimate

SERNAM. Thus, it has managed better than its predecessors to resist attempts at party political and electoral co-option.

To what degree has the level of women's representation determined whether and how gender issues enter the legislative arena? The former remained modest in both countries, so I would argue that the key variable is actually the underlying political cleavage structure of a national polity, and the degree of party and party system institutionalization. It is not so much a question of critical *mass* as of critical *actors*, both inside and outside the formal political sphere. Whilst executive dominance and the institutional rules in both parliaments discriminate strongly against legislator-initiated bills, in Brazil it has been easier for feminists to get elected to the legislature through the PMDB, then the PT, and to shift policy preferences to those of the unified cross-party women's caucus as a result of factors such as the low degree of ideological definition in most Brazilian parties, absence of a religious–secular cleavage, consequent non-party politicization of gender issues and personal morality, and the diffuse nature of the evangelical *bancada* in Congress. The party co-option of the CNDM displaced feminist activity into a dense policy network composed of the *bancada feminina* and horizontally organized networks of feminists in representative and bureaucratic institutions, NGOS and grassroots organizations. This network has been able to influence policy and legislation at different levels of government (federal, state and municipal), thus creating multiple pressure points.

Party political competition and ideological differences, both inter- and intra-alliance, hinging on the issue of secular pluralism versus religious values, have strongly shaped and constrained SERNAM's gender policy agenda over the last 15 years. SERNAM has been most affected in the legislative arena and cross-bench unity among women politicians has been only sporadic. Those within the Concertación have been highly united because the female Christian Democrats, the party with the deepest schism, have tended to be feminist sympathizers, whilst the presence of liberals within RN has created dissent on the opposition benches. The most consistent parties on gender issues have been the PPD and UDI, albeit at opposite poles. RN and the DC suffer from both generational and religious–secular divisions, which their liberal members have been unable to overcome. Moreover, competition between radically opposed policy communities has affected the passage of gender legislation over reproductive rights, family and sexual freedom. On the one side, there is a 'progressive' alliance of SERNAM, its backers in the Concertación parties, and a small handful of legislators in Congress. However, the wider network required to sustain this is weak, comprising a handful of feminist NGOs and research institutes, an effect of SERNAM's crowding-out effect and of more general social demobilization. On the other side, the conservative policy community of right-wing integralists composed of UDI, elements of the Christian Democrats, and the hierarchy of the Catholic Church, has made full use of its political privileges and is well-supported by a wider network, including groups such as Opus Dei. As Chilean legislative activity is characterized by parsimony in comparison to Brazil's profligacy, the stakes are even higher; new laws, once passed, will be implemented and have a concrete, rather than symbolic, impact.

The political vision and strategy of the dominant party of the Concertación, the Christian Democrats, itself internally divided, left its imprimatur on SERNAM's agenda in the first two terms of office, a hegemony the PPD and PS permitted. This privileged economic and social rights, poverty and the family. Targeted anti-poverty measures, aimed at integrating economically vulnerable women into the labour market as 'market citizens', chimed with the needs of the Chilean economy, existing social policy and the neo-liberal approach of the Right, and were not politically contentious. On political rights, SERNAM notably failed to push for reform of the electoral system, aware that the male leaders of all the parties would oppose a measure with potential zero-sum implications, quite aside from their principled positions on affirmative action. On sexual and reproductive rights it imposed self-censorship, at least in the domestic political arena, where the integralist Right staked out an absolutist and uncompromising position aligned with that of the Catholic Church. The conservatives' assertive veto and agenda-setting role succeeded in restricting both SERNAM's substantive mandate and its institutional reach and resources, and created an environment of politicized morality more radical than public opinion, in the face of which the secular Left, especially the still class-based Socialists, remained reactive and uncertain. In the Chilean party system, valence issues focused on the private sphere have ended up determining much of the parties' tactical, spatial positioning.

By comparison, welfare and poverty issues have been of minor importance in Brazil because there was little coherent government policy in this area, and the right-wing parties have been more inclined to oppose social policy with redistributive implications rather than private sphere gender issues. On the other hand, the feminist policy community was able to set a gender-progressive agenda with a rights focus and less fear of tackling sexual, reproductive and political citizenship. For example, the Brazilian Catholic Church's focus on social justice, rather than personal morality, and its political association with the PT allowed the feminist movement to frame 'legal' abortion as a public health and maternal rights issue. In Chile, the Church and UDI succeeded in defining it an issue of foetal rights and homicide, regularly invoking it in order to undermine the moral authority of the Concertación government.

Parties in both countries have also been permeable in different degrees to the international gender rights regime. Successive Brazilian governments have been happy to align themselves with the normative requirements of international rights regimes, and all the main parties are pluralist. The Chilean government has been more ambivalent, as the religiously inclined Right remains suspicious of universal rights talk, invokes static notions of moral nationalism and presents this as a clash of values, drawing on the counter-hegemony of the Vatican. This legacy of the Pinochet regime has been hard to counter, despite the international linkages of the centre-left parties and the feminist technocrats. However, SERNAM has also attempted to make use of the 'boomerang' effect, using the international gender rights regime to legitimize domestically its programme of gender equity and equality (Keck and Sikkink, 1998).

State agencies can come to reflect the organizational as well as the ideological cast of the party in government, particularly in their relationship to state and society. The PT's foundational, horizontal relationship with the social movements, based on mutual autonomy, is visible in the collaboration and negotiations over the women's councils, forums and other government gender units, especially at the sub-national level. The PT has also been better able to handle plural views because, as a political party rather than a state institution, its core function is to represent and aggregate interests rather than to form policy. This pluralism is, of course, a function of its origins and composition, sheltering diverse political movements and tendencies, with differing identities, goals, and social insertion, as well as officially sanctioned factions. Although SERNAM's status as a relatively well-resourced and centralized state agency may have helped its gender-mainstreaming mission, its size and technocratic cast distanced it from grassroots women's organizations. The latter are not able to participate as equals in a horizontal policy network, such as appeared in Brazil to substitute a hollowed-out CNDM; they are viewed by government as convenient vehicles for policy delivery, not design, reflecting the current disengagement of the Concertación parties from their constituencies. Departisanization of SERNAM has been beneficial, but depoliticization in a wider sense has not.

The gender politics of location

Party behaviour in sub-national government is conditioned by another element of the political opportunity structure, the degree of centralization or federalism. Internal party organization also determines patterns of recruitment at this level, the relationship of local party structures to the national party and local civil society, and the approach to local governance. Political agency may also be differently gendered at distinct levels of government. In Chile, the municipal sphere was constructed as a feminine terrain, a *casa grande* requiring a good housekeeper, through the Catholic Right's deployment of marianist discourse, and the secular Left's fear of women's electoral preferences, manifest in the two-stage extension of suffrage. When the Chilean military regime came to depoliticize local government, it deployed maternal tutelage of local government. By contrast, the localized character of Brazilian politics ensured that the grammar of municipal politics has remained that of clientelism and dynasty, not of gender and household. Not a single woman was appointed mayor under Brazil's military regime, which instead encouraged electoral colonization of the municipality by its own party, ARENA.

The municipality can be both opportunity and ghetto for women. During periods of electoral politics, the municipality has not been a privileged site of feminized political activity, as is shown by the low FSI rates in the countries. The statutory quota in Brazil and party quotas within the Concertación have had almost no effect on the proportion of women candidates or the final level of representation; in neither country have female candidates for city councillor outperformed their male counterparts. In Brazil, the PT runs and elects the most women for city councillor, a recruitment effect of its roots in the social movements. It also runs the highest percentage of women mayoral candidates, but elects a below-average number of women mayors and has a very poor FSI whilst the conservative, catch-all parties, dominant in the interior and poorer areas, have elected most, often on their family name. Conversely, in Chile, the ultra-conservative UDI, the only party whose genesis lay principally in local government under military rule, now runs and elects most female candidates for both city councillor and mayor, showing the persistence of a right-wing pragmatism and promotion of municipal maternalism that dates back to the Conservatives in the 1930s. The appeal of its female candidates, evidenced in their female vote advantage, surely lies in the party's own anti-party, populist, technocratic discourses. This has resulted in Chile now electing more than double Brazil's percentage of women mayors, even though the proportion has not reached that appointed by the military regime.

The view of municipal government to which each party subscribes, be it the managerial-technocratic, radical participatory or clientelistic one, will affect its approach to local gender policymaking and to women's participation in that process. Traditionally in Brazil, social policy in the municipality, as party politics, obeyed the logic of atomization, paternalism and party patronage, with the mayor's wife wielding a social welfare fund for electoral purposes. In contrast, the PT has taken advantage of the way that Brazil's federal system replicates government structures and instruments at both state and municipal levels. It pioneered a range of sometimes innovative and award-winning gender policies, multiplied across its municipal governments and 'trickled up' to state and national level, although they have not spread horizontally and been adopted by other parties, which lack the PT's degree of institutionalization. In part, the PT has played this role due to the weakness of vertical linkages between levels of the federation. The evisceration of the CNDM under the PMDB and PSDB led to decentred and dispersed gender policy. These very localized efforts were amplified by the dense feminist policy community mentioned above, and by the PT, which provided feminist activists with institutional space to develop policy ideas.

Whereas in Brazil in the 1990s the women's councils and other gender policy initiatives were more dynamic at state and municipal level than at national level, the opposite was true of SERNAM, which consolidated first at national and then at the regional level. It lost any direct line-ministry influence in the municipality because of the Right's political anxieties. The vertical model of delivery of nationally-determined anti-poverty and social policies transmitted through a hierarchy of deconcentrated offices was also disrupted by incomplete decentralization and the lukewarm support given by the Concertación parties' representatives at regional, provincial and municipal levels. Therefore, the OMMs have neither been efficient channels for national policy, nor developed as a space to encourage local women's input into municipal gender policy. The indifference of the centre-left to the local sphere has allowed UDI to use the municipality as a contestational space, for example over reproductive rights, even though the Chilean municipalities have a very limited degree of autonomy in relation to social policy. As the mayor, rather than the city councillors, is the primary gatekeeper to the municipality, a UDI mayor with a deeply conservative gender ideology could eliminate from the OMM's role the more strategic items on SERNAM's agenda. The OMMs have tended to revert to a welfarist profile, tackling mainly practical, poverty-related issues, a default position that is due to the long legacy of the Mothers' Centres, echoed in its 'modern' successor, PRODEMU, and the broad ideological consensus among all parties over anti-poverty measures, such as childcare for low-income women, where none exists on areas such as reproductive, family and sexual rights.

Women's practical gender needs are more easily met at the local level, but tackling strategic gender interests requires a view of the municipality as a gendered political space, rather than a technocratic one that regards women as an effective conduit through which to meet social welfare targets. Building consultation into policy processes, quotas into elections, and strengthening women's organizations will begin to bridge the gap between local and national, practical and strategic gender issues, and in this the parties play a potentially very important role. While the PT and UDI are the two most distinctive parties in the municipal politics of their respective countries, they share only superficial similarities in their discourses on participation. Where UDI seeks to depoliticize the municipality, the PT emphasizes its character as a contestable space. UDI's hierarchical character and managerial approach treats the local populace as clients of predetermined policy, whilst the PT's origins and participatory internal ethos and culture have helped it develop a reflexive and consistent approach to promoting social development and more inclusionary and effective channels of representation and voice, such as the participatory budget, master plan consultations and sectoral councils. The PT has used the institutional framework, along with its strong organic relationship with social movements, to combine implementation (secretariats) with representation (councils) and open access (forums) to channel women's claims into the state. This model, tested and honed by the PT in its local administrations, resulted in systematic interaction between a range of local women's groups and city hall femocrats, as well as in the restructuring and revitalization of the CNDM. The division, in the transition years, between the *políticas* and *autônomas* inside and outside the parties, has been transfigured into a triadic relationship between the party of government, state apparatus and women's groups. By contrast, the other main parties lack the PT's institutional and political investment in municipal government and still generally regard the town hall as a site for clientelism, rent-seeking, or a ladder to higher office.

Conversely, the return to democracy in Chile decreased women's visibility as gendered actors within local politics and brought social demobilization. Although the Chilean state has much greater governance capacity than the Brazilian state, the technocratic model is still very top-down. The parties are now more organizationally centralized than ever, with previously mass parties such as the DC and the PS transformed into increasingly electoral-professional machines. With the exception of UDI, they are unsure how to occupy sub-national political space. The Chilean Left has failed to emulate the PT's enthusiastic embrace of local government for reasons that are historical (the nature of party political engagement with the municipality pre-1973 and the effects of military rule), meta-institutional (centralism and the constraints of the 1980 Constitution) and party-cultural. Historically, the Socialists have not had the same reach into the poor neighbourhoods as the Christian Democrats or the Communists, whilst the PPD is opportunistic in its espousal of the municipalist cause, which it sees as a popular issue that is ignored by the other parties. Chile's partial decentralization has increased state capacity, but undermined political devolution or citizen empowerment, and there is little pressure for change either from above or below. The recently initiated round-table dialogues with local women in Chile appear improvised compared to the PT's more tried and tested model.

The Brazilian case study demonstrated the generation of gender policy at the local, rather than the national, level by a single, distinctive opposition party, influencing the centre from the margins, through a process of trickle up, not down, from a radical oppositional perspective rather than a cautious governing one. The Chilean case, by contrast, shows how party politics has hampered both the transmission of national gender policy down to the municipal level, and the establishment of genuine dialogue on local gender policy between state, civil society and political actors.

In conclusion, in order to understand how women's movement demands translate into outcomes in political and policy arenas, we need a more nuanced understanding of the gendered dynamics of one of the most strategically placed players, the political parties. Parties are complex beasts, directed not just by their ideology, but also by their histories, leaders, members and organizational cultures. All of these factors shape their responses to the institutional environment – which is more permissive in Brazil, more restrictive in Chile – as well as to gender issues.

Ideology is important, but our analysis should not be restricted to the left–right axis. Not only is there considerable diversity among parties on each point of this spatial spectrum, but this axis also intersects with other cleavages, which vary from country to country. The degree of fragmentation, ideological intensity and depth and type of institution-alization appear more relevant for women's *voz y voto*, whilst cleavages within party *systems* are more significant in shaping party attitudes to gender policy. Parties with low ideological intensity may take on women's movement demands but for the wrong reasons, and their temporary commitment may just as easily turn to co-option and indifference. Highly ideological parties will have formed their own view of gender relations, some espousing fixed, traditional roles, which will lead them to take on a veto role in relation to movement demands, others privileging other sociological factors, such as class. The first will react with open hostility to gender-progressive policy, whereas the second are semi-permeable, with feminists encountering moderated scepticism as to the relative importance of gender issues. Their underlying political habitus may continue to conflict with explicit principled support for feminist agendas.

Party recruitment patterns and commitment to gender policy are also a function of the type of institutionalization. Horizontal institutionalization (strong but democratic relations with civil society) allows parties to recruit from a wider base and to respond to social movement demands, whilst vertical institutionalization allows the party to 'fix' commitments to these demands in the party's programme and policies. However, vertical institutionalization without much horizontal reach allows feminists little access. Parties that are weak on both dimensions will only be pushed towards higher female representation or gender policy positions by external actors or agents, such as quota laws, by a well-articulated women's movement or caucus in parliament or, indeed, by the anti-feminist voices such as the Church. In a region where women's political representation remains modest in many countries, and where certain kinds of gender policy are still heavily contested, it behoves feminists to acquire a fuller understanding of the internal dynamics of Latin America's key institutional gatekeepers, the political parties.

Notes

Introduction

1. See Lovenduski and Norris (1993), and numerous monographs and case studies.
2. On Christian Democratic parties, see Mainwaring and Scully (2003); on Conservative parties, Middlebrook (2000); on the Left, Carr and Ellner (1993).
3. One exception is Friedman (2000a).

1 Gendered and Gendering Parties

1. Von Beyme (1985) identified nine major European party groups, or 'spiritual families'. Here, we are interested in the Liberal and Radical, Conservative, Socialist and Social Democratic, Christian Democratic, and Communist parties, as well as the less ideologically defined category of populist-corporatist parties in Latin America.
2. Institutionalization is defined as follows: stability in the rules and nature of party competition, parties with roots in society, party independence with respect to leaders and other organizations, parties are valued in and of themselves, the electoral and party systems are accepted as the legitimate routes to power.
3. Argentina elected 22 per cent women deputies in 1955 due to the Peronist Party's unilateral quota, whilst in Cuba a quota for the national legislature pushed female representation up to 22.6 per cent by 1980.
4. Source: Inter-Parliamentary Union website www.ipu.org/wmn-e/world.htm.
5. That said, at the follow-up conference five years later only two countries (Argentina under Menem and Nicaragua under Alemán) were willing to follow the Vatican's line.
6. Since at least the mid-twentieth century, most countries in Latin America have permitted so-called 'therapeutic abortion' in the cases of danger to the mother's life or pregnancy resulting from sexual assault.
7. The FMLN criticized, but could not stop, this constitutional amendment as it needed only 56 votes to pass. The party allowed a free vote and some of its 27 deputies voted in favour (Center for Reproductive Law and Policy, 2001).
8. Once appeals to national courts have failed, the Protocol enables individuals or groups of women to submit complaints to the Committee on the Elimination of Discrimination against Women, which itself may also undertake investigations of grave or systematic violations of women's rights.
9. They removed a quota provision for party lists and a guarantee of equity in the distribution of property after divorce.
10. Marianism is here used to refer to a set of Virgin Mary-like attributes, including purity, self-sacrifice and motherliness, discursively associated with women in Latin America.

11. In 1947, Gaitán's Colombian Liberals proposed the same, with female suffrage to be extended later to departmental and national elections only if the clergy were excluded from voting.
12. Argentine women won the right to vote in municipal elections in the province of Santa Fé (1921) and in municipal and provincial elections in San Juan (1927). The Mexican state of Yucatán allowed women to vote in local elections in 1922. In Brazil, the governor of Rio Grande do Norte state gave women political rights in 1927.
13. Direct elections for mayor are a relatively recent phenomenon in many Latin American countries, introduced in Peru in 1980, Colombia (1988), Venezuela (1989) and Bolivia (1994) (Willis *et al.*, 1999: Table 1; O'Neill, 2003: Table 1).
14. Some 52,000 Peronist base units were in operation by 1954 (Levitsky, 2003: fn. 9).

2 Porous Parties, Permeable State

1. Collor (1990–2) was impeached for corruption and replaced by Vice-President Itamar Franco. Cardoso served two mandates (1995–2002).
2. The president of the Republic was selected from the ranks of the military. The state legislatures indirectly elected the third senator allocated to each state in 1977 and the state governors who appointed the mayors of 120 cities (state capitals and 'national security areas'). Direct elections were eventually restored for state governors (1982), all mayors (1985), all senators (1986) and president (1989).
3. In São Paulo in 1978 and in Rio de Janeiro in 1982, the feminist movement made endorsement of their manifesto a condition for supporting candidates (Alvarez, 1990: 147–50; Tabak, 1994: 132).
4. Vargas established two parties to further his legacy, the urban labour-centred Brazilian Labour Party (*Partido Trabalhista Brasileiro* – PTB) and the more heterogeneous Social Democratic Party (*Partido Social Democrático* – PSD). Their main opponent was the National Democratic Union (*União Democrática Nacional*).
5. The PDT was constituted in 1980 by Leonel Brizola, a prominent PTB leader, after the courts granted rights over the latter party's name to the late president's niece, Ivete Vargas. The PTB is now a small right-wing party.
6. The PSB was revived in 1986 by the other grandee of the pre-1964 left, Miguel Arraes.
7. The Brazilian Communist Party (*Partido Comunista Brasileiro* – PCB) was historically much weaker than its Chilean counterpart. Founded in 1922, it was illegal for most of its existence until the mid-1980s, and ill-fated attempts at armed struggle during the military regime led to severe repression and internal schisms such as the formation of the Maoist PCdoB. In the 1990s, the pro-Soviet PCB evolved into the PPS, a European-style democratic socialist party.
8. Measures include the high level of party switching and party fragmentation, low internal discipline and party cohesion, and the fluidity of electoral coalitions.

9. Only the PCB consistently had female auxiliaries, such as the Women's Union, set up in 1934 to support the revolutionary National Liberation Alliance movement, and the Federation of Brazilian Women, formed in 1947 to demand the release of imprisoned party activists and thus a precursor of the Women's Amnesty Movement of the 1970s (Teles, 1993). The far-right Integralist movement also had a women's division (McGee Deutsch, 2001).

10. Both the PSDB and PMDB, once in government, attracted opportunists migrating from other parties, including former *arenistas* (Power, 2000).

11. Thirteen parties had women's sections (Grossi and Miguel, 2001: fn. 14).

12. The CFEMEA survey covered employment guarantees for pregnant women, maternity and paternity rights, childcare provision, non-discrimination and labour rights, sexual harassment, penalties for rape, family planning, sterilization, abortion and de facto unions.

13. The coalition parties voted in a disciplined manner in Congress not because of their internal structures and rules, but rather due to the executive's skilful management of institutional incentives, and 'pork-barrel' distribution through the party leaders (Figueiredo and Limongi, 1999).

14. The same pattern was visible in the attempted constitutional revision of 1993–4. Amendments that were regressive in gender terms tended to be aimed at cutting state expenditure; for instance, on childcare provision.

15. Even so, right-wing parties whose lifeblood has been the resources of the state bureaucracy do not wholly embrace downsizing of the state. The PT is equally ambivalent on this issue, as many of its supporters are employed in that same bureaucracy, even as it criticizes misuse of public funds.

16. In the period 1995–8, 57 deputies and 11 senators belonged to the Catholic group (*Jornal da Rede Feminista de Saúde*, 21 September 2000).

17. Following the 2002 elections, the born-again Christian group membership rose from 46 to 48, with 13 from the Liberal Party, the party of the new vice-president (INESC, 2002: 11).

18. The 'legal abortion' movement in Brazil is attempting to enforce the existing law as a precursor towards eventual decriminalization (a termination can currently only be granted under very limited circumstances by a court order) and liberalization (Htun, 2003: 156–61). Even Catholic members of the Committee on Social Security and the Family approved a bill in favour of legal abortion in 1995.

19. Rede Feminista de Saúde and CFEMEA (2001).

20. In 2000, the Brazilian government announced it would grant gay and lesbian couples the right to inherit each other's pension and social security entitlements, the first Latin American country to do so.

21. It passed unopposed in the Chamber of Deputies and, after some debate, in the Senate, where the Catholic Church attempted to intervene.

22. From 1951 to 1976 only two women held seats in Congress.

23. For example, in a constituency represented by 70 federal deputies, each party is now allowed to run 105 candidates. If the 30 per cent quota were respected, 32 would be women and 73 men. Under the previous rules, the party could only have run 70 candidates in all.

24. Votes are counted for individual candidates and for the party or parties in a coalition. Together, they determine the total for each party or coalition, and

the electoral quotient. Seats are assigned to parties or coalitions using the d'Hondt distributor, and then to individuals on the basis of their personal vote (Nicolau, 1996).

25. District magnitude is between eight and 70 (electoral districts coincide with state boundaries).
26. By May 2000, there were 13 quota-related bills in parliament, only one of them sponsored by a PT legislator (Grossi and Miguel, 2001: fn. 12).
27. The senators are elected for an eight-year term on a rolling basis. Two thirds of the 81 seats were renewed in 1994, one third in 1998 and two thirds in 2002.
28. Data from the state legislatures are not available.
29. From 1951 to 1987, she served as PTB federal deputy for six terms, during three of which she was the only woman.
30. One survey characterized the cohort of female deputies in the Constitutional Assembly as harder working, with a greater legislative success rate than their male counterparts (DIAP, 1988).
31. My calculations on the basis of data in *Fêmea*, 23, 72, 120, and Miguel (2000).
32. *Fêmea*, 120.
33. Cross-party interest groups include state delegations, born-again Christians, Catholics, large landowners, supporters of the rural workers and professionals involved in particular policy areas such as health or education.
34. Some 84 per cent of respondents would vote for a woman for mayor, 80 per cent for governor and 72 per cent for president, with ratings improving over time in the Instituto Vox Populi polls carried out in 2000 and 2001 (*Fêmea*, 85: 108).
35. The 1934 Charter included a statement of the legal equality of men and women, whereas the 1946 Constitution was written only by male legislators and omits mention of women's rights.
36. *Jornal da Rede Feminista de Saúde*, op. cit.
37. A new civil code, from which nearly all discriminatory provisions have been removed, entered into force in 2003. For the history behind this revision, see Htun (2003: 127–9).
38. She was the first woman directly elected to Congress (1934–7). Lutz served as a stand-in (1935–7).
39. The women's councils encompass both advisory and executive functions, whereas the other social sector councils tend to exercise one or the other (Costa, 1997: 92).
40. There are three main types of councils: statutory, overseeing ongoing social policies (health, education, children's welfare); ad hoc, set up to deliver special government policies such as school meals or employment; and thematic, founded on local initiative, addressing issues such as race (Tatagiba, 2002: 49).
41. Interview, 24 October 1995.
42. His 1994 manifesto promised to evaluate and redefine the role of the CNDM (Cardoso, 1994: 236).
43. Eva Blay, interview, 9 May 1994.
44. The women's movement has lobbied the principal presidential candidates at every election since 1989.

45. In preparation for Cairo, Rio de Janeiro hosted a region-wide conference on 'Reproductive health and justice'.
46. After a number of earlier, abortive attempts to prepare and agree a report, the first governmental report was considered at the CEDAW Committee's 29th session in June 2003. Brazil similarly delayed reporting on the Conventions against Torture and on the Rights of the Child.
47. Of these, 90 per cent aimed to maintain existing provisions.
48. In 2000, the incumbents were returned in 14 state capitals, including all three women elected in 1996.
49. Roseana Sarney (MA, 1995–2002), Rosinha Garotinho (RJ, 2003–6), Wilma de Faria (RN, 1999–2002).
50. The first women's *conselhos* were established in Minas Gerais and São Paulo (1983), Curitiba (1984), Salvador, Bahia and Paraná (1985), Ceará, Rio Grande do Norte, Rio Grande do Sul, Belém do Pará and Natal (1986), Rio de Janeiro, Sorocaba and Mato Grosso do Sul (1987) and the Federal District (1988).
51. Some 20 municipal *conselhos* in São Paulo state were also disbanded after the 1992 elections.
52. Sub-national constitutions may amplify but not contradict the provisions of the Federal Constitution.
53. In 1985, the Rio de Janeiro state and municipal legislatures approved the provision of legal abortion, but the governor vetoed the state bill under pressure from the Catholic Church.

3 The Workers' Party, Gender and Feminism

1. This and the next chapter are based on some 80 qualitative interviews carried out in a wide cross-section of PT administrations 1994–2003. For ease of reference, the acronym is given (in brackets) for each party activist's and each city's state in the federation, when first mentioned.
2. In 1982, a straight ticket voting system required parties to run candidates for all posts up for election in a given locality – mayor, state and federal deputy, governor – an almost impossible requirement for a newly formed party.
3. By 2004, branches of the party existed in 83 per cent of Brazilian municipalities.
4. In 1982, the PT crossed the 3 per cent threshold only in São Paulo and Acre states with 9.9 per cent and 5.4 per cent of the vote respectively.
5. Since 1995, the PT has chaired almost continuously the parliamentary standing committee on human rights in the Chamber of Deputies as well as equivalents in municipal and state legislatures.
6. Organized every year since 2001 to coincide with the World Economic Forum in Davos, the WSF highlights the human cost of – and alternatives to – globalization.
7. By 2003, the PT had held 13 national conferences and two Congresses (in 1991 and 1999). In the eight months preceding the 1999 Congress, over 260,000 members participated in preparatory meetings. Rank-and-file members also vote directly in party primaries, on conference resolutions and for the party leadership, executive and ethics boards at national, state, municipal and neighbourhood levels. Of 340,000 registered members, over 220,000 voted in 2,834 municipalities in September 2001, according to the Fundação Perseu Abramo.

8. Only Trotskyite factions have been expelled from the party.

9. The public has ranked the PT high on values and low on personalism, and PT voters had the highest level of non-electoral civic participation (the PSDB's had the lowest). Moreover, 65 per cent of those who identified with a party chose the PT (Samuels, 2004a).

10. This study was completed halfway through the Lula government, when it appeared that the party's ethics and internal democracy were coming under considerable strain from the pressure of national administration and a number of corruption scandals.

11. The Fundação Perseu Abramo and the Instituto Cidadania.

12. The PT started with around 215,000 members. Accurate figures for the intervening period are hard to find, but by March 2003 it had 400,000, which had doubled to 826,275 by September 2005 due to a membership drive. The party has 27 state committees, 2,957 municipal committees (and an additional 1,666 provisional committees), 177 zonal committees and 40,000 local party leaders (data from Fundação Perseu Abramo).

13. The PT had a membership-to-voter ratio of just under 3 per cent in 2002 (the same as the Spanish Socialist Party), compared to 58 per cent for AD and 54 per cent for the PJ (Levitsky, 2003: 61).

14. Unfortunately, some political sociologists continue to think that class and occupation are the only relevant variables; Rodrigues (2002) completely ignores both race and gender in his analyses of the PT leadership and of the relationship between ideology and social composition in Brazil's parties.

15. She was an early PT leader, previously a PMDB state deputy.

16. It called for a 'wide, general and unrestricted' amnesty that would allow the thousands of exiles and those stripped of their political rights by the military to return to national political life. The government draft of the bill added a clause extending immunity to state security agents and this version was approved under protest.

17. Iriny Lopes (ES), Maninha (DF), Maria do Carmo Lara (Betim), Neyde Aparecida (GO) and Ideli Salvatti (SC).

18. Her father was a stevedore and PTB union militant, whose place as city councillor her mother took over after 1964 (RHUDO-SA and USAID, 1993: 73).

19. Interview, 25 April 1994.

20. Maria do Carmo Lara, interview, 30 May 1994.

21. Interview, 24 April 1994, and published testimony at www.fpabramo.org.br/especiais/anistia

22. She was the only (substitute) female member of the 1983 National Executive Committee.

23. Sandra was a founder of the oil workers' union, lost her political rights and become involved in a clandestine left-wing group. She helped found the PT in several states and draft its first statutes, becoming its third woman federal deputy and first gubernatorial candidate and party leader in Congress. Interview, 28 April 1994.

24. This status change was never actually formally approved, it was more a de facto shift, causing some resentment in the Secretariat for Popular Movements that feminists had acquired backdoor privileges.

25. Held in São Paulo (1982), Espírito Santo (1988), Minas Gerais (1991, 1995 and 1997), Rio de Janeiro (1993).
26. In 2004, the PT had 15 internal divisions, of which seven were concerned with sectoral or thematic issues (women, youth, race, agrarian matters, culture, environment, popular movements).
27. This is the average reported to the SNM. No sex-disaggregated figures are currently available.
28. Survey by the Fundação Perseu Abramo.
29. All but one of the factions supported the quota before it was implemented. Neide Aparecida, DN member from Franca (SP), interview, 29 April 1994.
30. Sônia Hippólito, Secretary of Popular Movements, DN and CEN member, interview, 16 May 1994.
31. This is confirmed by my interviews and those conducted by Godinho (2000) and Sacchet (2002).
32. By 2001 the PDT had a quota of 20 per cent, the PPS and PV 30 per cent, the PSDB 25 per cent (Sacchet, 2002: fn. 162).
33. The CUT, General Confederation of Workers (CGT), Union Strength (*Força Sindical*) and Confederation of Rural Workers (CONTAG).
34. Neide Aparecida (ibid.), a view confirmed by Isabel Conceição Silva, head of the CUT Women's Committee, interview, 18 February 1994.
35. Marta Suplicy proposed the bill along with the women's caucus in Congress. She had failed to persuade the party to include the gender quota in the bill on electoral reform being drawn up at the time by the left-wing parties. The PT was allowed to put forward four recommendations and did not want to 'waste' one on the gender quota if the other parties did not support it (Sacchet, 2002: fn. 113).
36. This law originated in bills presented by women legislators from other parties (Grossi and Miguel, 2001: fn. 12).
37. The parties sometimes struggle to find enough candidates, especially women, to meet the quota. Only in the most populous states, where the ratio of population to elected representatives is much larger, do party leaderships actively select candidates.
38. Data for 1996 are too unreliable to make a cross-party comparison, and there are no figures for earlier elections.
39. Brazilian electoral law requires that candidacies be approved in municipal, state and national conventions. The PT has used primaries more than its rivals, although not required to by law, when there is a clear contest between pre-candidates. In 2004, the party switched to choosing candidates by consensus, which is less divisive but involves much more intra-party, factional bargaining.
40. She joined the PSB, for which she was then elected federal deputy.
41. Maria José Rocha, state deputy for Bahia, similarly related how she had been elected on a coalition ticket as the only representative of the PCdoB. That party then asked her to 'stand aside' to allow a male colleague further down the list to occupy the seat. Infuriated, she switched to the PT. Interview, 19 March 1994.
42. Arlete Sampaio (DF, 1994) Benedita da Silva, (RJ, 1994) and Dalva Figueiredo (AP, 1998).

43. The PT elected one female mayor in 1985, two in 1988, two in 1992, seven in 1996, nine in 2000 and 26 in 2004.

44. These include Maria Luiza Fontenelle and Luizianne de Oliveira Lins in Fortaleza 1986–8 and 2005–8; Mario do Carmo Lara, Betim, 1993–6; Telma de Souza, Santos, 1989–92; Angela Guadagnin, São José dos Campos, 1993–6; Stela Beatriz Farias Lopes, Alvorada (RS), 1997–2004; Marília Campos, Contagem (MG), 2005–8. The only women to reach the second round in 2004 in 44 of the largest cities were six *petistas*.

45. The PT has also elected more black politicians, although this represents a smaller proportion than that of women.

46. Through her leadership of grassroots movements she was elected city councillor, federal deputy, senator and deputy governor.

47. The most common trade union sectors in which PT women tend to hold elected office are education and banking, less frequently industry or rural unions.

48. Respectively, Sandra Starling, Ivete Garcia, Neide Aparecida (who helped unionize the Franca footwear industry, over half of whose workers are women), and Ana Júlia Carepa.

49. Irma Passoni, Luci Choinacki and Telma de Souza.

50. Interviews with Sônia Hipólito (ibid.), and Vera Gomes, Secretariat for Union Affairs, 27 May 1994.

51. PT administrations that have provided legal abortions include São Paulo, Porto Alegre and the Federal District.

52. PT women have twice persuaded the leadership in Congress to remove avowedly anti-choice deputies from representing the party on a congressional committee addressing abortion liberalization.

53. Lula himself has been influenced by supporters of sexual pluralism such as radical theologian Frei Betto. Interviews with William Aguiar, PT gay and lesbian sector campaigner, 10 June 1994 and Rose Souza, state deputy (RJ), 6 April 1994.

54. Nilmário Miranda, appointed state secretary for human rights in 2003, drafted a bill to this effect.

55. The PT had 2,009 active proposals in Congress, and had submitted a staggering 8,100 between 1982 and 2002. Source: PT's technical advisory office in Congress, www.informes.org.br

56. During the legislative term 1999–2002, the PT got 59 of its bills passed into law compared to 50 for the PSDB, 28 (PFL) and 40 (PMDB), even though the first two were the parties of the government coalition.

57. In its annual survey of 100 most influential politicians, DIAP, a trade union lobbying organization, cites more representatives from the PT than from any other party.

58. First Benedita, then Emilia Fernandes, co-ordinated the women's caucus in the Senate.

59. The PMDB elected three women in 1982 and ten in 1986.

60. In 1990, the distribution was: PDT (6), PT (5), PMDB (5), PDS (4), PDS and PFL (8), minor parties (8).

61. In 1994, three parties dominated: PMDB (8), PT (7), PSDB (5), seven other parties (12).

62. In 1998, the party system reconsolidated: PMDB (8), PSDB (7), PT (5), PFL (5), minor parties (4).

63. In 2002, the other women were elected as follows: PFL (6), PSDB (6), PMDB (4), PCdoB (4), minor parties (8).
64. She also submitted bills on racial equality, and set up parliamentary inquiries into death squad killings of children (1991) and trafficking in children (1994).
65. Ribeiro was previously the co-ordinator of the women's unit in the PT's Santo André administration.
66. The Figueiredo and Sarney governments appointed one woman minister apiece, Collor two and Franco four. Cardoso made only one female ministerial appointment, towards the end of his presidency.
67. Interview conducted by CFEMEA, December 2002.
68. The CNDM has been retained as a collegiate, mixed state–civil society, oversight body.

4 *O Modo Petista*: Local-Level Gender Policy

1. These studies have been produced by the party itself, Brazilian and foreign academics, and Brazilian think-tanks (Capistrano Filho, 1991; Keck, 1992: 199–215; Pinto, 1992; Simões, 1992; Couto, 1995; Macaulay, 1996; Singer, 1996; Nylen, 1997; Baiocchi, 2003b).
2. For a full list see www.pt.org
3. The most famous national welfare agency was the Brazilian Welfare League (*Legião Brasileira de Assistência*), founded by President Vargas' wife. Although at one time it performed a useful role in assisting low-income women and children (Allen, 1985), it had become a byword for corruption by the 1990s and was dissolved by the Cardoso administration.
4. Through the 1980s, the PT debated the status of the 'popular councils' that it advocated to represent the voices of marginalized sectors, with radicals arguing that they should form a 'parallel power' to the liberal, representative institutions of government, whilst others urged that they could only be advisory. The PB process resolved the issue in favour of the latter position. This debate did not refer to the women's *conselhos*, as they were already in existence, with a hybrid status and associated with the PMDB.
5. They were closed down in Londrina and Goiânia.
6. Maria Liège, PCdoB staff member of CEM, interview, 26 April 1994.
7. Nylen (2003b) compares the PB process in two towns in Minas Gerais to discover the conditions under which increased local activism can endure after a PT administration, noting the dangers of party politicization of these spaces.
8. This process was also assisted by the preparations for the Beijing Conference and Beijing Plus 5 and Plus 10.
9. Many mayors were unaware of the SNM's critique of the *conselhos* and did not understand that they were constituted differently from the other, statutory councils (Tatau Godinho, conversation, July 1999).
10. When the PT returned to power (2001–4) it set up a CEM instead.
11. PT administrations that have set up a *conselho* and no other gender units include Imperatriz (MA), Aracajú, Ipatinga (MG) and Belém do Pará.
12. She noted that there was no autonomous women's movement, although the local neighbourhood association and homeless movement were run predominantly by women. Interview, 30 May 1994.
13. Joana Leal Garcia, interview, 11 May 1994.

14. Joana D'Arc Aguiar, ADM director, interview, 6 November 1995.
15. Marina Sant'Anna, city councillor and president of PT Municipal Directorate, interview, 17 November 1995, and Joana D'Arc Aguiar, ibid.
16. Ivete Garcia, the Santo André ADM co-ordinator, organized the roundtable on which the chapter was based.
17. Cristovam Buarque, interview, 23 January 2002. Women's rights are not mentioned in the overview of his government (Government of the Federal District n.d.).
18. Maria Ricardina, director of the Federal District's *Conselho*, interview, 10 October 1995.
19. Interviews with Vânia Araújo Machado, CEM director, Margareth Nunes, ADM director, July 1999, and Márcia Bauer, assistant to Helena Bonumá, 11 November 1995.
20. Every city with more than 20,000 inhabitants is required to draw up a master plan for zoning purposes.
21. According to the plan's author, Sonia Calió, this was due not to vested economic interests but rather to the plan's element of grassroots participation. Presentation at Instituto Cajamar, 11 November 1995.
22. Ivete Garcia, interview, 18 May 1994. Also Carvalho and Ribeiro (2001), Suárez *et al.* (2001), IBAM/ISER (2002) and municipal website www.santoandre.sp.gov.br
23. She was not a *petista* as she was subsequently elected city councillor for the PCdoB, then the PMDB.
24. Interviews with Elza Pereira Correia Muller, CEM co-ordinator, 31 October 1995, and Maria José Barbosa, *secretaria* co-ordinator, July 2003. See Costa (1997: 49–87).
25. Amélia Naomi, city councillor, São José dos Campos, interview, 11 November 1995.
26. Tatau Godinho, interview, 21 May 2002.
27. In one PT town, the mayor's wife greatly expanded the work of the local charitable fund.
28. She was elected city councillor in 1992.
29. Other key city councillors included Joana Leal Garcia, Iara Bernardi, Ana Júlia Carepa, Amélia Naomi, Neusa Santos (Belo Horizonte), Lygia Pupatto (Londrina), Francisca Marinheiro (Rio Branco), Gilsa Barcellos (Vitória) and Selma Schons (Ponta Grossa, PR).
30. Interview, 6 April 1994.
31. My calculations based on data from the Fundação Perseu Abramo.
32. *Fêmea*, 96: 8–9.
33. My calculations based on data in Bittar (1992).
34. Andrea dos Santos, CEM director, interview, 11 November 1995.
35. These include Aracajú, Goiânia, and Campinas.
36. Eduardo Jorge and Sandra Starling (Htun, 2003: 158–9).
37. *Fêmea*, 63. Of the 26 state constitutions, eight refer to the state's obligation to provide legal abortion via the public health service.
38. Women constituted 86.2 per cent of the beneficiaries of the Minimum Income scheme in São Paulo and 71 per cent of the 'Fresh Start' scheme. Some 90 per cent of households benefited in 1997 by Belém do Pará's *bolsa escola* scheme were headed by women.

39. www.maringa.pr.gov.br/assessoriamulher/index.htm
40. www.goiania.go.gov.br/html/comurg
41. Women also constituted 45 per cent of the municipal bus drivers and ticket collectors in Santos.
42. Joana Leal Garcia, ibid.
43. Filomena Emilia Ramos, Casa Rosa Mulher co-ordinator, interview, 16 October 1995.
44. Unusually, both the superintendent of public security and head of the prison system were both women. Acre also appointed a female head of public security – a post that often goes to retired military officials.
45. The 'Light up Campinas' project is a similarly integrated approach to assisting victims of sexual violence, regardless of age, sexuality or sex.
46. Raimunda Ferreira de Almeida, interview, July 2003.
47. In 1990, Erundina allowed women to serve for the first time. The Municipal Guard is intended primarily to protect the city's buildings and parks, but PT governments such as Santo André, Diadema and São Paulo have begun to bolster it as a community-style alternative to the state military police.
48. Interview with Maria Conceição dos Santos, women's unit co-ordinator, Volta Redonda, 11 November 1995, and IBAM/ISER (2002).
49. Information from Fundação Abrinq, and Suárez *et al.* (2001).
50. In the run-up to the 1996, 2000 and 2004 municipal elections, the PT organized workshops on municipal gender policy for party activists, accompanied by a checklist of policies, including work, violence, transport, health, abortion, education, domestic work, social infrastructure and 'preventive action against urban violence'.
51. For example, Belo Horizonte and Angra dos Reis. Accounts of 'participatory' master plan consultations, such as that in Recife (under a non-PT government) in the early 1990s, omit mention of women participants or gender issues (Cabral and Moura, 1996).
52. Campinas already had a *conselho*, set up under the first PT government in 1992.
53. Andrea dos Santos, CEM director, interview, 11 November 1995 and *Dicas: idéias para a ação municipal*, 155.

5   In Their Place: The Political Uses of Women

1. Scully (1995), Siavelis (1997), Valenzuela and Scully (1997) and Angell (2003) stress the continuities in the party system and electoral preferences, whilst others emphasize discontinuities and change, arguing that Chile has experienced high electoral volatility, periodic outbursts of personalism and a sequence of quite distinct party systems (Valenzuela, 1995; Montes *et al.*, 2000: 796).
2. The right-wing alliance assumed a different name in each election: Democracy and Progress (1989), Union for the Progress of Chile (1993), Union for Chile (1997) and Alliance for Chile (2001).
3. For a classification of the political orientation of Chilean parties, see Montes *et al.* (2000), who use only a left–right axis, and Coppedge (1997), who combines this with the secular–religious cleavage.
4. Maza Valenzuela (1995) gives the fullest account of women's participation in Church–State conflicts.

5. On suffrage campaigns, see Gaviola *et al.* (1986) and Lavrin (1995: 286–320).
6. The Videla government also purged all Communist and 'subversive' women from the electoral roll (Antezana-Pernet, 1994: 181).
7. This is not, however, true of the 1952 or 1964 elections.
8. The second round was introduced in 1989 to increase legitimacy and governability.
9. It is only in municipal elections, where the district magnitude is higher, that voters get a full choice of parties. Only two of the four Concertación parties can compete in any given district, whilst the right-wing alliance has taken to running only one candidate in senatorial contests, dividing the districts between UDI and RN.
10. The lack of new blood in the women's departments of both parties was quite striking; in 1992, the Radical Party's was headed by an octogenarian. Interviews with Fresia Urrutia and Lilian Valencia, women's officers for the PR and DC respectively, 12 August 1992.
11. Mariana Aylwin, DC National Executive member and head of Women's Technical Commission, interview, 1 September 1992.
12. In 1994, the main parties had the following levels of female party affiliation: PC 42.6 per cent, PS 41.2 per cent, PPD 44.5 per cent, DC 41.7 per cent, PRSD 49.4 per cent, RN 51 per cent, UDI 61.7 per cent (Servicio Electoral, 1994).
13. The PPD's party statute includes a similar 10 per cent quota for ethnic minorities.
14. A quota of 25 per cent was first suggested to the party's congress in 1991. Mariana Aylwin, President Aylwin's daughter, a feminist and senior figure in the DC, was a key proponent of this measure.
15. Personal communication from Angel Soto Gamboa, April 2004.
16. Lomnitz and Melnick (1998) note the influence of Christian Democratic mothers in the political socialization of their families.
17. The term *gremialista* refers to a corporatist, communitarian form of social organization based on 'guilds' and civic associations.
18. UDI did not elect any women to Congress until 2001.
19. The DC has a number of divisions by generation and clan: the Aylwinistas (older) versus Freístas (younger), *guatones* (more right-wing) versus *chascones* (more left-wing), and conservatives (more religious and integralist) versus modernizers (more secular and pluralist). See Huneeus (2003: 147–50).
20. This translates roughly as 'promoting the interests of ordinary people'.
21. The faction most reconciled to neo-liberalism is represented by the Renewal group or 'mega-tendency'; the centre or Third Way by *tercerismo*; and the radicals by the New Left, led by Camilo Escalona.
22. María Angélica Ibáñez, interim Women's Vice-President, interview, 5 July 1994. See also Hite (2000: 79 fn. 8). Aylwin had also complained about the lack of female nominees.
23. Soledad Alvear, Foreign Relations; Mariana Aylwin, Education; Michelle Bachelet, Health; Alejandra Krauss, Planning; Adriana Delpiano, SERNAM.
24. Before 1975, there were ten senatorial districts, each returning five members. Since 1989, two senators have been elected for each of 19 districts in staggered elections.
25. The two-member districts are also referred to as a 'binomial' or 'binominal' system.

26. For debate on the effects of the binominal system on the party system and governability, see Rabkin (1996), Siavelis (1997), Magar *et al.* (1998), Rahat and Sznajder (1998), Siavelis and Valenzuela (1999).
27. By my calculations, since 1989 this over-representation has amounted to 10 per cent on average, in both national and municipal elections.
28. The parties use a variety of selection procedures, from complete central committee control to open primaries. They can be ranked from the most centralized (UDI), through the PPD, PS, DC to the most decentralized (RN) (Navia, 2004).
29. For an account of the party selection processes, see Siavelis (2002) and Navia (2004). Many of the women politicians that I interviewed complained about the insular 'boys club' culture of their party's leadership.
30. Marina Prochelle, who had represented District 55 for RN since 1989, was deselected in 2001. Forced to run as an independent, she lost her seat.
31. Interview, 27 July 1994.
32. Over 75 per cent of constituencies return one deputy from each of the two main coalitions (Magar *et al.*, 1998: 717).
33. PPD Senator Laura Soto complained bitterly about being ousted by a Christian Democrat former minister.
34. In 1997 and 2001, some 60 per cent of both men and women deputies returned for another term.
35. Lists would be disqualified if they failed to comply.
36. The Left ran an average of 12.1 per cent women candidates, the Right 7.5 per cent and the Centre 6 per cent.
37. The DC runs candidates in nearly all districts, thus giving it a bigger pool into which it could potentially absorb more women candidates.
38. In 1968, a law covering the Neighbourhood Councils and other community groups allowed the Mothers' Centres to become legally constituted community organizations.
39. See Maza Valenzuela (1995) on Catholic women's benevolent societies that also pressed for suffrage and social reform in the early decades of the twentieth century.
40. The DC women's department prioritized the organization of the centres in both the cities and rural areas as part of the party's election strategy (Valdés and Weinstein, 1993: 55).
41. The council was composed of three types of groups: socio-economic, socio-communitarian, and socio-'gremial'.
42. The UP promised, but failed, to set up a Ministry for the Protection of the Family.
43. Reflecting his party's origins in the student movement, Guzmán was more interested in building up the Youth Department than in the SNM.
44. At various points, Pinochet's suggestion of a pro-regime party was rejected for a number of reasons.
45. It raised funds through the lottery, selling handicrafts, and government grants.
46. Until 1973, Chile was organized administratively into eight regions, 25 provinces and 302 municipalities, which the military government replaced with the Metropolitan Area and 12 regions, subdivided into 51 provinces and 334 municipalities. After 1990, seven new municipalities were created in densely inhabited urban areas.
47. They have little clout by comparison to Brazil where state governors control a major source of patronage.

48. Municipalities with under 75,000 registered voters (about 85 per cent) elect six councillors, those with over 75,000 eight, and those with over 150,000 ten. This very low ratio of legislators to population was further reduced as one councillor became mayor.
49. Interview, 13 July 1994.
50. I calculate, from an internal government document listing all mayors appointed under the military (Departamento Administración Municipal, 1988), that the average percentage over the whole period 1973–92 was around 10 per cent.
51. Interview, 21 August 1992.
52. In 1992, only women two (28.1 per cent) were elected outright, whilst 23 (71.9 per cent) held a split term.
53. The Concertación's mayoral candidates for 2004 were allocated as follows: DC 46.5 per cent, PRSD 11.9 per cent, PS 22.7 per cent, PPD 18.9 per cent. Source: www.electoral.cl
54. Interview, 26 August 1992.
55. Ibid.
56. In the legislative elections 1989–97, RN won 17.1 per cent of votes and 22.5 per cent of seats, compared to UDI's 12 per cent of both. However, in 2001, UDI's share jumped to over 25 per cent, nearly double that of RN.
57. Marta Cousiño, head of UDI's Women and Family section, and María Inés Suárez Montoya, mayor of Pudahuel, interviews, 27 August 1992.
58. This worked very well; Lavín polled 77.8 per cent in 1996 and Francisco de la Maza Chadwick, his successor, 57.7 per cent in 2000.
59. *Cosas*, 741, and interview, 11 August 1992.
60. In 2000, 45.6 per cent of male city representatives ran for re-election, compared to 32.6 per cent of women. Over 92 per cent of mayors ran for re-election. I am grateful to Magda Hinojosa for gender-disaggregated data for the 2000 elections. Neither SERNAM nor the Electoral Service could provide such data for 1996 or 2004.
61. In 2000, women constituted 18.2 per cent of UDI's candidates for re-election compared to 10.3 per cent in the Socialist Party (Hinojosa, 2002).
62. In these first direct elections for mayor, the Concertación ran 11 per cent women candidates, whilst the opposition ran 20 per cent. The three main government parties elected an average of 8.7 per cent women mayors, whilst UDI and RN managed more than double that, with 19.6 per cent.
63. Pilar Urrutia in Conchalí (1.267), Vicky Barahona in Renca (1.203) and Carolina Plaza in Huechuraba (1.261) (the last two faced strong female opponents – the incumbent PPD mayor, Sofia Prats, and socialist Carmen Gloria Allende). However, in one of UDI's flagship municipalities, Concepción, the gender advantage of their candidate Jacqueline van Rysselberghe was only 1.029, less than the party's average. The same pattern persisted for these first three in 2004.

6 Between Ideologies: The National Women's Ministry

1. By the late 1990s, it had around 340 staff members, with around 150 in the central office and 190 in the regions.
2. He had also been cautious in the first round on this issue, as his Concertación opponent in the primaries was the high Catholic Christian Democrat Senator Zaldívar.

3. 'Twenty-four points of the Falange'.
4. Declaration of Principles, Article 7.
5. There is a significant influence of freemasonry in RN, as there was in the Radicals, which may account for its greater agnosticism on faith-related matters.
6. Declaration of Principles, Article 9.
7. For example, two leading PPD politicians, Guido Girardi and Jorge Schaulsohn, lent their legal services to the gay group Opus Gay to fight a court case brought by Opus Dei in 2002.
8. Jaime Guzmán (UDI), Jacques Maritain (DC), and a pantheon of Marxist thinkers (PS).
9. Instituto Libertad y Desarrollo, Fundación Jaime Guzmán (UDI), CERC and ICHEH among others (DC), Fundación Salvador Allende (PS).
10. For an account of women organizing against military rule in Chile, see Waylen (1992), Valdés and Weinstein (1993), Chuchryck (1994), Gaviola *et al.* (1994) .
11. 'El "feminismo", otra arma política', RN newsletter, February–March 1989.
12. 'The new face of Marxism', Article 12 of UDI's Declaration of Principles.
13. The original text gave SERNAM power of decision over all matters specific to women and over all areas concerning planning, implementation and evaluation of national development policies, with the power to require, not merely recommend, the modification of any discriminatory regulation or norm.
14. The head of SERNAM is thus accorded the title *Ministra-Directora* (Minister Director).
15. All previous mechanisms had fallen under the aegis of the General Secretariat of the Republic. Aylwin, in his May 1990 speech to the Chamber of Deputies in support of the SERNAM bill, noted that such a location would not satisfy the requirements of the CEDAW in terms of the functions, attributes, budget and legal status required of such a government mechanism.
16. In the Chamber of Deputies, the PPD–PS voted against this item whilst one socialist senator abstained.
17. These were: Soledad Alvear, the first minister from 1991 to 1994 (married to Gutenberg Martínez, DC), Soledad Larraín, deputy minister (partner of Jorge Arrate, PS) and María Eugenia Hirmas, head of communications (married to Sergio Bitar, PPD), plus other prominent party activists such as Délia del Gatto (DC), and María Teresa Chadwick (wife of José Antonio Viera-Gallo, PS).
18. A businessman, not a politician, Frei was selected as presidential candidate on the strength of his family name. He tended to appoint from his circle of confidants or trusted professionals, rather than satisfy strictly party or factional criteria.
19. María Angélica Ibáñez, interim PS Women's Vice-President, interview, 5 July 1994.
20. As is the coalition's practice, the Christian Democrat minister was counterbalanced by socialist deputy ministers: Soledad Larraín, Maria Teresa Chadwick, Paulina Veloso and Natacha Molina (the first feminist movement appointee). The Lagos government inverted this pattern with Christian Democrat deputy ministers Karen Herrera Esparza and Lisette Garcia Bustamente.

21. Delpiano was replaced in February 2003 by Socialist Cecília Perez.
22. Alvear is a lawyer, strongly Catholic and traditional on sexual and reproductive issues.
   Larraín is a psychologist, and a member of the national directorate of the PS, with a history of feminist activism and a much more informal style.
23. *La Nación*, 28 October 1992.
24. However, Article 5 of the 1980 Constitution already gives international conventions the status of national law.
25. Only the third prompted a 'shadow' report to the UN treaty body, a common practice among NGOs. See La Morada *et al.* (1999).
26. Instituto Libertad y Desarrollo Newsletter, no. 563, 11 January 2002.
27. A survey of hostile press articles from May to July 1995 found 259 items on SERNAM with 37 per cent of the criticisms directed at the EOP and 58.7 per cent at the Beijing document, with the majority published in *El Mercurio*, whose editorials have reflected UDI's animosity (SERNAM, 1995).
28. *El Mercurio*, 27 and 29 August 1995. The head of the DC's Women's Department took the Vatican's view.
29. In the period 1990–8, 24 bills relating to women's rights were introduced (Haas, 1998).
30. In 1994, left-wing legislators had submitted a bill that would have incorporated into the Constitution the following modifications: the CEDAW norms, a definition of 'discrimination against women', a guarantee of workplace equality, elimination of sexist images in state education, recognition of childcare as a social function rather than the sole responsibility of women and a commitment by the state to protect women's health and reproductive rights.
31. A man must 'commit a scandal' or enter into concubinage, whereas a woman need only have sexual relations with a man who is not her husband.
32. The proportion of children born out of wedlock rose from 16 per cent in 1960 to nearly 50 per cent in 2000.
33. PPD deputy Adriana Muñóz and Socialist Sergio Aguiló Melo.
34. 'Informe nacional de Chile sobre violencia' (1999), downloadable at www.cladem.com/espanol/nacionales/CHILE/informe_violencia.asp
35. The civil code allowed for divorce on very specific grounds and did not dissolve the union or permit remarriage, except in the case of death or annulment.
36. Annulments accounted for 3.6 per cent of marriages in 1980 and 8.5 per cent in 1998. SERNAM website: www.sernam.gov.cl/estadisticas/familia/05/05.php
37. Soledad Larraín commented 'I don't remember any tacit or explicit agreement to that effect, and I was heading the inter-party working group on the government programme', interview, 4 September 1995. For the socialist party positions on this and other gender-related matters during the transition, see Molina (1989).
38. Speaking as a much-respected elder statesman, his successor guaranteed, Aylwin condemned annulment as a fraud that undermined the legal system. *El Mercurio*, 11 January 1994.
39. Source in PS.
40. The leaders of the other coalition parties did not sign the manifesto but attended the launch event.

41. For an account of the debates over divorce, see Blofield (2001) and Htun (2003: 102–10).

42. In the final version, the judges have less discretion to deny unilateral petitions, except where the petitioner has failed to pay maintenance during the separation period. There are further protections for women as alimony must be paid by the financially weaker spouse.

43. María Angélica Cristi and Adriana Muñóz's domestic violence bill would have made rape in marriage grounds for separation, but SERNAM probably feared that any linkage with divorce would scuttle the bill. A bill on property in marriage was presented by RN women deputies (Cristi, Prochelle and Evelyn Matthei), and on equality for all children by PPD Senator Laura Soto.

44. The PS argued for a national referendum on divorce, but never pushed hard for it.

45. Patricia Provoste, Instituto de la Mujer, interview, 14 July 1994.

46. In 1993, she lost her seat to an anti-choice Christian Democrat and a UDI candidate, even though she received more votes than in 1989. In 1997, she moved to the PPD and was elected for a different district, winning the highest vote of any woman in Chile, with no change in her abortion stance (Hite, 2000: 85).

47. The bill would have allowed women to plea bargain for a reduction in sentence in exchange for information on abortion providers. It also defined abortion as 'homicide' rather than as an offence against public morals.

48. She must have at least four living children, be over 32 years of age and have her husband's consent.

49. She notes that the SERNAM budget is small, under 0.1 per cent of the national budget, and heavily dependent on foreign funding, and claims that the government capitulated to opposition demands for cuts as 'punishment' for the Beijing report (Baldez, 2001: 18–20).

7   Decentralization Deficits: Delivering Policy at the Local Level

1. Article 1 of Law 19.023.

2. The information in this chapter is based mainly on interviews conducted with SERNAM staff, and on written responses to two questionnaires sent to all 13 regional offices in September 1995 and October 2002, to which the response rate was 53.8 per cent and 61.5 per cent respectively. Questionnaire responses are cited by region and date. I also interviewed representatives from NGOs to which SERNAM contracts out particular services, and municipal staff with responsibility for implementing gender-related policies. Questionnaire responses are cited by region and date.

3. Gladys Gómez, Head of Regional Development, interview, 31 August 1995.

4. Each ministry has about six or seven departments under its auspices, but none has SERNAM's hybrid national status, which it should also have been granted automatically at regional level.

5. The CIDEMs can only offer advice, not resolve individual problems. However, their analysis of clients' enquiries helps identify women's priorities in the region.

6. The regions had 193 staff in total by 1998, an average of 14 staff members per region. Three (Metropolitan Region, Concepción and Valparaíso) were allocated an extra staff member due to their relative population density.

7. The Metropolitan Region enjoys a geographically compact area with a relatively highly developed infrastructure. The proximity of SERNAM's headquarters tends to overshadow the regional office, even as it gives it more access to central power.

8. SERNAM established regional committees in 1996 and a national ministerial committee on equal opportunities policies in 2000.

9. Spain's autonomous regions provided the inspiration for decentralization in Chile and the advisor on Múrcia's Equal Opportunities Plan became a consultant to SERNAM.

10. Region V, 2002.

11. Five PPD, three PS, four DC and one independent linked to the governing coalition in 2002.

12. Region XII, 2002.

13. Region XII, 1995.

14. Alba Gallardo Velásquez, Region VI Director, interview, 6 September 1995.

15. Region III, 2002.

16. Region V, 1995.

17. Region XII, 1995.

18. The new Region V Director noted in 2002 that her first job was to overturn the local perception that SERNAM was very distant from the community and the OMMs.

19. Region VII, 1995.

20. Region IX, 1995.

21. The Mothers' Centres were not closed down, out of respect for the thousands of women for whom they had become a way of life, but were allowed to go into decline.

22. Law 18.695 (Article 4, paragraph k) states that municipalities may carry out activities related to 'the promotion of equal opportunities between men and women'. A previous draft had specifically attributed this task to the Municipal Development Office.

23. Many of the data in this section are based on the survey by Valdés *et al.* (1995).

24. In 1997, SERNAM put the number of OMMs at 132 in 1994, decreasing to 115 in 1995 and was 120 in 1996. However, there was a sharp increase in the number of towns with a centre for victims of domestic violence, from 11 in 1994 to 177 in 1995, undoubtedly due to the passage of the Family Violence law.

25. Region II, 2002.

26. Region V, 1995.

27. Region II, 2002.

28. Region III commented in 2002 that 'the authorities give the issue very little importance, regardless of their sex or political affiliation'.

29. Katrina Sanguinetti, Region V Director, interview, 5 September 1995.

30. Delia del Gatto, Head of Regional Development and DC activist, interview, 25 July 1994.

31. Region XII, 2002.

32. Valeria Ambrosia, Metropolitan Region Director, interview, 25 July 1994.

33. In 1989, Aylwin appointed the mayors of the 15 largest municipalities.

34. Others also date from the early 1990s. Viña del Mar's was founded in 1992 in one of the most important towns in the region, with the mayor's backing, a decent infrastructure and sufficient municipal resources to contract four workers.

35. Saa was one of only two woman appointed by Aylwin after pressure from the CMD and women in the PPD. The other was Sofia Prats, whose father, General Prats, was murdered in 1974 by the military regime.
36. See Provoste (1995) for a study of gender policy in these municipalities.
37. In 2004, the PPD won back Conchalí but the other two stayed under the control of the Right.
38. Coty Silva, head of domestic violence programme, Metropolitan Region, interview, 7 September 1995.
39. Valeria Ambrosia, ibid.
40. Despite the row, an estimated 17,000 doses were distributed to municipalities nationwide.
41. Region VI, 1995.
42. This is most reminiscent of the Santo André experience in Brazil.
43. Region VII, 2002.
44. Ibid.
45. Region III, 2002.
46. Region VII, 2002.
47. Region VII, 1995.
48. Region IX, 1995.

References

Abers, Rebecca N. (2000) *Inventing Local Democracy: Grassroots Politics in Brazil*, Boulder, CO: Lynne Rienner.

Allen, Elizabeth (1985) *Poverty and Social Welfare in Brazil: A Challenge for Civilian Government*, Glasgow: University of Glasgow Institute of Latin American Studies, Occasional Paper no. 44.

Alvarez, Sonia E. (1990) *Engendering Democracy in Brazil: Women's Movements in Transition Politics*, Princeton, NJ: Princeton University Press.

Alvarez, Sonia E., Evelina Dagnino and Arturo Escobar (eds) (1998) *Cultures of Politics, Politics of Cultures: Re-visioning Latin American Social Movements*, Boulder, CO: Westview Press.

Ames, Barry (2001) *The Deadlock of Democracy in Brazil: Interests, Identities and Institutions in Comparative Politics*, Ann Arbor: Michigan University Press.

Angell, Alan (1993) *What Remains of Pinochet's Chile?*, London: Institute of Latin American Studies, Occasional Paper no. 3.

Angell, Alan (2003) 'Party change in Chile in comparative perspective', *Revista de Ciencia Política*, 23(2): 88–108.

Angell, Alan, Pamela Lowden and Rosemary Thorp (2001) *Decentralizing Development: The Political Economy of Institutional Change in Colombia and Chile*, Oxford: Oxford University Press.

Angell, Alan and Benny Pollack (2000) 'The Chilean presidential elections 1999–2000 and democratic consolidation', *Bulletin of Latin American Research*, 19(3): 357–78.

Antezana-Pernet, Corinne (1994) 'Peace in the world and democracy at home: The Chilean women's movement in the 1940s', in Rock (1994).

Araújo, Clara (2001) 'Potencialidades e limites da política de cotas no Brasil', *Revista Estudos Feministas*, 9(1): 231–52.

Aslanbegui, Nahid, Steven Pressman and Gale Summerfield (eds) (1994) *Women in the Age of Economic Reform: Gender Impact of Reforms in Post-Socialist and Developing Countries*, London and New York: Routledge.

Auyero, Javier (2001) *Poor People's Politics: Peronist Survival Networks and the Legacy of Evita*, Durham, NC: Duke University Press.

Baiocchi, Gianpaolo (2003a) 'Participation, activism, and politics: the Porto Alegre experiment in participatory governance', in Fung and Wright (2003).

Baiocchi, Gianpaolo (ed.) (2003b) *Radicals in Power: The Workers' Party (PT) and Experiments with Urban Democracy in Brazil*, London: Zed Press.

Baldez, Lisa (2001) 'Coalition politics and the limits of state feminism in Chile', *Women and Politics*, 22(4): 1–28.

Baldez, Lisa (2002) *Why Women Protest: Women's Movements in Chile*, Cambridge: Cambridge University Press.

Barreira, Irlys A. Firmo (1993) 'Ideologia e gênero na política: estratégias de identificação em torno de uma experiência,' *Dados*, 36(3): 441–68.

Barrera Bassols, Dalia and Alejandra Massolo (eds) (2003) *Memoria del primer encuentro de presidentas municipales*, Mexico City: Instituto Nacional de las Mujeres.

Barrientos, Stephanie, Anna Bee, Ann Matear and Isabel Vogel (1999) *Women and Agribusiness: Working Miracles in the Chilean Fruit Export Sector*, Basingstoke: Macmillan.

Barros, Mauricio Rands (1999) *Labour Relations and the New Unionism in Contemporary Brazil*, Basingstoke: St Antony's/Macmillan.

Benjamin, Medea and Maisa Mendonça (1998) *Benedita da Silva: An Afro-Brazilian Woman's Story of Politics and Love*, London: Latin America Bureau.

Bento, Maria Aparecida Silva and Jurema Polycarpo (2001) 'Raça e gênero no programa de modernização administrativa', in Carvalho and Ribeiro (2001).

Bianchi, Susana and Norma Sanchis (1988) *El Partido Peronista Femenino (1949–55)*, Buenos Aires: Centro Editor de América Latina.

Bittar, Jorge (ed.) (1992) *O modo petista de governar*, São Paulo: Cadernos de Teoria e Debate.

Bland, Gary (2003) 'The impetus for decentralization in Chile and Venezuela', in Montero and Samuels (2003).

Blandón, Maria Teresa (2001) 'The Coalición Nacional de Mujeres: an alliance of left-wing women, right-wing women and radical feminists in Nicaragua', in Kampwirth and González (2001).

Blay, Eva (1979) 'The political participation of women in Brazil: the female mayors', *Signs: Journal of Women in Culture and Society*, 5(1): 42–59.

Blofield, Merike Helena (2001) *The Politics of 'Moral Sin': A Study of Abortion and Divorce in Catholic Chile since 1990*, Santiago: FLACSO.

Blofield, Merike H. and Liesl Haas (2005) 'Defining a democracy: reforming the laws on women's rights in Chile 1990–2002', *Latin American Politics and Society*, 47(3): 35–68.

Blondet, Cecilia (2002) 'The devil's deal: women's political participation and authoritarianism in Peru', in Molyneux and Razavi (2002).

Borba, Angel, Nalu Faria and Tatau Godinho (eds) (1998) *Mulher e política: gênero e feminismo no Partido dos Trabalhadores*, São Paulo: Editora Fundação Perseu Abramo.

Branford, Sue and Bernard Kucinski (1995) *Carnival of the Oppressed: Lula and the Brazilian Workers' Party*, London: Latin America Bureau.

Bruhn, Kathleen (2003) 'Whores and lesbians: political activism, party strategies and gender quotas in Mexico', *Electoral Studies*, 22(1): 101–9.

Buarque, Cristovam (1999) *A segunda abolição: um manifesto-proposta para a erradicação da pobreza no Brasil*, São Paulo: Paz e Terra.

Cabral, John and Alexandrina Sobreira de Moura (1996) 'City management, local power, and social practice: an analysis of the 1991 Master Plan process in Recife', *Latin American Perspectives*, 23(4): 54–70.

Caccia Bava, Silvio (1998) *Programas de renda mínima no Brasil*, São Paulo: Revista Pólis no. 30.

Capistrano Filho, David (1991) *Santos: mil dias de Governo Popular*, São Paulo: Editora Brasil Urgente.

Cardoso, Fernando Henrique (1994) *Mãos à obra, Brasil: proposta de governo*, Brasília: n. p.

Carr, Barry and Steve Ellner (eds) (1993) *The Latin American Left: From the Fall of Allende to Perestroika*, Boulder, CO: Westview Press.

Carvalho, José Murilo de (1997) 'Mandonismo, coronelismo, clientelismo: uma discussão conceitual', *Dados*, 40(2): 229–50.

Carvalho, Maria do Carmo A. A. and Débora Felgueiras (2000) *Orçamento partici-pativo no ABC*, São Paulo: Revista Pólis no. 34.

Carvalho, Maria do Carmo A. A. and Matilde Ribeiro (eds) (2001) *Gênero e raça nas políticas públicas: experiências em Santo André*, São Paulo: Revista Pólis no. 39.

Casas, Lidia and Claudia Chaimovich (1997) *El aborto: un problema de salud pública*, Santiago: CLADEM.

Castro, Vanessa de (2002) 'Educação um sonho possível: conversando com as mães bolsistas', Brasília: unpublished report prepared for the NGO Missão Criança.

Center for Reproductive Law and Policy (2001) *Persecuted: Political Process and Abortion Legislation in El Salvador – a Human Rights Analysis*, New York.

Center for Reproductive Law and Policy, and Open Forum on Reproductive Health and Rights (1998) *Women behind Bars: Chile's Abortion Laws – a Human Rights Analysis*, New York and Santiago.

CFEMEA (1993) *Direitos da mulher: o que pensam os parlamentares*, Brasília: CFEMEA.

Chalmers, Douglas, Carlos M. Vilas, Katherine Hite, Scott B. Martin, Kerianne Piester and Monique Segarra (eds) (1997) *The New Politics of Inequality in Latin America: Rethinking Participation and Representation*, Oxford: Oxford University Press.

Chaney, Elsa (1979) *Supermadre: Women in Politics in Latin America*, Austin: University of Texas Press.

Chavez, Daniel (2004) 'Montevideo: from popular participation to good governance', in Chavez and Goldfrank (2004).

Chavez, Daniel and Benjamin Goldfrank (eds) (2004) *The Left in the City: Partici-patory Local Government in Latin America*, London: Latin America Bureau.

Chuchryck, Patricia (1994) 'From dictatorship to democracy: the women's movement in Chile', in Jaquette (1994).

Clulow, Michael (2003a) *The Central American Women's Movement and Public Policy: Analysis by Five Feminist Organizations*, London: One World Action.

Clulow, Michael (2003b) *Gender Equity and Local Governance: A Study of the San Salvador Municipal Gender Equity Policy*, London: One World Action.

Committee on the Elimination of Discrimination against Women (1991) *Initial Reports of States Parties: Chile*, CEDAW/C/CHI/1.

Committee on the Elimination of Discrimination against Women (1995) *Second Periodic Report of States Parties: Chile*, CEDAW/C/CHI/2.

Committee on the Elimination of Discrimination against Women (1999) *Third Periodic Report of States Parties: Chile*, CEDAW/C/CHI/3.

Committee on the Elimination of Discrimination against Women (2003a) *Combined Initial, Second, Third, Fourth and Fifth Periodic Reports of States Parties: Brazil*, CEDAW/C/Bra/1–5.

Committee on the Elimination of Discrimination against Women (2003b) *Consideration of Reports of States Parties: Brazil Combined Initial, Second, Third, Fourth and Fifth Periodic Reports*, CEDAW/C/2003/II/CRP.3/Add.2/Rev.1.

Coppedge, Michael (1997) *A Classification of Latin American Political Parties*, Notre Dame, IN: Kellogg Institute Working Paper no. 244.

Corcoran-Nantes, Yvonne (1993) 'Female consciousness or feminist consciousness in community based struggles in Brazil', in Radcliffe and Westwood (1993).

Costa, Ana Alice Alcântara (1998) *As donas no poder: mulher e política na Bahia*, Salvador: Núcleo de Estudos Interdisciplinares sobre a Mulher FFCH/UFBA.

Costa, Delaine Martins (ed.) (1997) *Democratização dos poderes municipais e a questão de gênero*, Rio de Janeiro: Instituto Brasileiro de Administração Municipal/ Fundação Ford, Serie Experiências Inovadoras vol. 7.

Costa Benavides, Jimena (2003) 'Women's political participation in Bolivia: progress and obstacles', Paper presented at the International IDEA workshop, 'The implementation of quotas: the Latin American experiences', Lima, Peru, 23–24 February.

Couto, Cláudio Gonçalves (1995) *Os desafios de ser governo: o PT na Prefeitura de São Paulo (1989–92)*, São Paulo: Paz e Terra.

Craske, Nikki and Maxine Molyneux (eds) (2002) *Gender and the Politics of Rights and Democracy in Latin America*, Basingstoke: Palgrave.

Dagnino, Evelina (ed.) (2002) *Sociedade civil e espaços públicos no Brasil*, São Paulo: Paz e Terra.

Dandavati, Annie (1996) *The Women's Movement and the Transition to Democracy in Chile*, New York: Peter Lang.

Deere, Carmen Diana (2004) 'Married women's property rights in Mexico: a comparative, Latin American perspective and research agenda', Paper presented at the conference 'Law and Gender in Contemporary Mexico', Institute of Latin American Studies, London, 19–20 February.

Della Cava, Ralph (1988) *The Church and the Abertura in Brazil 1974–85*, Notre Dame, IN: Helen Kellogg Institute for International Studies, University of Notre Dame.

Departamento Administración Municipal (1988) *Nomina de alcaldes*, Santiago: Republic of Chile.

DIAP (1988) *Quem foi quem na constituinte*, São Paulo: Cortez Editora.

Dore, Elizabeth and Maxine Molyneux (eds) (2000) *The Hidden Histories of Gender and the State in Latin America*, Durham NC and London: Duke University Press.

Downs, Anthony (1957) *An Economic Theory of Democracy*, New York: Harper.

Draibe, Sônia Miriam (1998) *A nova institucionalidade do sistema brasileiro de políticas sociais: os conselhos nacionais de políticas sectoriais*, Campinas: UNICAMP Caderno de Pesquisa no. 35.

Drake, Paul W. and Iván Jaksic (eds) (1991) *The Struggle for Democracy in Chile 1982–90*, Lincoln: University of Nebraska Press.

Eaton, Kent (2004a) 'Risky business: decentralization from above in Chile and Uruguay', *Comparative Politics*, 37(1): 1–22.

Eaton, Kent (2004b) 'Designing subnational institutions: regional and municipal reforms in post-authoritarian Chile', *Comparative Political Studies*, 37(2): 218–44.

Ellner, Steven and Daniel Hellinger (eds) (2003) *Venezuelan Politics in the Chavez Era: Class Polarization and Conflict*, Boulder, CO: Lynne Rienner.

Ensalaco, Mark (1994) 'In with the new, out with the old? The democratising impact of constitutional reform in Chile', *Journal of Latin American Studies*, 26(2): 409–30.

Escobar, Arturo and Sonia Alvarez (eds) (1992) *The Making of Social Movements in Latin America: Identity, Strategy and Democracy*, Boulder, CO: Westview Press.

Esmeraldo, Gema Galgani S. L. and Magnólia Azevedo Said (2002) 'O conselho cearense de direitos da mulher: espaço de interlocução entre as demandas dos movimentos de mulheres e o estado', in Dagnino (2002).

Fêmea, monthly newsletter published by CFEMEA, Brasília, various issues.

Figueiredo, Argelina Cheibub and Fernando Limongi (eds) (1999) *Executivo e legislativo na nova ordem constitutional*, São Paulo: Fundação Getúlio Vargas.

Figueres, Karen Olsen de (1998) 'The road to equality – women in parliament in Costa Rica', in International IDEA (1998).

Franceschet, Susan (2001) 'Women in politics in post-transitional democracies: the Chilean case', *International Feminist Journal of Politics*, 3(2): 207–36.

Franceschet, Susan (2003) 'State feminism and women's movements: the impact of Chile's Servicio Nacional de la Mujer on women's activism', *Latin American Research Review*, 38(1): 9–40.

Franco, Jean (1998) 'Defrocking the Vatican: feminism's secular project', in Alvarez, Dagnino and Escobar (1998).

Fraser, Nicholas and Marysa Navarro (1980) *Eva Perón*, London: Andre Deutsch.

Friedman, Elisabeth Jay (1998) 'Paradoxes of gendered political opportunity in the Venezuela transition to democracy', *Latin American Research Review*, 33(3): 87–136.

Friedman, Elisabeth Jay (2000a) *Unfinished Transitions: Women and the Gendered Development of Democracy in Venezuela 1936–1996*, University Park: Pennsylvania State University Press.

Friedman, Elisabeth Jay (2000b) 'State-based advocacy for gender equality in the developing world: assessing the Venezuelan National Women's Agency', *Women and Politics*, 21(2): 47–80.

Friedman, Elisabeth Jay (2002) 'Getting rights for those without representation: the success of conjunctural coalition-building in Venezuela', in Craske and Molyneux (2002).

Friedman, Elisabeth Jay, Kathryn Hochstetler and Ann Marie Clark (2001) 'Sovereign limits and regional opportunities for global civil society in Latin America', *Latin American Research Review*, 36(3): 7–36.

Fries, Lorena and Verónica Matus (1999) *El derecho: trama y conjuntura patriarchal*, Santiago: LOM Ediciones.

Frohmann, Alicia and Teresa Valdés (1993) *'Democracy in the Country and in the Home': The Women's Movement in Chile*, Santiago: FLACSO Social Studies Series Working Paper no. 55.

Fundación Jaime Guzmán (1995) *Nuestro aporte a la IV Conferencia Mundial sobre la Mujer*, Santiago: Fundación Jaime Guzmán.

FUNDAPEM (2004) *Towards the Incorporation of the Gender Perspective in Local Governments in Costa Rica: Perspectives and Challenges of the Municipal Women's agencies*, San José: Fundación para la Paz y la Democracia.

Fung, Archon and Erik Olin Wright (eds) (2003) *Real Utopias IV: Deepening Democracy: Innovations in Empowered Participatory Governance*, London: Verso.

Furlong, Marlea and Kimberley Riggs (1999) 'Women's participation in national level politics and government: the case of Costa Rica', *Women's Studies International Forum*, 19(6): 633–43.

Gadotti, Moacir and Otaviano Pereira (1989) *Pra que PT: Origem, Projeto e Consolidação do Partido dos Trabalhadores*, São Paulo: Cortez Editora.

Garretón, Manuel Antonio (ed.) (1989) *Propuestas políticas y demandas sociales Vol. III*, Santiago: FLACSO.

Garretón, Manuel Antonio (2000) 'Atavism and democratic ambiguity in the Chilean Right', in Middlebrook (2000).

Gaviola, Edda, Ximenia Jiles, Lorella Lopresti and Claudia Rojas (1986) '*Queremos votar en las próximas elecciones': historia del movimiento femenino chileno 1913–1952*, Santiago: Centro de Análisis y Difusión de la Condición de la Mujer.

Gaviola, Edda, Eliana Largo and Sandra Palestro (1994) *Una historia necesaria: mujeres en Chile 1973–1990*, Santiago: Akí y Aora Ltda.

Godinho, Tatau (1996) 'Ação afirmativa no Partido dos Trabalhadores', *Revista Estudos Feministas*, 4(1): 148–57.

Godinho Delgado, Maria do Carmo (2000) 'Desigualdade de gênero e participação política das mulheres: a experiência do Partido dos Trabalhadores', unpublished masters dissertation, Pontifical Catholic University (PUC), São Paulo.

Gómez de la Torre, Maricruz and Verónica Matus M. (1994) *Balance de los derechos de la mujer en el período de la transición*, Santiago: Programa de Mujeres, Comisión Chilena de Derechos Humanos.

González, Victoria (2001) 'Somocista women, right-wing politics and feminism in Nicaragua, 1936–79', in Kampwirth and González (2001).

Government of the Federal District (no date) *Creative Solutions*, Brasília.

Governo do Distrito Federal (1995) *Programa de governo: Brasília de todos nós*, Brasília.

Green, James N. (1994) 'The emergence of the Brazilian gay liberation movement', *Latin American Perspectives*, 21(1): 38–55.

Grossi, Míriam Pillar and Sônia Malheiros Miguel (2001) 'Transformando a diferença: as mulheres na política', *Revista Estudos Feministas*, 9(1): 167–206.

Guidry, John A. and Pere Petit (2003) 'Faith in what will change: the PT administration in Belém', in Baiocchi (2003b).

Guzmán, Virginia, Sandra Lerda and Rebeca Salazar (1994) *La dimensión de género en el quehacer del estado*, Santiago: Centro de Estudios de la Mujer.

Haas, Liesl (1998) 'The effects of institutional structure on policymaking: an examination of women's rights legislation in Chile 1990–1998', Paper presented at the conference of the Latin American Studies Association, Chicago, 24–26 September.

Haas, Liesl (2001) 'Changing the system from within? Feminist participation in the Brazilian Workers' Party', in Kampwirth and González (2001).

Hahner, June. E. (1990) *Emancipating the Female Sex: The Struggle for Women's Rights in Brazil, 1850–1940*, Durham, NC: Duke University Press.

Heiss, Claudia and Patricio Navia (2002) 'Institutional design and decentralization: the case of Chile', Paper presented at the Midwest Political Science Association Congress, Chicago, 25–27 April.

Hinojosa, Magda (2002) 'Se buscan candidatas mujeres', published electronically at www.electoral.cl

Hipsher, Patricia (2001) 'Right and left-wing women in post-revolutionary El Salvador: feminist autonomy and cross-political alliance building for gender equality', in Kampwirth and González (2001).

Hite, Katherine (2000) *When the Romance Ended: Leaders of the Chilean Left, 1968–1998*, New York: Columbia University Press.

Hola, Eugenia and Gabriela Pischedda (1995) *Mujeres, poder y política: nuevas tensiones para viejas estructuras*, Santiago: Centro de Estudios de la Mujer.

Htun, Mala (2003) *Abortion, Divorce and the Family under Latin American Dictatorships and Democracies*, Cambridge: Cambridge University Press.

Htun, Mala and Mark Jones (2002) 'Engendering the right to participate in decisionmaking: electoral quotas and women's leadership in Latin America', in Craske and Molyneux (2002).

Huneeus, Carlos (2000) 'Technocrats and politicians in an authoritarian regime: the "ODEPLAN Boys" and the "Gremialists" in Pinochet's Chile', *Journal of Latin American Studies*, 32(3): 461–501.

Huneeus, Carlos (2001) *La derecha en el Chile después de Pinochet: el caso de la Unión Demócrata Independiente*, Notre Dame, IN: Kellogg Institute Working Paper no. 285.

Huneeus, Carlos (2003) 'A highly institutionalized political party: Christian Democracy in Chile', in Mainwaring and Scully (2003).

Hurrell, Andrew (1996) 'The international dimensions of democratization in Latin America: the case of Brazil', in Whitehead (1996).

IBAM (2000) *Participação feminina na construção da democracia*, Rio de Janeiro: Instituto Brasileiro de Administração Municipal.

IBAM/ISER (2002) *Violência contra mulheres e as ações municipais das mercocidades brasileiras*, Rio de Janeiro: Instituto Brasileiro de Administração Municipal.

INESC (2002) *Revista parlamento: previsão eleitoral 2003–06*, Brasília: INESC.

Inter-American Dialogue (2001) *Women and Power in the Americas: A Report Card*, Washington, DC: Inter-American Dialogue.

International IDEA (1998) *Women in Parliament: Beyond Numbers*, Stockholm: International IDEA.

ISIS International (1993) *El espacio posible*, Issue no. 19 of *Ediciones de las Mujeres*, Santiago.

Jaquette, Jane (1994) *The Women's Movement in Latin America: Participation and Democracy*, Boulder, CO: Westview Press.

Johnson, Niki (2002) 'In pursuit of the right to be free from violence: the women's movement and state accountability in Uruguay', in Craske and Molyneux (2002).

Joignant, Alfredo and Patricio Navia (2003) 'De la política de los indivíduos a los hombres de partido: socialización, competencia política y penetración electoral de la UDI (1989–2001)', *Estudios Públicos*, 89: 129–71.

Jones, Mark P. (1998) 'Gender quotas, electoral laws and the election of women: lessons from the argentine provinces', *Comparative Political Studies*, 31(1): 3–21.

Jornal da Rede Feminista de Saúde, no. 21, September 2000.

Kampwirth, Karen and Victoria González (eds) (2001) *Radical Women in Latin America: Left and Right*, University Park: Pennsylvania State University Press.

Keck, Margaret E. (1992) *The Brazilian Workers' Party and Democratization in Brazil*, New Haven: Yale University Press.

Keck, Margaret E. and Katherine Sikkink (1998) *Activists beyond Borders: Advocacy Networks in International Politics*, Ithaca: Cornell University Press.

Kingstone, Peter R. and Timothy J. Power (eds) (2000) *Democratic Brazil: Actors, Institutions and Processes*, Pittsburgh: University of Pittsburgh Press.

Klubock, Thomas (1996) *Contested Communities: Class, Gender and Politics in Chile's El Teniente Copper Mine 1904–1951*, Durham, NC: Duke University Press.

La Morada, CLADEM and CRLP (1999) *Alternative Report to the Third Periodic Report of Chile on the Status of Compliance with the Women's Convention*, Santiago.

Lavinas, Lena (1999) 'Renda mínima: práticas e viabilidade', *Novos Estudos*, 53: 65–83.

Lavinas, Lena and Maria Ligia de Oliveira Barbosa (2000) 'Combater a pobreza estimulando a freqüência escola: o estudo de caso do programa bolsa-escola de Recife', *Dados*, 43(3): 447–77.

Lavrin, Asunción (1995) *Women, Feminism, and Social Change in Argentina, Chile, and Uruguay, 1890–1940*, Lincoln, Neb.: University of Nebraska Press.

Lehmann, Carla (2003) *Women, Work, and Family: Reality, Perceptions, and Challenges*, Santiago: Centro de Estudios Públicos, Series Puntos de Referencia no. 269.

Levitsky, Steven (2003) *Transforming Labor-based Parties in Latin America: Argentine Peronism in Comparative Perspective*, Cambridge: Cambridge University Press.

Levy, Susana and Norbert Lechner (1986) 'CEMA-Chile y Secretaría Nacional de la Mujer', in Meza (1986).

Lipset, Seymour Martin and Stein Rokkan (1967) *Party Systems and Voter Alignments*, New York: Free Press.

Lomnitz, Larissa Adler and Ana Melnick (1998) *La cultura política chilena y los partidos de centro: una explicación antropológica*, Federal District, Mexico and Santiago, Chile: Fondo de Cultura Económica.

Londregan, John (2000) *Legislative Institutions and Ideology in Chile*, Cambridge: Cambridge University Press.

Lovenduski, Joni and Pippa Norris (eds) (1993) *Gender and Party Politics*, London: Sage.

Luna, Lola G. (2001) 'El logro del voto femenino en Colombia: la violencia y el maternalismo populista, 1949–1957', *Boletin Americanista* 51: 81–94.

Macaulay, Fiona (1996) ' "Governing for everyone": the Workers' Party administration in São Paulo 1989–1992', *Bulletin of Latin American Research*, 15(2): 211–29.

Macaulay, Fiona (2000) 'Getting gender on the policy agenda: a study of a Brazilian feminist lobby group', in Dore and Molyneux (2000).

Macaulay, Fiona (2004) 'La política de género en el gobierno del PT', *América Latina Hoy*, 37: 101–20.

Macaulay, Fiona and Guy Burton (2003) ' "PT never again": Success and failure in the PT's state governments in Espírito Santo and the Distrito Federal', in Baiocchi (2003b).

Machado, Leda Maria Vieira (1988) 'The participation of women in the health movement of Jardim Nordeste', *Bulletin of Latin American Research*, 7(1): 47–63.

MacRae, Edward (1992) 'Homosexual identities in transitional Brazilian politics', in Escobar and Alvarez (1992).

Magar, Eric, Marc R. Rosenblum and David Samuels (1998) 'On the absence of centripetal incentives in double-member districts: the case of Chile', *Comparative Political Studies*, 31(6): 714–39.

Mainwaring, Scott (1986) *The Catholic Church and Politics in Brazil, 1916–1985*, Stanford: Stanford University Press.

Mainwaring, Scott (1999) *Rethinking Party Systems in the Third Wave of Democratization: The Case of Brazil*, Stanford: Stanford University Press.

Mainwaring, Scott, and Timothy Scully (eds) (1995) *Building Democratic Institutions: Party Systems in Latin America*, Stanford: Stanford University Press.

Mainwaring, Scott and Timothy Scully (eds) (2003) *Christian Democracy in Latin America: Electoral Competition and Regime Conflicts*, Stanford: Stanford University Press.

Marcondes, Celso (1991) *Em algum lugar do passado: o PT na Prefeitura de Campinas*, São Paulo: Editora Pagina Aberta.

Massolo, Alejandra (1998) 'Women in the local arena and municipal power', in Rodríguez (1998).

Massolo, Alejandra (2003) 'Participación de las mujeres en los gobiernos locales de América Latina', in Barrera Bassols and Massolo (2003).

Matear, Ann (1996) ' "Desde la protesta a la propuesta": Gender politics in transition Chile', *Democratization*, 3(3): 246–63.

Matear, Ann (1999) 'Gender relations, authoritarianism and democratization in Chile', *Democratization*, 6(3): 100–17.

Maza Valenzuela, Erika (1995) *Catholicism, Anticlericalism and the Quest for Women's Suffrage in Chile*, Notre Dame, IN: Kellogg Institute Working Paper no. 214.

Maza Valenzuela, Erika (1998) 'Liberales, radicales y la ciudadania de la mujer en Chile (1872–1930)', *Estudios Públicos*, 58: 319–56.

McGee Deutsch, Sandra (2001) 'Spreading right-wing patriotism, femininity, and morality: women in Argentina, Brazil and Chile, 1900–1940', in Kampwirth and González (2001).

Meneguello, Rachel (1989) *PT: A formação de um partido 1979–1982*, Rio de Janeiro: Paz e Terra.

Meza, Maria Angélica (1986) *La otra mitad de Chile*, Santiago: CESOC.

Middlebrook, Kevin J. (ed.) (2000) *Conservative Parties, the Right and Democracy in Latin America*, Baltimore, Md.: Johns Hopkins University Press.

Miguel, Sônia Malheiros (2000) *A política de cotas por sexo: um estudo das primeiras experiências no legislativo brasileiro*, Brasília: CFEMEA.

Ministerio del Interior (1992) *Listado oficial de intendentes, de gobernadores, de alcaldes*, Santiago: Republic of Chile.

Molina, Natacha (1989) 'Propuestas políticas y orientaciones de cambio en la situación de la mujer', in Garretón (1989).

Molyneux, Maxine (2001) *Women's Movements in International Perspective: Latin America and Beyond*, Basingstoke: Palgrave.

Molyneux, Maxine and Shahra Razavi (eds) (2002) *Gender Justice, Development and Rights*, Oxford: Oxford University Press.

Montaño, Sonia, Jacqueline Pitanguy and Thereza Lobo (eds) (2003) *As políticas públicas de gênero: um modelo para armar: o caso de Brasil*, Santiago: CEPAL Series Women and Development no. 45.

Montecino, Sonia and Josefina Rossetti (eds) (1990) *Tramas para un nuevo destino*, Santiago: Concertación de Mujeres por la Democracia.

Montecinos, Verónica (1994) 'Neoliberal economic reforms and women in Chile', in Aslanbegui *et al.* (1994).

Montecinos, Verónica (2001) 'Feminists and technocrats in the democratization of Latin America: a prolegomenon', *International Journal of Politics, Culture and Society*, 15(1): 175–99.

Montero, Alfred P. (2000) 'Devolving democracy: political decentralization and the new Brazilian federalism', in Kingstone and Power (2000).

Montero, Alfred P. and David Samuels (eds) (2003) *Decentralization and Democracy in Latin America*, Notre Dame, IN: Notre Dame University Press.

Montes, J. Esteban, Scott Mainwaring and Eugenio Ortega (2000) 'Rethinking the Chilean party systems', *Journal of Latin American Studies*, 32(3): 795–824.

Mosovich Pont-Lezica, Diana (1997) 'Local politics and depoliticisation in Chile', *Bulletin of Latin American Research*, 16(2): 197–217.

Moulian, Tomás (1998) *El consumo me consume*, Santiago: LOM Ediciones

Munizaga, Giselle (1988) *El discurso público de Pinochet: una análisis semiológica*, Santiago: CESOC/CENECA.

Myers, David J. and Henry A. Dietz (eds) (2002) *Capital City Politics in Latin America: Democratization and Empowerment*, Boulder, CO: Lynne Rienner.

Navia, Patricio (2004) 'Legislative candidate section in Chile', published electronically at pages.nyu.edu/~pdn200

Nelson, Barbara J. and Najma Chowdhury (eds) (1994) *Women and Politics Worldwide*, New Haven: Yale University Press

Neuhouser, Kevin (1995) 'Worse than men: gendered mobilization in an urban Brazilian squatter settlement, 1971–91', *Gender and Society*, 9(1): 38–59.

Nickson, R. Andrew (1995) *Local Government in Latin America*, Boulder, CO: Lynne Rienner.

Nicolau, Jairo (1996) *Multipartidarismo e democracia*, São Paulo: Fundação Getúlio Vargas.

Nogueira, Helena, Tatau Godinho and Vera Soares (2000) *Gênero nas administrações: desafios para prefeituras e governos estaduais*, São Paulo: Friedrich Ebert Stiftung.

Norris, Pippa (2004) *Electoral Engineering: Voting Rules and Political Behaviour*, Cambridge: Cambridge University Press.

Nylen, William (1997) 'Reconstructing the Workers' Party (PT): lessons from northeastern Brazil', in Chalmers *et al.* (1997).

Nylen, William (2003a) 'An enduring legacy? popular participation in the aftermath of the participatory budget in João Monlevade and Betim', in Baiocchi (2003b).

Nylen, William (2003b) *Participatory Democracy versus Elitist Democracy: Lessons from Brazil*, New York: Palgrave Macmillan.

O'Neill, Kathleen (2003) 'Decentralization as an electoral strategy', *Comparative Political Studies*, 36(9): 1068–91.

Oxhorn, Phillip (1994) 'Where did all of the protesters go? Popular mobilization and the transition to democracy in Chile', *Latin American Perspectives*, 21(3): 49–68.

Oxhorn, Phillip (1995) *Organizing Civil Society: The Popular Sectors and the Struggle for Democracy in Chile*, University Park: Pennsylvania State University Press.

Oyarzún, Kemy (2000) 'Engendering democracy in the Chilean university', *NACLA*, 33(4): 24–7.

Paley, Julia (2001) *Marketing Democracy: Power and Social Movements in Post-Dictatorship Chile*, Berkeley: University of California Press.

Panebianco, Angelo (1988) *Political Parties: Organization and Power*, Oxford: Oxford University Press.

Partido dos Trabalhadores (1980) *Manifesto*, São Paulo.

Partido dos Trabalhadores (1994) *Uma revolução democrática no Brasil: Programa de governo: Projeto para discussão*, São Paulo.

Partido dos Trabalhadores (1998) *Resoluções de encontros e congressos 1979–1998*, São Paulo.

Partido Socialista de Chile (1995) *Program Socialista de la Mujer*, Santiago: Vice-Presidencia de Asuntos de la Mujer.

Pateman, Carol (1989) *The Disorder of Women: Democracy, Feminism and Political Theory*, Cambridge: Polity Press.

Pinheiro, Paulo Sérgio (2000) *Brazil and the International Human Rights System*, Oxford, Centre for Brazilian Studies, University of Oxford, Working Paper no. 15.

Pinto, Valeska P. (1992) *Prefeitura de Fortaleza: administração popular 1986–88*, São Paulo: Pólis.

Pitanguy, Jacqueline (2003) 'Movimento de mulheres e políticas de gênero no Brasil', in Montaño *et al.* (2003).

Plumb, David (1998) 'El Partido por la Democracia: the birth of Chile's postmaterialist catch-all left', *Party Politics*, 4(1): 93–106.

Poire, Alejandro and Jorge I. Domiguez (eds) (1999) *Towards Mexico's Democratization: Parties, Campaigns, Elections and Public Opinion*, New York: Routledge.

Pollack, Marcelo (1999) *The New Right in Chile 1973–97*, Basingstoke: Macmillan.

Posner, Paul W. (1999) 'Popular representation and political dissatisfaction in Chile's new democracy', *Journal of Interamerican Studies and World Affairs*, 41(1): 59–85.

Power, Margaret (2002) *Right-Wing Women in Chile: Feminine Power and the Struggle against Allende 1964–1973*, University Park: Pennsylvania State University Press.

Power, Timothy (2000) *The Political Right in Post-Authoritarian Brazil*, University Park: Pennsylvania State University Press.

Prá, Jussara Reis (1992) 'A representação da mulher no Brasil (1982–1990): a articulação de gênero e a questão institucional', unpublished doctoral dissertation, University of São Paulo.

Prefeitura Municipal Santo André (1992) *Mulher e espaço urbano*, Santo André.

Provoste, Patricia (1995) *La construcción de las mujeres en la política social*, Santiago: Instituto de la Mujer.

Provoste, Patricia and Alejandra Valdés (2000) 'Democratización de la gestión municipal y ciudadania de las mujeres: sistematización de experiencias innovadoras', Santiago: Fundación Nacional para la Superación de la Probreza and the Centro de Análisis de Políticas Públicas, Universidad de Chile, Working Paper no. 22.

Rabkin, Rhoda (1996) 'Redemocratization, electoral engineering and party strategies in Chile, 1989–1995', *Comparative Political Studies*, 29(3): 335–56.

Radcliffe, Sarah A. and Sallie Westwood (eds) (1993) *'Viva': Women and Popular Protest in Latin America*, London: Routledge.

Rahat, Gideon and Mario Sznajder (1998) 'Electoral engineering in Chile: the electoral system and limited democracy', *Electoral Studies*, 7(4): 429–42.

Rai, Shirin and Geraldine Lievesley (eds) (1996) *Women and the State: International Perspectives*, London: Taylor & Francis.

Ramos Escandón, Carmen (1998) 'Women and power in Mexico: the forgotten heritage, 1880–1954', in Rodríguez (1998).

Rede Feminista de Saúde and CFEMEA (2001) 'Direito ao aborto no parlamento', published electronically at www.redesaude.org.br

RHUDO-SA and USAID (1993) *Brasil: mujeres en el poder local: proyectos y contextos*, Quito: IULA/CELCADEL.

Richards, Patricia (2003) 'Expanding women's citizenship? Mapuche women and Chile's National Women's Service', *Latin American Perspectives*, 30(2): 41–65.

Rocha, Sonia (2001) *Applying Minimum Income Programmes in Brazil: Two Case Studies*, Geneva: International Labour Organization.

Rock, David (ed.) (1994) *Latin America in the 1940s: War and Postwar Transitions*, Berkeley, CA: University of California Press.

Rodrigues, Leôncio Martins (2002) *Partidos, ideologia e composição social*, São Paulo: EDUSP.

Rodríguez, Victoria E. (ed.) (1998) *Women's Participation in Mexican Political Life*, Boulder, CO: Westview Press.

Rosemblatt, Karin Alejandra (2000) *Gendered Compromises: Political Cultures and the State in Chile 1920–1950*, Chapel Hill, NC: University of North Carolina Press.

Rule, Wilma and Joseph F. Zimmerman (1994) *Electoral Systems in Comparative Perspective: Their Impact on Women and Minorities*, Westport, CT: Greenwood Press.

Saa, Maria Antonieta (1993) 'Desacralizar el poder', in ISIS International (1993).

Sacchet, Teresa (2002) 'Making women count: campaigns for quotas in Brazil', unpublished doctoral dissertation, University of Essex.

Sader, Emir and Ken Silverstein (1991) *Without Fear of Being Happy: Lula, the Workers' Party and Brazil*, London: Verso.

Saffioti, Heleieth I.B. (1978) *Women in Class Society*, New York and London: Monthly Review Press.

Saint-Germain, Michelle and Martha Morgan (1991) 'Equality: Costa Rican women demand "the real thing" ', *Women and Politics*, 11(3): 23–74.

Samuels, David (2000) 'Reinventing local government', in Kingstone and Power (2000).

Samuels, David (2001) 'Money, elections and democracy in Brazil', *Latin American Politics and Society*, 43(2): 27–48.

Samuels, David (2003) *Ambition, Federalism and Legislative Politics in Brazil*, Cambridge: Cambridge University Press.

Samuels, David (2004a) 'Bases do Petismo', Paper presented at the fourth Annual Conference of the Brazilian Political Science Association, Rio de Janeiro, 21–24 July.

Samuels, David (2004b) 'From socialism to social democracy: party organization and the transformation of the Workers' Party in Brazil', *Comparative Political Studies*, 37(9): 999–1024.

Savage, Michael and Ann Witz (eds) (1992) *Gender and Bureaucracy*, Oxford: Blackwell.

Schedler, Andreas (1995) *Under- and Overinstitutionalization: Some Ideal Typical Propositions Concerning New and Old Party Systems*, Notre Dame, IN: Kellogg Institute Working Paper no. 213.

Schild, Veronica (1998a) 'Market citizenship and the "new democracies": the ambiguous legacies of the contemporary Chilean women's movement', *Social Politics*, 5(2): 232–49.

Schild, Veronica (1998b) 'New subjects of rights? Women's movements and the construction of citizenship in the "new democracies" ', in Alvarez *et al.* (1998).

Schild, Veronica (2000) 'Neo-liberalism's new gendered market citizens: the "civilising" dimensions of social programs in Chile', *Citizenship Studies*, 4(3): 275–305.

Schneider, Cathy Lisa (1995) *Shantytown Protest in Pinochet's Chile*, Philadelphia: Temple University Press.

Schumaher, Schuma and Erico Vital Brazil (2000) *Dicionário mulheres do Brasil de 1500 até a atualidade*, Rio de Janeiro: Jorge Zahar.

Scully, Timothy (1992) *Rethinking the Center: Party Politics in Nineteenth- and Twentieth-Century Chile*, Stanford: Stanford University Press.

Scully, Timothy (1995) 'Reconstituting party politics in Chile', in Mainwaring and Scully (1995).

SERNAM (1995) 'Análisis de las informaciones de prensa respecto a las críticas negativas a SERNAM y/o el gobierno en los meses de mayo, junio y julio de 1995 a partir de los recortes', internal document, Santiago.

SERNAM (2000) *Plan de igualdad de oportunidades entre mujeres y hombres*, Santiago.

Servicio Electoral (1994) *Partidos políticos*, Santiago: Republic of Chile.

Siavelis, Peter (1997) 'Continuity and change in the Chilean party system: on the transformational effects of electoral reform', *Comparative Political Studies*, 30(6): 651–74.

Siavelis, Peter (2000) *The President and Congress in Post-Authoritarian Chile: Institutional Constraints to Democratic Consolidation*, University Park: Pennsylvania State University Press.

Siavelis, Peter (2002) 'The hidden logic of candidate selection for Chilean parliamentary elections', *Comparative Politics*, 34(4): 419–38.

Siavelis, Peter and Arturo Valenzuela (1999) 'Electoral engineering and democratic stability: the legacy of authoritarian rule in Chile', in Waisman and Lijphart (1999).

Siavelis, Peter M., Esteban Valenzuela Van Treek, and Giorgio Martelli (2002) 'Santiago: municipal decentralization in a centralized political system', in Myers and Dietz (2002).

Silva, Patricio (2001) 'Towards mass technocratic politics in Chile? The 1999–2000 elections and the "Lavín" phenomenon', *European Review of Latin American and Caribbean Studies*, 70: 25–39.

Silva, Patricio (2004) 'Doing politics in a depoliticised society: social change and political deactivation in Chile', *Bulletin of Latin American Research*, 23(1): 63–78.

Silveira, Maria Lúcia da (2001) 'Perspectiva de gênero e raça no Programa de Renda Mínima de Santo André', in Carvalho and Ribeiro (2001).

Simões, Júlio Assis (1992) *O dilema da participação popular: a etnografia de um caso*, São Paulo: Editora Marco Zero.

Simões, Solange de Deus (1985) *Deus, pátria e família: as mulheres no golpe de 1964*, Petrópolis: Vozes.

Singer, Paul (1996) *Um governo de esquerda para todos: Luiza Erundina na Prefeitura de São Paulo (1989–92)*, São Paulo: Editora Brasiliense.

Soares, Vera (2001) 'Banco do Povo de Santo André', in Carvalho and Ribeiro (2001).

Soto Gamboa, Angel M. (2001) 'La irrupción de la UDI en las poblaciones, 1983–1987', Paper presented at the meeting of the Latin American Studies Association, Washington DC, 6–8 September.

Souza, Celina (1997) *Constitutional Engineering in Brazil: The Politics of Federalism and Decentralisation*, Basingstoke: Macmillan.

Suárez, Mireya, Marlene T. Rodrigues and Ana Julieta T. Cleaver (2001) *Considerando as diferenças de gênero: para uma política de igualdade entre homens e mulheres*, São Paulo: Pólis and Fundação Getúlio Vargas.

Subsecretaría de Desarrollo Regional y Administrativo (2001) *Género y desarrollo municipal*, Santiago: Ministério del Interior.

Sugiyama, Natasha Borges (2002) 'Gendered budget work in the Americas: selected country experiences,' published electronically at www.international-budget.org

Tabak, Fanny (1989) *A mulher brasileira no Congresso Nacional*, Brasília: Câmara dos Deputados.

Tabak, Fanny (1994) 'Women in the struggle for democracy and equal rights in Brazil', in Nelson and Chowdhury (1994).

Tatagiba, Luciana (2002) 'Os conselhos gestores e a democratização da políticas públicas no Brasil', in Dagnino (2002).

Teles, Maria Amélia de Almeida (1993) *Breve história do feminismo no Brasil*, São Paulo: Brasiliense.

Tinsman, Heidi (2002) *Partners in Conflict: The Politics of Gender, Sexuality, and Labor in the Chilean Agrarian Reform, 1950–1973*, Durham, NC: Duke University Press.

Todaro Williams, Margaret (1976) 'Church and State in Vargas's Brazil: the politics of cooperation', *Journal of Church and State*, 18(3): 443–62.

UNIFEM (1998) *Bringing Equality Home: Implementing CEDAW*, New York: United Nations Development Fund for Women.

Valdés, Teresa and Marisa Weinstein (1993) *Mujeres que sueñan: las organizaciones de pobladoras en Chile: 1973–1989*, Santiago: FLACSO.

Valdés, Teresa, Marisa Weinstein and Marcela Díaz (1995) *Análisis y evaluación de experiencias municipales dirigidas a la mujer*, Santiago: FLACSO.

Valenzuela, Arturo (1977) *Political Brokers in Chile: Local Government in a Centralized Polity*, Durham NC: Duke University Press.

Valenzuela, J. Samuel (1985) *Democratización via reforma: la expansión del sufragio en Chile*, Buenos Aires: IDES.

Valenzuela, J. Samuel (1995) *The Origins and Transformations of the Chilean Party System*, Notre Dame, IN: Kellogg Institute Working Paper no. 215.

Valenzuela, J. Samuel and Timothy R. Scully (1997) 'Electoral choices and the party system in Chile: continuities and changes at the recovery of democracy', *Comparative Politics*, 29(4): 511–27.

Valenzuela, María Elena (1991) 'The evolving roles of women under military rule', in Drake and Jaksic (1991).

Verucci, Florisa (1991) 'Women and the new Brazilian constitution', *Feminist Studies*, 17(3): 551–6.

Vigna, Edélcio (2001) *Bancada ruralista: um grupo de interesse*, Brasília: INESC.

Von Beyme, Klaus (1985) *Political Parties in Western Democracies*, Aldershot: Gower.

Waisman, Carlos and Arend Lijphart (eds) (1999) *Institutional Design in New Democracies*, Boulder, CO: Westview Press.

Walker, Ignacio (2003) 'The future of Chilean Christian Democracy', in Mainwaring and Scully (2003).

Watson, Sophie (1992) 'Femocratic feminisms', in Savage and Witz (1992).

Waylen, Georgina (1992) 'Rethinking women's political participation and protest: Chile 1970–1990', *Political Studies*, 40(2): 299–314.

Waylen, Georgina (1996) 'Democratization, feminism and the state in Chile: the establishment of SERNAM', in Rai and Lievesley (1996).

Waylen, Georgina (2000) 'Gender and democratic politics: a comparative analysis of consolidation in Argentina and Chile', *Journal of Latin American Studies*, 32(3): 765–94.

Waylen, Georgina (2003) 'Gender and transitions: what do we know?', *Democratization*, 10(1): 157–78.

Whitehead, Laurence (1996) *The International Dimensions of Democratization: Europe and the Americas*, Oxford: Oxford University Press.

Willis, Eliza, Stephan Haggard and Christopher Garman (1999) 'The politics of decentralization in Latin America', *Latin American Research Review*, 34(1): 7–56.

Index